Wissenschaftliche Untersuchungen
zum Neuen Testament · 2. Reihe

Herausgeber / Editor
Jörg Frey (Zürich)

Mitherausgeber / Associate Editors
Markus Bockmuehl (Oxford) · James A. Kelhoffer (Uppsala)
Tobias Nicklas (Regensburg) · Janet Spittler (Charlottesville, VA)
J. Ross Wagner (Durham, NC)

596

Monique Cuany

Proclaiming the Kerygma in Athens

The Argument of Acts 17:16–34
in Light of the Epicurean and Stoic Debates
about Piety and Divine Images
in Early Post-Hellenistic Times

Mohr Siebeck

Monique Cuany, Born 1980; studied history and theology in Switzerland, China, the USA, and the United Kingdom; 2019 PhD in New Testament studies, University of Cambridge, UK; Professor of History of Christianity, Haute Ecole de Théologie, St-Légier, Switzerland.
orcid.org/0000-0001-7198-8907

ISBN 978-3-16-161427-9 / eISBN 978-3-16-161428-6
DOI 10.1628/978-3-16-161428-6

ISSN 0340-9570 / eISSN 2568-7484
(Wissenschaftliche Untersuchungen zum Neuen Testament, 2. Reihe)

The Deutsche Nationalbibliothek lists this publication in the Deutsche Nationalbibliographie; detailed bibliographic data are available at *https://dnb.de*.

© 2023 Mohr Siebeck Tübingen, Germany. www.mohrsiebeck.com

This book may not be reproduced, in whole or in part, in any form (beyond that permitted by copyright law) without the publisher's written permission. This applies particularly to reproductions, translations and storage and processing in electronic systems.

The book was printed on non-aging paper and bound by Gulde-Druck in Tübingen.

Printed in Germany.

To my parents
Jacqueline and Dominique Cuany

To my parents,

Preface

This study is a slightly revised version of my PhD thesis, submitted at the University of Cambridge in 2018.

I would like to thank my supervisor, Prof Simon Gathercole, for reading my work with so much care, and providing me with helpful feedback and encouragement during those years, including on many pieces which never made it into this thesis. His expertise, attention to detail and precision in thinking has often challenged and inspired me, and made my thesis a much better work. Likewise, Prof Judith Lieu provided helpful criticism and advice at various stages of this project, especially during the first and second year of my research, challenging me to reflect on my methodology and the broader implications of my proposal. I also wish to thank the examiners of my thesis, Prof Sean Adams and Dr James Carleton Paget, for their helpful criticisms, remarks and suggestions.

My research has been made possible by a scholarship from the Faculty of Divinity, Cambridge, and by grants from my college, Corpus Christi. I am truly grateful for this institutional support. My appreciation also goes to the members of the Acts Seminar of the British New Testament Society and the European Association of Biblical Scholarship for giving me feedback on some of the ideas which helped to shape this thesis.

My time in Cambridge has been greatly enriched by the friendship and support of many friends. In particular I would like to thank Ruth Norris, Hannah Robinson, Nicki Wilkes, and Onesimus Ngundu for their friendship, as well as the Gurry Family for so generously opening their home to me on many occasions. The Cambridge Chinese Christian Church has been a very supportive and kind community of friends. In Switzerland, I would like to express a special thanks to Lucette et Danilo Hasler, Simone et Jean-Marc Tapernoux, Niki and Damaris Conzelmann, as well as to my siblings and their families: Thérèse and Philippe Cuany, Carmen and Joël Deriaz, and Francine and Mathieu Grandjean.

Finally, I would like to thank my parents, Jacqueline and Dominique Cuany, for their unwavering support in so many ways during those years of research. Words fail me to express my gratitude for their encouragements and kindness at every stage, and for the enthusiasm and patience with which they have shared the joys and doubts of this journey. I dedicate this work to them, in gratitude.

St-Légier, 21 August 2023 *Monique Cuany*

Table of Contents

Preface VII
Table of Contents IX
Abbreviations XV

Chapter 1: Introduction 1

1.1 The Areopagus Speech in Acts and Scholarship 1

1.2 Some Maine Lines in Past Scholarship 5

    1.2.1 Jewish-Christian *Grundmotiv* and Stoic *Begleitmotiv* (Norden) 5
    1.2.2 A Philosophical Sermon on the Knowledge of God
         (Dibelius, Pohlenz, Balch) 6
    1.2.3 A Thoroughly Jewish Speech: Downplaying the Importance of
         Greek Material (Gärtner) 8
    1.2.4 The Mixed Nature of the Speech and Hellenistic Jewish
         Preaching (Nauck) 10
    1.2.5 A Christian Speech: Reinterpreting Greek Philosophy Within a
         Christian Framework (Conzelmann) 12
    1.2.6 *Anknüpfung und Widerspruch*: Philosophy as Criticism of
         Graeco-Roman Religion 14
    1.2.7 The Search For 'Common Ground' and 'Points of Contact'
         in the Service of Apologetic 16
    1.2.8 Christianity and Greek Philosophy as Rival Traditions (Rowe) 18
    1.2.9 Conclusion: Making Sense of the Hellenization of the Speech
         and Its 'Christian' Conclusion 22

1.3 A New Approach to the Areopagus Speech 23

    1.3.1 Recent Research on Hellenistic Judaism and Hellenization 23
    1.3.2 Narrative and Verisimilitude in Acts 25
    1.3.3 A Re-Examination of the Teachings of Stoicism
         and Epicureanism 29

X   Table of Contents

1.4   Outline and Structure of the Argument 30

Chapter 2: Setting Up the Debate – The Immediate Context and Beginning of the Speech (Acts 17:16–23) 32

2.1   The Occasion of the Speech: Collision and Newness in Athens 32

      2.1.1   Paul's Reaction to Athenian Worship (vv. 16–17) 33
      2.1.2   The Athenians' Perception of Paul and His Message (v.18) 34
      2.1.3   The Setting of the Speech (vv.19–21) 38

2.2   The Philosophical Context: Debating with Stoic
      and Epicurean Philosophers 40

      2.2.1   Debating With Stoic and Epicurean Philosophers 40
      2.2.2   The Socratic Allusions 42
      2.2.3   The *Deisidaimonia* of the Athenians and Their
            Ignorant Worship 44

2.3   Conclusion 45

Chapter 3: Neither 'Piety,' nor 'Superstition' – Redefining *Deisidaimonia* in the Context of Graeco-Roman Religious Grammar (c. 100 BCE–120 CE) 48

3.1   Methodological Concerns in the Study of *Deisidaimonia* 51

      3.1.1   The Lack of Semantic Study of the Terminology
            of *Deisidaimonia* 51
      3.1.2   The Assumption of Anachronistic Conceptual Frameworks in the
            Study of Ancient Religion and Philosophy 53
      3.1.3   Ancient Definitions of *Deisidaimonia* 56
      3.1.4   Methodology of this Chapter 58

3.2   The Use of *Deisidaimonia* in Historians and Geographers 60

      3.2.1   Diodorus Siculus (90–30 BCE) 60
      3.2.2   Strabo (c. 64 BCE–c. 24 CE) 65
      3.2.3   Josephus (37–100 CE) 69

3.3   The Use of *Deisidaimonia* in Plutarch of Chaeronea
      (c. 45 CE – Before 125) 74

3.3.1 Plutarch's *De Superstitione* and His Religious Thought 74
3.3.2 Plutarch's Use of *Deisidaimonia, Eusebeia* and *Eulabeia* 76
3.3.3 Plutarch's Use of *Deisidaimonia* in *De superstitione* and His
Religious Thought 78

3.4 Conclusion 80

3.4.1 The Use of *Deisidaimonia* Between the 1st c. BCE
and the Early 2nd c. CE 80
3.4.2 *Deisidaimonia* and the Grammar of Graeco-Roman Religion 81
3.4.3 *Deisidaimonia* in Acts 17 83

Chapter 4: *Deisidaimonia*, Piety and the Gods in Debate – Polemics Between Epicurean and Stoic Philosophers Around the First Century CE 85

4.1 Epicureans on Deisidaimonia, *the Gods, and Piety* 87

4.1.1 *Deisidaimonia* and Piety in Epicurean Philosophy 87
4.1.2 Epicurean Theology in Debate: The 'Harms' of Gods
Who Are Not Wrathful nor Favourable 96
4.1.3 Summary: The Epicureans on *Deisidaimonia* and Proper Piety ... 103

4.2 The Stoics on Deisidaimonia, *the Gods, and Piety* 104

4.2.1 *Deisidaimonia* and Piety in Stoic Philosophy 104
4.2.2 Stoic Theology in Debate: The Problems of Stoic Providence 116
4.2.3 Summary: The Stoics on *Deisidaimonia* and Proper Piety 120

4.3 Conclusions 120

4.3.1 The Philosophical Criticism of *Deisidaimonia* in Early
Post-Hellenistic Times 121
4.3.2 Stoic and Epicurean Philosophers on Traditional Religion
and Piety 126

Chapter 5: Something New in Athens – Godlikeness and Divine Justice in Light of the Resurrection (Acts 17:22–31) 130

5.1 Introducing the Subject: Deisidaimonia *and the
Unknown God (17:22–23)* 130

5.1.1 The Altar to the Unknown God and the Concern About
Hostile Gods 130

5.1.2 The Unknown God and the Subject of the Speech 132
5.1.3 Summary vv. 23–22 138

5.2 The Creator God's Relationship to Humanity (17:24–28) 138

5.2.1 The Impossibility to Serve the Creator God Along Traditional
Means (vv.24–25) 138
5.2.2 God's Arrangement of Humanity's Conditions to Seek Him
(vv. 26–27) 140
5.2.3 The Witness of Human Life (v. 28) 145
5.2.4 Summary vv. 24–28 152

5.3 False Divine Representations (17:29) 153

5.3.1. Preliminary Remarks on the Logic of Verse 29 153
5.3.2 The Divine and Man-Made Images 157

5.4 Divine Justice and Divine Representation (17:30–31) 160

5.4.1 The Universal Call to Repentance 162
5.4.2 Divine Judgment in Righteousness and the Risen Man 163
5.4.3 The Resurrection and the Proclamation of True Divine
Representation 168

5.5 Conclusion 171

Chapter 6: Conclusions – A New Interpretation of the Argument in Athens and Its Relation to Greek Philosophy 174

6.1 A New Reading and Coherence for the Speech:
Proclaiming the True Image of God 175

6.1.1 The Argument of the Speech 176
6.1.2 The Immediate Narrative Context 178
6.1.3 The Philosophical Teaching in Early Post-Hellenistic Times 178

6.2 The Speech and the Greeks: A Rapprochement with
Greek Philosophers? 179

6.2.1 No 'Significant' Rapprochement From a Philosophical
Point of View 180
6.2.2 A Speech 'at Home' in – and Engaged With – the Debates
About *Deisidaimonia*, Piety and Peace With the Gods
Among Stoic and Epicurean Philosophers 182

      6.2.3 A New Teaching in Athens: The Challenge of the Speech to
              Greek Philosophies..184

6.3   *Christology and the Proclamation of the Kerygma
      to the Gentiles in Acts* 187

6.4   *The Christian Movement, Graeco-Roman Culture and
      the Purpose of Acts* 191

Bibliography..195

Index of References.. 207

Index of Authors 216

Subject Index.. 218

Abbreviations

Abbreviations of biblical and other ancient writings generally follow the conventions in P. H. Alexander et al., eds., *The SBL Handbook of Style: For Ancient Near Eastern, Biblical and Early Christian Studies* (Peabody, MA: Hendrickson, 1999), and can be found in the index of references at the end of the present volume.

The additional abbreviations used are provided here for the reader's convenience.

EOD	"English Oxford Living Dictionaries." Oxford University Press, https://en.oxforddictionaries.com/english.
LSJ	Liddell, Henry George/Scott, Robert/Stuart Jones, Henry. *A Greek-English Lexicon*. 9th ed. with revised supplement. Oxford: Clarendon. 1996.
MC	Personal translation [Monique Cuany]
OCD	Hornblower, Simon/Spawforth, Antony, eds. *Oxford Classical Dictionary*. 3rd rev. ed. Oxford: Oxford University Press. 2005.
PHI	"Searchable Greek Inscriptions: A Scholarly Tool in Progress." The Packhard Humanities Institute, https://epigraphy.packhum.org/.
TLG	"Thesaurus Linguae Graecae: A Digital Library of Greek Literature." University of California, http://stephanus.tlg.uci.edu/.
TDNT	Kittel, Gerhard and Gerhard Friedrich, eds. *Theological Dictionary of the New Testament*. 10 vols. Translated and edited by Geoffrey W. Bromiley. Grand Rapids: Eerdmans. 1964.
TLNT	Spicq, Ceslas. *Theological Lexicon of the New Testament*. 3 vols. Translated and edited by James D. Ernest. Peabody: Hendrickson. 1994.
SVF	Arnim, Hans Friedrich August von. *Stoicorum veterum fragmenta*. 4 vols. Leipzig: Teubner. 1903–24.
Usener	Usener, Hermann, ed. *Epicurea*. Cambridge: Cambridge University Press. 2010 [1887].

Greek and Latin authors

Arius Didymus
Epit. *Epitome of Stoic Ethics*

Cicero
ND *De natura deorum (On the Nature of the Gods)*

Epicurus
Ep. Hdt. *Epistle to Herodotus*
Ep. Men. *Epistle to Menoeceus*
Ep. Pyth. *Epistle to Pythocles*
KΔ *Kuriai Doxai (Principal Doctrines)*

Lucretius
RN *De rerum natura*

Philodemus
P. Herc. 1251[On Choices and Avoidances]

Seneca
[Superst.] *[De superstitione]*

1. Introduction

1.1 The Areopagus Speech in Acts and Scholarship

The passage in Acts (17:16–34) depicting the apostle Paul debating with Epicurean and Stoic philosophers and delivering a speech to the Areopagus in Athens constitutes the oldest account of a confrontation between Christianity and Graeco-Roman religion and philosophy.[1] Situated in the ancient cultural capital of Greece and penned with literary skills which have often drawn superlatives from exegetes,[2] this well-known scene has become a symbol of the encounter between Christianity and Graeco-Roman culture and its wisdom.[3]

In the book of Acts, this pericope is indeed one of the two *sole* descriptions of a Christian speech delivered to a broader Gentile audience.[4] This quasi-unique status in a narrative which describes the spread of Christianity from Jerusalem (Acts 1) to Rome (Acts 28) led many past and current exegetes to the conclusion that the speech in Athens is 'the' or at least 'a' climax in the whole book. For example, in his landmark article published in 1939, Martin Dibelius wrote:

> The scene in the book of Acts in which Paul preaches to the people of Athens (17.19-34) denotes, and is intended to denote, a climax in the book. The whole account of the scene testifies to that: the speech on the Areopagus is the only sermon reported by the author which is preached to the Gentiles by the apostle to the Gentiles.[5]

---

[1] Following the current convention in scholarship, the author of the gospel of Luke and the book of Acts will be referred to as 'Luke' in the present work. For the sake of convenience, the passage of Acts 17: 16–34 will sometimes be referred to simply as 'Acts 17.'

[2] E.g., Harnack 1906: 321: 'das wundervollste Stück der Apostelgeschichte.' Cf. Mason 2012: 165–166: 'an author of considerable worldly knowledge and literary ability.'

[3] Conzelmann 1966: 217. Cf. Johnson 1992: 318: Luke made this account 'the exemplary meeting between Jerusalem and Athens, and the anticipation of the Christianized Hellenistic culture for which it provided the symbol.'

[4] Cf. the brief words addressed to the crowds in Lystra (Acts 14:15–17). As Soards (1994: 11) points out, the categorization of the speeches between mission- and trial- speeches in Acts is largely artificial, since the judicial speeches often contain the same elements as the *Missionsreden*. Hence the reference here to speeches to a 'broader' Gentile audience to distinguish them from speeches addressed to Gentile officials in trial narratives.

[5] Dibelius 1956a: 260. The German scholar also emphasized the style and compactness of the speech which suggest its importance.

Along the same lines, but proceeding more from an analysis of the structure of Luke's complete narrative and his theological purposes, Paul Schubert argued that the speech in Athens is 'the final climactic part of his exposition' because it 'is not only a hellenized but also a universalized version of Luke's βουλή-theology.'⁶ Less categorical about the climactic status of the speech in the book of Acts, Jacques Dupont nonetheless concluded that Luke had sought to make this pericope the climax of Paul's *missionary* career. For the Belgian scholar, the fact that Luke chose to situate Paul's discourse to the Gentiles in Athens, a city in which his ministry was clearly not as important as in Corinth and Ephesus, and which was not at all an important political place, shows that he wants to sketch a symbolic scene of significance: 'la rencontre du message évangélique avec la sagesse des Grecs.'⁷

Of course, past scholars have also been impressed by the compactness, the rhetorical flourish, and the sophisticated interaction with Greek philosophy displayed in the pericope of Acts 17. Clearly Luke seemed to have crafted this passage with particular care and thus given it a special importance. But above all, it is Acts' apparent concern with the spread of the gospel to the Gentiles and Paul as a 'light to the nations' (Acts 13:47) which played a crucial role in their assessment of the centrality of this pericope in the account of the first Christian historian.⁸

Today, few exegetes would argue that Acts 17 is *the* climax of Luke's narrative.⁹ There is indeed little in the overall structure of Acts to suggest that this pericope is climactic or even central in Acts.¹⁰ But it has remained a crucial text to assess how Luke situates or describes Christianity's position towards the Gentile world, a problematic which lies at the heart of the Lukan project and has been central in scholarship on Luke-Acts for at least two centuries. As Daniel Marguerat summarizes:

How does he situate Christianity between Jerusalem and Rome – or, alternatively, between Israel and the Roman Empire? Without exaggeration, one could say that the whole history of the interpretation of Luke-Acts unfolds from this problematic. Anyone who wants to

---

⁶ Schubert 1968: 260–61.

⁷ Dupont 1984: 384–385. Cf. Also Vielhauer (1966: 34) and Schneider (1982: 231).

⁸ The importance of this point is underestimated by Rowe, who concludes that the assessment of those scholars is due to 'the academic inclination of the interpreters in questions that has led them to value the explicitly philosophical speech above other parts of the narrative' (Rowe 2009: 191, n.82). For Luke as the first Christian historian, cf. Marguerat 2004.

⁹ See, however, Fitzmyer (1998: 601) who calls it a 'major speech,' and Schnabel (2005: 176) who describes it as 'a key passage in the Book of Acts.' Rothschild (2014: 1) speaks of 'a literary crest of the overall narrative.'

¹⁰ As Johnson (1992: 319) rightly notes: 'It is not the end of the book, not its singular climax, but another in a series of symbolic encounters between the word of the gospel and the many aspects of the world it was destined to transform.'

establish the theological aim of Luke's writing must first determine how the author positions Christianity in relation to Judaism and in relation to the pagan world.[11]

The pericope of Acts 17 has thus played an important role in scholarship's attempt to understand Acts' attitude towards the Gentiles, the Graeco-Roman world more generally, and thus Luke's overall purpose in writing the Acts of the Apostles.

For example, for Marguerat, Acts 17 is window on Luke's purpose to present 'a Christianity between Jerusalem and Rome' and illustrates his 'theological programme of integration.'[12] According to the Swiss scholar, the author of Acts has composed a speech which can be read from a Greek and a Jewish perspective until verse 31, thus underscoring that God is the God of the Greek and the Jew.[13] Luke uses this device of semantic ambivalence several times in his work in the service of his theological project of presenting 'Christianity as both the fulfilment of the promises of Scriptures and as the answer to the religious quest of the Graeco-Roman world.'[14]

Very differently, Jacob Jervell sees the speech as wholly condemnatory of the Gentiles. Not only so, but the discourse – which is the only substantial speech delivered to a broader Gentile audience in Acts – is *not* a missionary speech, for it does *not* present the gospel. For Jervell this substantiates his thesis articulated since the 1970s over against the then general tendency among scholars to read Acts as an anti-Jewish and pro-Roman document. Indeed, according to him, the book of Acts is not concerned with the progress of the gospel among Gentiles outside of the synagogue, but only among Jews and God-fearers.[15] According to this interpretation then, Graeco-Roman culture cannot in any way serve as a preparation for, or an ally in, the proclamation of the gospel. Only the Jewish context – i.e. the synagogue – and the Jewish Scriptures serve this function for Luke.

Another reading has been advanced recently by Kavin Rowe in an article published in *NTS* in 2011. Arguing against the interpretation of the Areopagus speech (Acts 17:16–34) as an attempt at theological rapprochement (*Anknüpfungspunkt*) between Christianity and Greek philosophy, Rowe proposes that it describes a fundamentally different grammar for the whole of life which conflicts with pagan tradition. The message presented by the speech in Athens is

---

[11] Marguerat 2004: 65.

[12] Marguerat 2004: 65–66. Marguerat develops this thesis in his essay 'A Christianity between Jerusalem and Rome' in Marguerat 2004, and in his commentary (2015).

[13] Marguerat 2004: 71–72.

[14] Marguerat 2004: 76.

[15] Jervell 1998: 455: 'Dies liegt daran, dass die Heidenmission für Lukas nicht mit der Areopagrede und dem ausserjüdischen Heidentum zusammenhängt, sondern mit den Gottesfürchtigen in den Synagogen. Lukas hat also die knappen Nachrichten aus dem Bericht des Paulus in Athen VV 16f. und 34 zu einer Szene ausgestaltet, die das Nein der Kirche zum ausserjüdischen Heidentum darlegt.' Cf. Jervell 1972.

thus fundamentally in conflict with Greek philosophical teaching. Rowe's article was an extension of his treatment of the Areopagus speech in his book *World Upside Down* (2009), where he defends the thesis that the book of Acts depicts the early Christian movement as subversive of Graeco-Roman culture, but emphatically innocent of political sedition.

A final example is provided by Joshua Jipp's article published in *JBL* two years later, where he contends that Luke has composed a speech which resonates with *both* Jewish and Greek traditions, thereby appropriating elements of Greek culture both to criticize aspects of it, and to exalt 'the Christian movement as comprising the best features of Greco-Roman philosophical sensibilities.'[16] Jipp points out that this reading corroborates other scholarly contributions on Acts which have highlighted the way Luke appropriates elements of Graeco-Roman script and culture, mimicking aspects of it in order to demonstrate that the Christian movement contains the best aspects of Graeco-Roman tradition and criticize competing movements.[17]

As those examples show, Acts 17 has become a window or a test case through which Luke's view of early Christianity's relation to the Gentiles and Graeco-Roman culture – including its politics, philosophy, and piety – is assessed; this perspective then is thought to shed important light on his literary purpose. At the same time, the strong differences and even incongruity between those interpretations of Acts 17 draws attention to the enduring conundrum which has marked the history of interpretation of this fascinating episode: the tension between the discourse's criticism of the Athenians' religion as 'ignorance' and idolatry, and yet the speech's apparent appeal to Greek philosophical religious common places to articulate the Christian message. As a result, the Areopagus speech's stance towards the Graeco-Roman world and pagan religiosity in particular has long been interpreted in very different and even radically opposite ways. At one end of the spectrum interpreters argue that the speech is to be understood along the lines of an anti-idol polemic denouncing the idolatry of the Athenians. The discourse is thus critical of Athenian religiosity through and through.[18] At the other end, the speech is interpreted as a discourse on the true knowledge of God which, building upon the 'inkling' of the notion of the true God demonstrated by Athenian religiosity and/or philosophy, presents the true and only God to the Athenians and corrects their misunderstandings.[19]

To shed new light on this enduring debate, the present project suggests a fresh perspective on this pericope based on a different approach to the 'Greek' material included in the speech. Before describing the approach taken in the

---

[16] Jipp 2012: 576 and 568 respectively.
[17] Jipp 2012: 569.
[18] E.g. Gärtner 1955; Dunn 1996; Jervell 1998.
[19] E.g. Dibelius 1939; Haenchen 1971.

present work, however, it will be helpful to discusses some of the ways past scholarship has interpreted the speech's use and allusions to Greek philosophy, and to assess whether those approaches have led to a convincing interpretation of the discourse in Athens.

1.2 Some Maine Lines in Past Scholarship

At least since the time of Clement of Alexandria (c. 150–c. 215 CE), exegetes have noticed the presence of Greek material and echoes to philosophy in the Areopagus speech.[20] Apart from the explicit quote from Aratus who is referred to as 'one of the poets' of the Athenians in v. 28, several motifs of the speech recall Greek philosophical formulations, such as the assertion that the divinity does not live in temples, that it has no need, or the reference to the divine appointment of seasons. While the great majority of exegetes in the 20th century has concurred that the speech in Athens is hellenized, there has been wide disagreement as to the extent or nature of this hellenization, and how it is to be interpreted in this pericope.[21] This section discusses some of the main ways this phenomenon has been interpreted since the early 20th century, highlighting some of the problems and methodological concerns created by past approaches but also how some contributions point towards a new possibility to examine this question.[22]

1.2.1 Jewish-Christian Grundmotiv and Stoic Begleitmotiv (Norden)

It is Eduard Norden who, with *Agnostos Theos* (1913), brought the question of the relationship between Jewish and Greek material in the speech to the fore of scholarly discussion. Norden saw the discourse in Athens as reflecting a tradition of mission speeches on the true knowledge of God. Highlighting the many parallels between the speech in Athens and the other speeches in Acts, he argued that the discourse is composed of a basic '*jüdisch-christliches*

---

[20] Clement of Alexandria's *Stromata* 1.19 is the earliest attestation to an identification of a quotation from Aratus' *Phaenomena* in Acts 17:28.

[21] 'Hellenization' is used in a broad sense, and includes, for example, the adoption of Greek form, argumentation, terminology or authors.

[22] The literature on this pericope is almost endless, but reviews of past scholarship remain almost non-existent, even in the two unique (!) monographs consecrated to this passage (Gärtner 1955; Rothschild 2014). To my knowledge, the most complete overview of scholarship is found in Zweck's unpublished dissertation, where he traces what scholars have said about natural revelation in Acts 17 (1985: 1–37). See also the overview in Dupont 1984: 396–403. Our analysis neither seeks comprehensiveness nor to differentiate between all nuances adopted by past exegetes. Rather it focuses on some of the major interpretations which have been or are still influential in scholarship, or contributions which are particularly helpful for our methodological reflection in the next section.

Grundmotiv' into which has been inserted '*ein stoisches Begleitmotiv*' which represents an adaptation of this basic motif to the Hellenistic audience at hand. This *Begleitmotiv,* expressed in verses 26–28, refers to the assertion that although the divine is invisible, its existence is revealed through the visible world, a common theme in Hellenistic philosophy and especially in Stoicism. According to Norden, the author of the speech inherited the practice of including Greek knowledge about the divine from Hellenistic Judaism, which often used support from Greek philosophers who had criticized popular conceptions of the gods in their anti-idol polemics. In particular, the Stoa and its pantheism provided an easy bridge to Jewish and Christian monotheism. For Norden, this arrangement between Jewish-Christian and philosophical motifs reflects an adaptation of the apostolic preaching to its Hellenistic audience, a practice which was anticipated in Hellenistic Judaism.[23]

Although several of Norden's other proposals in *Agnostos Theos* failed to convince exegetes,[24] his explanation of the speech in terms of a Jewish-Christian main motif into which are integrated Stoic motifs set the debate on the relationship between Jewish and Greek material in the speech on the agenda of scholarly discussion on the Areopagus for much of the 20th century, and many scholars were to view the relationship between Jewish and Greek motifs along similar lines.

1.2.2 A Philosophical Sermon on the Knowledge of God (Dibelius, Pohlenz, Balch)

While Norden had interpreted the philosophical material of the speech as a *Begleitmotiv* integrated in a typical missionary speech, Dibelius (1939) argued that the whole speech is a *philosophical sermon* on the true knowledge of God.[25] Departing from Norden's form criticism and the question of the influence of tradition on the speech, Dibelius began his analysis with the discourse itself which he saw as a '*sinnvolles Ganzes*' whose composition had been significantly shaped by the author. Starting with verses 26–27, he interpreted them as a reference to the manifestation of divine providence in the arrangement of the seasons and the habitable zones of the earth which, in philosophy, serve as proofs of divine existence and providence and 'are intended to induce men to seek after God.'[26] He thus concluded that the rest of the speech must also be interpreted against this philosophical background to become intelligible.

---

[23] Norden 1913: 29.

[24] Norden's thesis that Acts 17 was inserted in Acts by a second-century writer who composed it based on a speech from Apollonius of Tyana failed to convince exegetes. See especially Harnack's refutation (1913).

[25] Dibelius 1956b: 26–77.

[26] Dibelius 1956a: 34.

1.2 Past Scholarship

Dibelius did not deny that some themes in the speech come originally from the Old Testament, such as the affirmation that God is the creator of the world or that he does not live in temples. But he argued that those themes have been hellenized. For example, the speech uses the terminology of *cosmos* rather than the terminology of 'heaven and earth' as does the Old Testament. Likewise, the *via negationis* way of talking about God, such as the assertion that he does not need anything, although it came to be used in Hellenistic Judaism and early Christianity, originates from Greek philosophy rather than from the Old Testament. Dibelius also saw verse v. 28 as affirming a panentheistic worldview and thus depicting humanity's relationship with God in a way which totally departs from the Old Testament.[27]

Importantly then, for Dibelius, it is 'not only subsidiary motifs' which are derived from Stoicism in the speech, but its main idea, which is that knowledge of God can be attained through nature and humanity's inner knowledge of God. He thus concluded that 'the Areopagus speech is a Hellenistic speech with a Christian ending.'[28] This led the German scholar to the strange and now famous conclusion that the speech is 'a foreign body' not only in Acts but in the whole New Testament. For stylistic reasons, however, Dibelius nonetheless believed that the speech is the composition of the author of Acts who thus pens a paradigmatic sermon on how one should preach to the Gentiles around 90 CE.

Following Dibelius, several scholars continued to interpret the speech in Acts 17 as essentially describing a philosophical argument about the knowledge of God, although they sometimes challenged his interpretation of parts of the speech.[29] Most influentially, Max Pohlenz, who argued that the speech has strong similarities with the teachings of the Stoic Posidonius (c. 135 BCE – c. 51 BCE), presented several modifications to Dibelius' interpretation but concurred with him that the subject of the speech is 'eine heidnische Theorie der natürlichen Gotteserkenntnis.'[30] For him, the Christian speech simply overtakes this Stoic doctrine as an attempt to seek common ground with his Gentile audience, as its mention of the verse from Aratus in v. 28 demonstrates.[31]

In the decades which followed, Dibelius and Pohlenz were regularly criticized for underestimating the importance of the Old Testament background of the speech.[32] Furthermore, later scholars confirmed that the 'Greek' or 'Stoic' ideas identified in the speech were already present in Hellenistic Jewish

---

[27] Dibelius 1956a: 52. For Dibelius, what the speech affirms at this point has nothing to do with the OT idea that humanity is created in God's image.

[28] Dibelius 1956a: 57–58.

[29] Pohlenz 1949, Vielhauer 1950–1951, Eltester 1957, Hommel 1955.

[30] Pohlenz 1949: 95.

[31] Pohlenz 1949: 89–90. Note that Pohlenz points out that the speech uses Stoic teaching to teach the Christian God and not the Stoic one. The speech thus reinterprets Aratus theistically.

[32] See 1.2.3 and 1.2.4 below.

sources and apologetic, thereby suggesting a different context than Stoicism for their origin and their interpretation. With the move of scholarship away from source to redaction and narrative criticism, several exegetes also criticized this interpretation for reading the speech's argument within a Stoic framework and not within the new framework suggested by the speech and its context.[33] In particular, this interpretation overlooks the new framework of the speech created by the anti-idol polemic and its Christological climax.

Despite this criticism, some commentators still claim that Paul's speech is 'a reflection on Stoic theology'[34] or that the general 'intellectual background of the speech' is Stoic.[35] Furthermore, in recent years, a similar reading which takes better into account the polemical context of the speech has been advanced by David Balch. Balch argues that the speech presents a Posidonian Stoic argument over against contemporary Stoicism – represented by Dio Chrysostom (c. 40 – c. 120 CE) – which was characterized by a rapprochement with popular religion. He concludes that 'Luke-Acts guards the legitimate philosophical tradition against the Athenians who delight in novelties.'[36] This thesis, however, does not avoid all the criticisms mentioned earlier. In addition to these, it can also be pointed out that this interpretation does not explain why the Athenians perceived Paul to be propagating a 'new teaching' (v.19) if he was simply propounding Stoic doctrine, nor how the resurrection of a man who would judge the world would fit well with the attempt to 'guard the legitimate philosophical tradition.'

1.2.3 A Thoroughly Jewish Speech: Downplaying the Importance of Greek Material (Gärtner)

At the opposite of Dibelius' thesis, some exegetes have downplayed the importance of Greek elements in the speech, and interpreted the discourse as making an essentially Jewish argument.[37]

In 1955, Bertil Gärtner published a dissertation which, over against Dibelius and Pohlenz's interpretation, argued that the speech is to be interpreted against a Jewish and especially an Old Testament background. Gärtner contended that the adduced parallels with Stoic arguments and theology are deceiving because those arguments need to be examined in their contexts before they can be considered appropriate parallels. Methodologically then, Gärtner proceeded to

---

[33] E.g., Dupont 1984: 414.
[34] Walaskay 1998: 166.
[35] Pervo 2009: 430.
[36] Balch 1990: 79.
[37] In a different manner, in her recent book on *Paul in Athens* (2014), Clare K. Rothschild also downplays the importance of Greek philosophy but argues that the speech is rather to be interpreted in light of the traditions associated with Epimenides. Rothschild's thesis is idiosyncratic in scholarship and will not be discussed here. For a brief assessment, see Cuany 2016.

1.2 Past Scholarship

analyse different themes of the speech – such as the knowledge of God from nature, the conception of God or the polemic against idolatry – in the Old Testament, Hellenistic Jewish literature and Stoic writings, paying particular attention to their function and context in the theology represented in each literature. He concluded that while some of those themes and corresponding terminology can be found in both Jewish and Stoic literature, they do not function in the same way in both. Most importantly, the reference to the knowledge of God available from nature functions in Jewish literature to criticize false worship and idolatry (e.g. Wis 13–15) and not to build arguments about the existence of God as in Stoicism. Likewise, knowledge of God from nature in the Areopagus speech is not used to prove the existence of God like in Stoic arguments as claimed by Dibelius, but to build an anti-idol polemic.[38]

For Gärtner then, the matrix out of which the speech comes is clearly the Old Testament and Judaism more generally. Without denying that the speech contains philosophical terminology, nor that it displays a rapprochement with philosophical ideas which is otherwise not found in the New Testament,[39] Gärtner emphasizes the necessity to distinguish between the '*assimilation* between Christian and Gentile-philosophical doctrines' and 'a clear-headed *adaptation* to the listeners' phraseology that does not overshadow the specifically Jewish-Christian content.'[40] For Gärtner the speech in Athens clearly falls in the second category, an interpretation which he saw as confirmed by the Athenians' perception of Paul as a *spermologos*, which shows that they perceived him to be some kind of 'eclectic.'[41] The convergence of the argument with Greek philosophy is thus very limited and can be explained by the preaching style of diaspora Judaism.

Gärtner's contribution, with the article of Wolfgang Nauck discussed in the next section, played an important role in highlighting the importance of the Old Testament and Jewish background of the speech, and in challenging Dibelius' interpretation. He was, however, frequently criticized for underestimating the importance of the 'Greek' elements of the speech and his attempt to trace almost the entirety of the speech to a Jewish-biblical background failed to convince many exegetes.[42]

More importantly for our purposes, and although this has not often been pointed out, Gärtner examines the way those motifs are used in two traditions – the Old Testament/Jewish and Stoic – and does not consider the possibility that the speech could be doing something totally different and new with them

---

[38] Gärtner 1955: 169.
[39] Gärtner 1955: 71.
[40] Gärtner 1955: 72 (my emphasis).
[41] Gärtner 1955: 72.
[42] See, however, Stenschke (1999: 203–224) who interprets the speech almost with no reference to the Greek material.

in a Christian speech. Methodologically, it is not so much the *origin* of the different motifs and ideas of the speech which is key here to interpret it, but how the discourse *as it stands in Acts 17* compares to the teachings of Hellenistic philosophy at this time.[43] In this light, and from a narratival perspective, Gärtner's interpretation of the Greek material as reflecting a purely 'formal' or terminological adaptation does not sufficiently take into account the fact that the final form of the speech does sound strangely similar to some of the things said by Hellenistic philosophers and that in the narrative it is addressed *to an audience at least partly made of Hellenistic philosophers*. Not only so, but the speech itself appeals to the poets of the audience, thereby seeking some kind of common ground at least explicitly at one point. Consequently, interpretations of the speech which – like Gärtner's – seek to explain its elements by appealing to a Jewish or Christian framework which would have been unknown to the audience of the speech depicted by the author all create tensions for the narrative realism of the pericope.

1.2.4 The Mixed Nature of the Speech and Hellenistic Jewish Preaching (Nauck)

In his long article published in 1956, Wolfgang Nauck moved back to tradition and form criticism, and argued that both the content and the structure of the speech can be explained against the tradition of Hellenistic Jewish preaching.[44] His publication defended three major points.

First, criticizing Dibelius for going too far in attempting to explain some motifs against the background of Greek philosophy, Nauck argued that the speech is mixed and shows a very close connection between Old Testament and Greek motifs. Furthermore, the speech hellenizes Old Testament teaching, sometimes to the point that this teaching has been reinterpreted within a Greek framework. Thus, in v. 28 the Old Testament motif of the creation of humanity in God's image has been reinterpreted along the lines of the Greek motif of the divine kinship of humanity. For Nauck, Luke is not the author of this convergence and hellenization of motifs, but he inherited it from Hellenistic Judaism.[45]

Furthermore, Nauck argued that the Areopagus speech is structured along the schema of 'creation, conservation and salvation' (*Schöpfung – Erhaltung – Heil*), and claimed that this model can be found in the missionary practice of Hellenistic Judaism.[46] For him, the presence of this schema taken over from Hellenistic Judaism excludes the validity of Dibelius' proposal about the subject of the speech being Stoic theology, for it shows that the framework of the

---

[43] Pervo 2009: 430, n.51, mentions this problem.
[44] Nauck mentions that he finished his article before seeing Gärtner's publication.
[45] Nauck 1956: 122–23.
[46] Nauck 1956: 31. For a similar kind of argument, cf. Lebram 1964.

speech is Jewish, as Norden had claimed.⁴⁷ It also shows that the Stoic motifs of the speech probably came to Luke through the intermediary of Hellenistic Judaism, rather than through a reflection on Stoic philosophy directly.

Finally, Nauck argued that there were different theological currents in Hellenistic Judaism, some of them being very critical of paganism (e.g. *Sibylline oracles*), while others were more conciliatory (e.g. Aristobulus). For Nauck, Paul, in Romans 1, follows the first current, while Luke, in the Areopagus speech, follows the latter. The Areopagus speech thus differs from many antiidol Jewish polemics not only in tone, but also in theology, by showing more willingness to connect to Gentile knowledge about God and a more positive view on the possibility of knowing God among the gentiles.⁴⁸

Nauck's article played an important role in the history of interpretation of this pericope. After his publication, most exegetes accepted the mixed character of the speech, and criticized Dibelius for having underestimated the Old Testament and Jewish background of several motifs of the speech and Gärtner for not taking its Hellenistic material enough into account.⁴⁹ Consequently, most scholars moved away from attempts to explain the totality of the speech against a single interpretative background as Dibelius and Gärtner had done. Instead, continuing to try to trace the background of the different motifs of the speech, they debated the way those different backgrounds and this different material relate to each other. This sometimes took the form of trying to determine whether the Stoic or the Jewish background is dominant. In this respect, many scholars concurred with Norden and Nauck's conclusion of a Jewish *Grundmotiv* and a Stoic *Begleitmotiv*.⁵⁰

Another development since Nauck's article is that exegetes now usually trace the background or origin of the 'Greek' material of the speech to Hellenistic Judaism and not directly to Stoic philosophy.⁵¹ While this had already been suggested or assumed by Norden and Gärtner, it became a consensus after Nauck's publication.

What has convinced exegetes less in the long run is Nauck's attempt to explain the succession of motifs of the speech by the existence of a traditional

---

⁴⁷ Nauck 1956: 33.

⁴⁸ While Nauck criticizes Dibelius' thesis that the speech is a reflection on Stoic theology then, his interpretation of the argument of the speech remains very close to Dibelius', whom he frequently cites. For him, the speech is mild polemic and the Gentiles' worship is not singled out as darkness and total error. On the contrary, natural revelation has led them 'zum ahnenden "Begreifen" und Verehren Gottes' (Dibelius 56 f.; Nauck 43). As for the repentance called for, as Dibelius had argued, 'sie besteht letzlich in der Besinnung auf jene Gotteserkenntnis, die dem Menschen von Natur eigen ist' (Dibelius 55; quoted in Nauck 34).

⁴⁹ For the mixed nature of the discourse, e.g., Dupont 1984: 403; Fitzmyer 1998: 603; Marguerat 2015: 152.

⁵⁰ Schneider 1982: 235; Conzelmann 1987: 147.

⁵¹ E.g., Balch 1990: 53; Pervo 2009: 430; Dunn 1992: 230.

scheme in Jewish missionary preaching. Either they have questioned the existence of such a scheme in Jewish preaching,[52] or the assessment that the speech in Acts 17 follows such a scheme,[53] or they have drawn attention to the author's role in shaping the speech as a literary creation. This last element became more and more important in the latter part of the 20th century and influenced the way scholars approached the examination of the function of the Greek material in the speech. The next few sections discuss some of the ways they have understood this material to relate to the speech.

1.2.5 A Christian Speech: Reinterpreting Greek Philosophy Within a Christian Framework (Conzelmann)

Several exegetes could be examined under this category.[54] According to these scholars the Stoic or Greek motifs – already present in Hellenistic Judaism – are used in the service of the Christian message of the speech, and especially to proclaim Christian or Jewish monotheism. For several interpreters, this also means that the Greek motifs are given a new meaning within their Christian framework. Most obviously, the pantheism implicit in Stoicism, and implied by the quotation from Aratus, is interpreted in a theistic way. What happens in the speech is thus a kind of *interpretatio christiana* of the philosophical material, and this sometimes implies a modification of the meaning which it had in its original context.[55] To do so, the speech exploits 'points of contact' or 'points of congruence' between Greek philosophy and the Christian message. The congruence exploited, however, is limited to the first article of the creed, namely the doctrine of God.[56]

Thus, in his 1966 article Conzelmann concurs that the speech uses both OT and Greek motifs and that sometimes the speech capitalizes on the convergence of both traditions. Commenting on v. 28, the exegete argues that its pantheism refers to an idea which is not found in the New Testament at all and which is incompatible with the idea of creation. He suggests, however, that the author is unaware of the original meaning of Aratus' quotation and, like Aristobulus before him, has reinterpreted it to use it for 'the sake of the belief in the biblical story of creation.'[57]

---

[52] Conzelmann 1966: 226.
[53] Conzelmann 1966: 226; Conzelmann 1987: 148.
[54] E.g. Conzelmann 1966; Haenchen 1971; Dupont 1984.
[55] The phrase 'interpretatio christiana' is from Haenchen 1971: 529. For Haenchen this type of reinterpretation already took place in Hellenistic Judaism and was borrowed by early Christian authors. Although their interpretation of the speech differs on several points, Haenchen, Conzelmann and Dupont all suggests that such a reinterpretation takes place.
[56] Haenchen 1971: 530.
[57] Conzelmann 1966: 224, cf. 225.

Furthermore, in his conclusion Conzelmann draws attention to the role of the author in shaping the speech and the new Christian framework in which the different motifs appear. Asking how the different elements of the speech, including its Christian conclusion, are related to each other, Conzelmann is unconvinced by Nauck's proposal that there exists a scheme of *creatio-conservatio-salvatio* in Jewish literature.[58] Furthermore, for him the analogy with such a pattern breaks at the crucial point of the Areopagus speech which focuses on anthropology – namely man's proximity with God and his kinship with him. Rather, the structure of the speech is Luke's literary product and reflects his particular concern. It is constructed on the Christian confession of faith: 'one God, one Lord.' Conzelmann explains this structure by the context at hand: whereas to a Jewish audience it is sufficient to present Jesus since belief in one God is assumed, in a polytheistic context, the first article of faith needs to be affirmed. At the same time, this tripartite division also reflects Luke's concern in his work with the three parts of history, Jesus' resurrection inaugurating a new stage.

Conzelmann's explanation of the structure of the speech as the reflection of a Christian confession of faith and Luke's specific concerns had an important consequence on his assessment of the meaning of the Stoic and Jewish motifs in the speech. Indeed, the placement of those motifs within the 'framework of a given pattern of belief' has the result that those motifs' meaning undergoes a change and is now to be understood within Luke's Christian framework.

> By the literary application of current motifs within the framework of a given pattern of belief, the meaning of the various motifs themselves undergoes a change. Accessibility of the world in the philosophical gnostic sense is replaced by access to the relation with God through μετάνοια (repentance), knowledge of God in the sense of πίστις (faith). Luke evidently is fully aware of this change. We cannot miss the conscious harshness with which he stresses the strangeness of the doctrine of the resurrection at the end.[59]

Thus, for Conzelmann, not only does Luke not share the Stoic view of history, but, although he takes over some elements of the view of history expressed in Jewish apocalyptic, he also simplifies the division of history into three periods. Thus, Jesus' resurrection 'introduces a historical epoch fundamentally new compared with the former one' and in which salvation through repentance is proclaimed and required to avoid perdition.[60]

Conzelmann is representative of exegetes who underscore the particular Lukan new framework of the speech whose combination of motifs – independent of their origin – is used to serve the author's purpose. He thus notes not

---

[58] In his 1987 commentary, however, Conzelmann concedes that such a schema can be discerned in the *Prayer of Manasseh* (1987: 148).

[59] Conzelmann 1966: 228.

[60] Conzelmann 1966: 228–229; on this tripartite view of history in Luke's work, see Conzelmann 1960.

only important discontinuity with Stoic philosophy but also with Judaism. As he expresses in his 1987 commentary, this means that the speech cannot be understood simply through comparative material.

> We must also take note of the reduction which has occurred in the literary setting where these motifs now appear. The Stoic motifs, in other words, cannot be interpreted without some attention to the singular framework into which they have been inserted [...][61]

For Conzelmann, the 'Stoic' motifs are used for establishing points of contact with the audience in a missionary endeavour.

> It is clear that Luke enlists the service of philosophy in establishing a point of contact between the missionary message and the non-Christian world; it is also apparent that he goes considerably further than Paul in establishing the connection.[62]

Conzelmann thus advocates a reinterpretation of the 'Stoic' motifs along Christian lines in the speech, but still claims that the speech seeks common ground with the audience.

Conzelmann's insistence on the new 'Christian framework' of the speech to interpret its motifs is a crucial development in the assessment of the meaning of the 'Greek' elements of the speech and the relationship of the discourse with Hellenistic philosophy. The question Conzelmann fails to ask, however, is whether such a radical reinterpretation of 'Stoic' motifs would still have been perceived as a search for common ground by a *Stoic audience*. This is the crucial question which is raised by Rowe's recent publications (cf. 1.2.8).

1.2.6 Anknüpfung und Widerspruch: *Philosophy as Criticism of Graeco-Roman Religion*

Several scholars have emphasized that the connections the speech makes with Greek philosophy are at least partly used to *criticize* the Athenians' religiosity.[63] In particular the three main sentences of the speech – that God does not live in temples made by human hands, that he is not served by human hands, and that he is not similar to gold, silver and stone – are all negative and critical, and parallels to those assertions can be found in Hellenistic philosophy. For some scholars, then, one of the obvious functions of Graeco-Roman philosophy is to criticize Athenian religion. They have, however, drawn different conclusions on the speech's attitude towards *Hellenistic philosophers*.

---

[61] Conzelmann 1987: 148.
[62] Conzelmann 1987: 148.
[63] E.g. Haenchen 1971; Barrett 1974; Schneider 1982; Jipp 2012. The phrase 'Anknüpfung und Widerspruch' is the title of one of Bultmann's well-known essays (1946), where he discusses the connection (*Anknüpfung*) the New Testament makes with the natural theology of the Stoa, mystery religions and the gnosis.

Thus, some exegetes have argued that the speech's criticism is directed against Athenian religion rather than against the philosophers.[64] The speech uses Greek philosophy as an ally to criticize and denounce pagan religion. For example, Haenchen writes:

> What the speech attacks, with arguments from the philosophy of the Greek enlightenment, is the heathen popular belief and not the religion of the philosophers. If the speech is nonetheless directed to these philosophers, it is because Greek culture is to be exhibited in its highest representatives.[65]

As Haenchen's comment shows, one tension created by this reading is that the narrative seems to suggest that the speech is addressed to philosophers, or at least to an audience containing philosophers. For Haenchen, however, this is not an issue because Luke has not composed a 'real' but an 'ideal' account.

Other exegetes, however, have interpreted this as a sign that Luke uses Hellenistic philosophy not only against Athenian religion, but also to some degree against Hellenistic philosophers themselves. For Barrett, for example, the speech uses elements of Epicurean philosophy against Athenian religion, and then Stoics elements against the Epicureans, even though in the end both philosophical systems are condemned:

> Paul enlists the aid of the philosophers, using in the first place the rational criticism of the Epicureans to attack the folly and especially the idolatry of popular religion, and then the theism of the Stoics to establish (against the Epicureans) the immediate and intimate nearness of God, and man's obligation to follow the path of duty and of (true) religion, rather than that of pleasure. But all these propaedeutics come in the end under judgment: men must repent, for God has appointed a day in which he means to judge the world in righteousness, by a Man whom he has appointed, and raised from the dead (17:31).[66]

Differently, Jipp and Balch interpret the use of philosophy as a criticism of Athenian religion which includes the philosophers because they often continued to engage in traditional cultic practices themselves. The criticism therefore serves to ironically highlight and denounce the philosophers because they failed to hold consistently to their own teaching (Jipp) or to the teachings of a more 'orthodox' form of Stoicism (Balch).[67]

This later interpretation fits better the narrative setting of the pericope, which suggests that the speech's audience includes philosophers. It also makes better sense of the call to repentance in v. 30, which is addressed to *all*, and thus would have included the philosophers. Finally, this interpretation is also attractive because denouncing the self-contradiction and inconsistencies of

---

[64] Schneider 1982: 235.
[65] Haenchen 1971: 528. Cf. 525.
[66] Barrett 1974: 75.
[67] Jipp 2012; Balch 1990.

one's opponent was a very common rhetorical and philosophical practice in the ancient world.[68]

There are, however, two problems with this analysis of the Greek material. First, the reactions of the philosophers, both before the speech and at the end of it, do not seem to corroborate the hypothesis that Paul was using philosophical arguments against the philosophers. Rather, their first perception of him is that he is a *spermologos*, 'a proclaimer of foreign divinities,' and a teacher of 'a new doctrine' (vv. 18–19), and most react to the speech with laughter or loss of interest. This suggests that the philosophers did not understand the speech to be making mainly – or at least powerfully – such an accusation of self-contradiction.

More importantly, however, this interpretation fails to take into account that both Stoic and Epicurean philosophers advanced philosophical reasons not only for tolerating some traditional religious practices but sometimes even for encouraging them. They could thus claim that the divinity does not live in temples, that it is not served by human hands and that idols themselves are not gods, and yet find good reasons for expressing piety *at least partly* along those ways.[69] From the perspective of narrative realism then, it is questionable that the kind of arguments advanced by the speech would have confounded the Stoics or the Epicureans of inconsistency because they still engaged in some traditional cultic practices.

1.2.7 The Search For 'Common Ground' and 'Points of Contact' in the Service of Apologetic

Many scholars speak of the speech in Athens as an attempt to seek 'common ground' or 'points of contact' with the philosophers or the audience, mainly for apologetic and communicative purposes.[70] For example, for Dunn the speech starts as an 'apology for the Jewish understanding of God' which builds on points of contact with Greek philosophy, a practice which is in continuity with the methodology of Hellenistic Jewish apologetic.[71]

> The language used builds as much as possible on contacts with the wider philosophies of the time (particularly Stoicism) but is basically Jewish monotheism and creation theology presented in its universal implications.[72]

---

[68] This is well illustrated by Plutarch's anti-Stoic and anti-Epicurean polemical works, several of which bear a title evocative of this strategy (e.g. *On stoic Self-contradictions*). On the importance of living according to one's doctrine as a philosopher, cf. Plutarch, *Stoic. rep.* 1033AB.

[69] This is discussed in chapter 4.

[70] Barrett 1974, 1998; Dunn 1996; Schnabel 2005; Jipp 2012; Marguerat 2004, 2015.

[71] Dunn 1996: 236.

[72] Dunn 1996: 230.

In addition, some of those scholars emphasize that while the speech contains affirmations which show continuity with Stoicism, it also makes assertions which are in direct contradictions with it and thus discontinuous. Barrett writes:

> The human race *is* one, it *was* made for a special relation with God, and it *is* man's business to discern this relation and to live in accordance with it. So far the Stoics are right, and they can be used against Athenian scepticism, atheism, and flippancy. They know that life is real and earnest, and that men must feel after God. But they worship God in ignorance, and what lies ahead of the human race is not (as they think) an ἐκπύρωσις and a new beginning of the age-old cycle, but the judgment of the world through Jesus Christ.[73]

Likewise, in his article Schnabel analyses the Stoic and Epicurean doctrines about God, providence and judgment and outlines continuities and discontinuities with Luke's teaching in the speech.[74]

A little different, but still advocating an apologetic reading of the speech are Marguerat and Jipp's proposals, who argue that the speech is consciously built to echo both Jewish and Greek traditions. For Marguerat, Luke thus creates an 'apologetic masterpiece' and presents Christianity not only as the fulfilment of the promises of Scriptures but also as the 'fulfilment' of the religious aspirations of the Graeco-Roman world.[75] He thereby seeks to integrate the best elements of Jewish tradition and Graeco-Roman culture within Christianity.[76] At the same time, the author also aims to demonstrate the intellectual respectability of the Christian message, by showing that the knowledge and argumentation of its spokesman stands up to a comparison with Hellenistic philosophers.[77]

For Jipp, the echoes which resonate with both Jewish and Greek traditions in the speech serve both to criticize Gentile religion and to 'exalt the Christian movement as comprising the best features of Graeco-Roman philosophical sensibilities and therefore as a superior philosophy.'[78] In particular, like the philosophers, the speech rejects the veneration of images as 'superstition,' and demonstrates, by its argumentation, that Christianity is no 'crass superstition.'[79] Not only so, but because the philosophers usually still engaged in cultic practices even though they often criticized them, Luke demonstrates that 'the Christian movement embodies the philosophical elite's ideals better and more consistently than do the Athenians.'[80] The speech thus serves both as criticism and as 'a form of legitimation or propaganda' of Christianity.[81]

---

[73] Barrett 1974: 73–74. In his commentary he notes that Luke restricts 'the use of philosophy to those themes which it shares with the OT.' (2004: 826).
[74] Schnabel 2005.
[75] Marguerat 2004: 76.
[76] Marguerat 2015: 152–153.
[77] Marguerat 2015: 167.
[78] Jipp 2012: 568.
[79] Jipp 2012: 581.
[80] Jipp 2012: 576.
[81] Jipp 2012: 588.

18   *Chapter 1: Introduction*

Despite its popularity, this interpretation of the Greek material is more problematic than is recognized. Key to the assessment of those proposals is what exegetes mean by 'apologetic' and how they envisage the 'apologetic audience' of the speech.[82] Unfortunately, scholars rarely clarify such elements in their discussion. But if this apologetic discourse is addressed to an audience of outsiders, then this reading appears rather problematic.

Indeed, while a modern scholar might be tempted to consider that Paul's philosophical allusions are the 'best aspects' of Graeco-Roman culture or even of Hellenistic philosophical teaching about the divine, it is far from evident that the philosophers, the Athenians, or any outsider generally, would have shared this assessment. In fact, some commentators have pointed out that much in the speech is simply philosophical common place. If this is the case, then it is unlikely to have embodied the 'philosophical ideals' of the elite. More importantly, if the use of Greek philosophy serves such an 'apologetic' purpose of convincing outsiders, then why does the speech end with the shocking proclamation of a coming judgment by a man risen from the dead without smoothing this claim by making the resurrection more palatable or convincing to the audience? In fact, the reaction of the Greek audience with laughter and loss of interest, which exegetes usually assess to be a very realistic description of what would have happened if such a speech was given to a Greek audience, strongly weakens the proposal that Greek philosophy in the speech serves apologetic purposes. If Luke's aim was to present a 'respectable' Christianity to outsiders, he certainly failed in the narrative world he is portraying!

A more convincing interpretation is that the speech serves an apologetic function for insiders, and that Luke seeks to show to his Christians readers that their 'religion' also embodies the best of Graeco-Roman philosophy or is the fulfilment of it. Through the speech, Luke thus contributes to building or solidifying Christianity's self-definition, or its 'internal' legitimization.[83] A weakness of this proposal, however, is that in light of its lack of convincing power towards outsiders, one might wonder how useful such an 'apologetic' would have been for insiders. At best, it might have comforted Christians that they shared *some teachings* about the divine with some venerable philosophical traditions of the Graeco-Roman world, and, for example, that it was also opposed to *deisidaimonia*.

1.2.8 Christianity and Greek Philosophy as Rival Traditions (Rowe)

Like some of the interpreters examined earlier, Rowe also represents an exegete who does not deny philosophical echoes in the speech, but downplays their

---

[82] For an excellent discussion of the issues with the use of this term with respect to Acts, see Alexander 1999.

[83] That the book of Acts aimed to build Christian self-identity has become a common assertion in scholarship. Cf. especially Sterling 1992.

significance.[84] However, unlike previous exegetes who do so because those echoes are included within a Jewish anti-idol polemic or because they are limited to points of convergence with Jewish material, Rowe argues from the *nature* of ancient philosophy.

Thus, in his article published in 2011, Rowe challenged the interpretation that the Areopagus speech represents an attempt at theological rapprochement (*Anknüpfungspunkt*) between Christianity and Greek philosophy by proposing that it describes a fundamentally different grammar for the whole of life which conflicts with pagan tradition. For Rowe, the elements of the speech which have usually been identified as Greek philosophical concepts and terms cannot be interpreted as an attempt to *translate* the Christian message with Greek philosophical language and thus a rapprochement with Greek philosophy, because those terms do not have a Stoic or Greek philosophical meaning in the Christian framework of the speech. By incorporating this philosophical material into the speech, the speech gives it a new meaning. In other words, Paul does not seek a common ground with Greek philosophy, but *redefines* – and thereby *transforms* – the meaning of Greek philosophical words and concepts by using them within a new Christian hermeneutical framework. As a consequence, what might appear as a Stoic concept needs to be understood with a Christian meaning because Paul is mentioning it in the framework of Christian history, as his allusion to Adam, Jesus and judgment show. Thus, Rowe speaks of *collision, appropriation* and *transformation* to describe the encounter between the Christian and the philosophical way of life.

> What is at stake in the appropriation and transformation of pagan tradition is not a simple difference in theoretical viewpoint but the difference in the total configuration of life that emerges out of conflicting claims to truth about the ultimate origin and destiny of humanity.[85]

The message presented by the speech in Athens is thus fundamentally in conflict with Greek philosophical teaching. Rowe's article was, as noted above, an extension of his treatment of the Areopagus speech in his book *World Upside Down* (OUP 2009), where he defends the thesis that the book of Acts depicts the early Christian movement as subversive of Graeco-Roman culture.

As the present overview of past scholarship on the Areopagus speech highlights, Rowe's claim that past interpretations have generally understood the speech as an act of *translation* of the Christian message into Stoic categories or terminology lacks nuancing.[86] In fact, few interpreters use the language of 'translation,' and many speak rather of a 'Christian *interpretation*' or '*re-*

---

[84] Rowe 2011 and Rowe 2009: 27–41.

[85] Rowe 2011: 46.

[86] In his conclusion, Rowe speaks of the 'long tradition of reading Paul's Areopagus speech as a "translation" of Christian theological convictions into pagan philosophical terms' (Rowe 2011: 49).

interpretation' of the pagan philosophical material which is necessitated by the new framework created by the speech.[87] Rowe's article thus overlooks the extent to which several past interpreters have already emphasized the element of transformation of the Greek material in the speech, and the reading of the speech he advocates is thus not as different from several past interpretations as he suggests.[88]

What is new and crucial in Rowe's contribution, however, is the consequence he draws from this, namely his assertion that the speech cannot reflect an attempt of *rapprochement* with the Greek audience *in light of the nature of Greek philosophy*. Admittedly, his claim that past scholarship has usually interpreted the speech as 'an attempt at theological rapprochement' would again have benefited from more nuancing.[89] Indeed, as the present overview has also demonstrated, there are important differences among past interpretations and exegetes have disagreed both on the *extent* of this rapprochement – whether it is purely terminological, or extends to some theology – and especially on its *purpose* – whether it is a rapprochement intended simply to enable cross-cultural communication, to criticize, to build an apologetic, or really to transmit a doctrine of God. Rowe's assessment is correct, however, in the sense that when exegetes have attempted to explain *the cause or the purpose of the hellenization of the speech* and its use of Greek material in it (and not of the speech as a whole as Rowe suggests), they have indeed generally explained it as an attempt of rapprochement with the audience at hand.

It is this traditional interpretation which Rowe challenges by drawing attention to the nature of ancient philosophy as traditions and embedded ways of life which covered the totality of life. His latest book on Christianity and Stoicism – *One True Life* (2016) – picks up this theme. In this publication, Rowe underscores that ancient Stoicism was a complex tradition with a vision of life which was ultimately incompatible and incommensurable with the *Weltanschauung* and the practical life advocated by Christianity. As Rowe rightly emphasizes both in his article on the Areopagus speech and in this book, what is crucial to measure is how the speech and Stoicism are related to each other is their *grammar*, and not just conceptual or terminological similarity.[90]

---

[87] See 1.2.5 and especially Haenchen 1971; Conzelmann 1966; Barrett 1974.

[88] Exegetes like Conzelmann, Barrett or Schnabel all show an awareness of the reinterpretation which takes place in the interpretative framework of the speech.

[89] Rowe 2011: 31, 34.

[90] This remark does not represent an endorsement without reserve of Rowe's arguments in *One True Life* (2016). For a discussion of some of the problems with his thesis, see, for example, Jipp's review (2017). Rowe (2011, 2016) repeatedly uses the terminology of 'grammar', but never defines it. In analogy to its meaning in linguistics, the word is used in the present study in the sense of 'the basic rules which govern the way the concepts relate to each other in a particular tradition or worldview' or 'the whole system or structure of a particular tradition,

1.2 Past Scholarship

What Rowe's assertion implies is that true theological rapprochement between the speech in Athens and Greek philosophy could hardly have happened simply by adducing a common terminology or even common concepts. As he writes:

> In the deepest sense, readers of Acts who advocate for translation as the interpretive lens through which to see Paul's speech either fail to take ancient philosophy seriously as philosophy or unwittingly mistake bits and pieces of verbal or conceptual overlap for a pattern of life – or, alas, do both at once.[91]

It is this larger point made by Rowe which is his crucial contribution to the debate at hand. *Contra* Rowe, it must be emphasized that some past exegetes *have* shown awareness that Stoicism and Christianity are different and even incompatible 'philosophical systems,'[92] but no one, to my knowledge, has ever thoroughly drawn the consequences of this state of affairs, namely the fact that this implies that bits and pieces of verbal and conceptual overlap *were unlikely to have been understood as a theological rapprochement or even a rapprochement of any kind* by a philosophical or a Christian audience. Rowe's studies, however, pointedly raise this issue.

Rowe's interpretation has two advantages. First, it fits with the narrative context of the speech in which the philosophers' assessment of Paul suggests that he is exposing a 'new teaching'; and second, it takes seriously into account the nature of ancient philosophy in which meaning lay in the *grammar* of the teaching rather than in the use of specific terminology or concepts. At the same time, however, Rowe's exegesis of Acts 17 remains problematic for two reasons. First, Rowe does not provide a convincing alternative explanation for the *abundance* of 'Greek' sounding material in this speech.[93] For Rowe, in Luke's narrative, Paul uses this material because of his precarious situation on trial and to help him refute the charge of newness, while also being part of his effort to communicate with pagans with words they understand.[94] Those suggestions, however, do not account well for the degree of hellenization of the speech, nor for the fact that Luke's Paul does indeed seem to seek some kind of common ground with the philosophical background of his audience when he cites Aratus.

In addition, like several other interpretations, Rowe's exegesis raises issues for the verisimilitude of the narrative world of the pericope. Rowe is emphatic

---

including not only the semantics of its terminology and concepts, but their articulation in relation to each other to express this system.'

[91] Rowe 2011: 49.

[92] See especially those who underscore the continuity but also discontinuity of the speech with Stoicism, but also those who underscores that a reinterpretation is taking place in it.

[93] Jipp (2012: 568, n. 3) rightly makes this remark and suggests that Rowe has not sufficiently 'explained *why and for what reason* Paul's speech utilizes pagan traditions to the extent that it does.'

[94] Rowe 2011: 41–42.

that *Luke*'s audience – i.e. his readers – would understand that the 'one' referred to in v. 26 is Adam and the man risen from the dead is 'Jesus.' But it is unlikely that the Athenians in the narrative world of Acts would have been able to make such links, or indeed grasp the Christian interpretation of the speech suggested by Rowe. Like exegetes who interpret the speech purely against a Jewish background, Rowe proposes an interpretation of the speech which might well have been accessible to the Christian reader of Acts, but not to the Athenians in the narrative. If then Luke is concerned to create a plausible story in which Paul seeks to communicate effectively with his audience, Rowe's interpretation remains problematic.

1.2.9 Conclusion: Making Sense of the Hellenization of the Speech and Its 'Christian' Conclusion

As this overview has highlighted, although all exegetes agree that the Areopagus speech is hellenized, they have disagreed both on the extent of this hellenization and what this means both in terms of the relationship of the speech with Greek philosophy and the interpretation of the speech itself. Most importantly, past approaches to the speech have struggled to provide an interpretation of the discourse which accounts both for its apparent attempt to seek common ground and communicate with the audience, and its unambiguous denunciation of Athenian religiosity as ignorance and proclamation of a shockingly new Christian message at the end of the speech. Indeed, the extent of the problem with current approaches is well illustrated by their failure to explain how a speech which seems so concerned with proper communication and seeking common ground with its audience suddenly announces a coming divine judgment by a man risen from the dead.[95] The speech's careful cross-cultural approach thus concludes with the sudden proclamation of events which would have been shocking – if understandable at all – by a Greek audience. As Dunn comments:

> But such a hopelessly brief allusion to the distinctive Christian claims regarding judgment and resurrection would have been bound to meet with incomprehension and dismissal, and a lengthier exposition would have demanded too great a leap in basic assumptions and conceptuality for most.[96]

F. C. Baur had already well perceived the problem. Pointing out that the speech seeks common ground with his audience and shows admirable wisdom in teaching, he asks how such a gifted teacher could possibly 'drop' a teaching as offensive as the resurrection the way the speech does.

> This speech is commonly praised as a model of the Apostle's apologetic method, and of his wisdom as a teacher. But has it been also considered that these merits ought to appear in

---

[95] The 'remarkable adjustment to the environment' of the speech in Athens (Mason 2012: 165) is generally accepted by exegetes.

[96] Dunn 1996: 238.

recommending the chief idea which the speaker was anxious to enforce? [...] The speaker appeals, in support of one of the principal ideas of the speech, to the words of a Greek poet, thus showing how much he wished to find a common ground between himself and his hearers for mutual approximation. [...] Up to this point the speech proceeded as well as possible; and the result it aimed at was all but won, when, by a word dropped incautiously by the speaker, all was changed and he was cut short, it appears in the middle of the sentence he had begun.[97]

For Baur, this total lack of tact in introducing a teaching as 'offensive' as the resurrection clearly shows that the apostle could not possibly have delivered such as speech.

The conclusion of the speech, and its connection with the rest of the speech which has been so carefully hellenized, has thus long been a key interpretative problem in the study of the Areopagus speech. In fact, the logic of the speech as a whole has remained a puzzle. Some older scholars explained the enchainment of motifs and its strange climax by arguing that it reflects the typical structure of a mission speech.[98] A more common explanation has been that the speech is not fully reported or that it is intended as a summary of a much longer and detailed exposition.[99] Pervo, however, comments: '[a] cultured Greek would dismiss these brief words as a stylistically inadequate and muddled collection of clichés with an unexpected and improbable conclusion'.[100]

Building on Rowe's latest challenge and insight about the nature of ancient philosophy, however, the present project takes a new approach to the Areopagus speech which illuminates the relationship of the speech and Greek philosophy. It further suggests that this approach also sheds new light on parts of its argument and, above all, on its Christological conclusion.

1.3 A New Approach to the Areopagus Speech

The present project suggests that an approach which takes into account recent research on hellenization, Luke's concern for a narrative reflecting verisimilitude and the nature of ancient philosophy sheds light on the relationship between the Christian message and Greek philosophy, and illuminate important parts of the argument of the speech, including its conclusion.

1.3.1 Recent Research on Hellenistic Judaism and Hellenization

One of the surprising shortcomings of past interpretations of the speech in Athens, is their lack of methodological reflection on, and integration of, recent

---

[97] Baur 1876: 175–176.
[98] Nauck 1956.
[99] E.g. Dunn 1996: 231.
[100] Pervo 2008: 430.

scholarship on 'hellenization' in diaspora and palestinian Judaism.[101] It is indeed very rare for exegetes of this pericope to address this question methodologically and to mention relevant scholarly literature on this subject. This has led to mistaken assumptions and premature conclusions about the way the hellenization of Acts 17 should be interpreted and led to problems of interpretation.

For example, past scholarship on Acts 17 has too often assumed that the hellenization – i.e. the adoption of Greek form, argumentation, terminology or sources – of the speech in Acts 17 implied a rapprochement with the Greek audience or Greek philosophy. But as studies of Jewish diaspora and post-colonial studies have shown, what is important to assess the attitude of a text towards Greek culture is not its degree of hellenization or use of Greek motifs, but *the use to which those motifs are put*. Indeed, a minority culture can use elements of the majority culture not only to integrate it, but also to resist and criticize it.[102] Despite this, while some studies of the Areopagus speech have argued that 'Greek philosophical ideas' in the speech are used to criticize Greek culture, there is still a tendency to interpret this at least as a partial endorsement of Greek philosophy or as a rapprochement with it. But this needs not to follow.

Furthermore, and even more fundamentally, despite the well-accepted fact since Nauck that the 'Greek' elements of the speech can also be found in diaspora Judaism, many scholars still focus on distinguishing between Jewish and Greek elements in the speech. But if, as studies on both diaspora Judaism in its Graeco-Roman environment and Judaism in the land of Israel have suggested, all or most of Judaism was more or less hellenized in the timeframe which concerns us, the question of the cultural origin of the motifs – a central preoccupation in much past scholarship on Acts 17 – is both *difficult* and, most importantly, *irrelevant* to assess the attitude of the speech towards Greek philosophy.[103] In a truly Hellenized cultural environment, the supposedly 'Greek' ideas and terminology of the speech are in fact no more Greek than Jewish.[104] In such a context, what we might today be tempted to classify as 'Greek' arguments were probably by the time which concerns us simply common ways of expression in a Hellenistic world, a world of which both Jewish and Christian

---

[101] On hellenization in the Jewish diaspora, see for example Collins 2000 [1983]; Barclay 1996; Gruen 1998. On the hellenization of Judaism in the land of Israel, see above all Hengel's landmark study *Hellenism and Judaism* (1974 [1969]), whose main thesis has been largely corroborated by later studies (cf. for example, the collection of essays in Collins and Sterling 2001).

[102] Cf. Barclay 1996: 98: 'acculturation could be used to construct either bridges or fences between Jews and their surrounding cultures.'

[103] This point is also made by Aitken (2004: 340) in his recent assessment of Hengel's contribution: '...the occasional drive to determine whether an idea is Jewish or 'Greek' becomes obsolete when it can be both at once.'

[104] On the problems of the divide Jewish/Hellenistic as analytical categories in the study of the Hellenistic world, see the collection of essays in Engberg-Pedersen (2001).

communities were an integral part.¹⁰⁵ They were cultural elements which by that time were common to the whole Graeco-Roman region and the larger Hellenistic culture of which Jewish and Christian communities were an expression.

Admittedly, the speech in Athens is different from the speeches addressed to a Jewish audience in Acts and shows indeed a clear adaptation to its Greek audience. But that does not make the speech in Athens more 'Greek' than the other speeches. It only means that the speakers in Acts' narrative speak differently and use different arguments when speaking with different audiences. If the environment is thoroughly hellenized then, even the question of the 'use' of such motifs becomes irrelevant, since they cannot be identified as specifically 'Greek' motifs anymore.

In light of such considerations, the present project will not at all focus on determining the Greek or Jewish origin of the motifs or terminology used, nor will it attempt to identify in any systematic way parallels to its ideas in Greek or Jewish literature as is generally done in scholarship on this pericope. Rather, it will proceed from the presupposition that the environment was sufficiently hellenized to make such questions irrelevant. Instead, the speech will be examined as a *Christian* speech which is addressed to a Greek audience. This brings us to the next methodological presupposition of this project, namely that Luke is concerned with the verisimilitude of his narrative.

1.3.2 Narrative and Verisimilitude in Acts

Following many scholars, this study takes a narratival approach to the book of Acts and presupposes that individual passages of the book find meaning within the broader context of Luke's literary project.¹⁰⁶ This has two important consequences for the study of the speech in Athens specifically. First, it implies that the immediate narrative context of the discourse plays a key hermeneutical role in the interpretation of Acts 17, something which recent studies have also underscored. And second, it means that the narrative of Acts *as a whole* provides an interpretative framework for the speech, since Acts 17 is part of a

---

¹⁰⁵ So Gruen 1998: 292: 'Jews remained true to ancestral traditions, the faith of their fathers, and the sanctity of the Scriptures. But they found themselves cheek by jowl with Hellenistic communities in Palestine, and they were part and parcel of Hellenistic societies in the Diaspora. The Jews were not as much permeated by the culture of the Greeks as they were an example of it. This made it all the more important to exhibit the features of their own legacy in the terms and language of their adopted one.'

¹⁰⁶ See, in particular, Rowe 2019, whose thesis is built on the study of a selection of individual passages in Acts, but from a narrative perspective. For a narratival approach applied to the whole book of Acts, see for example the commentary by Marguerat (2007, 2015), or the commentary on Luke-Acts by Tannehill (1986, 1990).

unified literary project. The reader thus encounters the pericope in Acts 17 with the hermeneutical lenses provided by the story.[107]

More specifically in the present case, this means that the speech in Athens is read with an awareness of the content of the narrative and apostolic preaching preceeding it. Scholars have long noticed that several themes are almost systematically repeated in the speeches.[108] Even Acts 17, which – as mentioned earlier – has been called a *Fremdkörper* in Acts, betrays similarities to the other speeches.[109] At the same time, exegetes sensitive to the narratival structure of Acts have noticed that the speeches also re-emphasize, complete or clarify the content of previous speeches in the narrative.[110] They seem to be intended to illuminate each other. A narrative approach to Acts 17 will thus assume that the reader encountering the speech has in mind the Christian message proclaimed by Paul and others characters elsewhere in Acts, and that the story as a whole informs his reading of this pericope.

In keeping with this narratival approach, then, this study begins with a chapter examining in detail the immediate narrative framework of the speech. Furthermore, while space constraints prevent a detailed comparison of Acts 17 with other passages of Acts, this project does appeal to other parts of Acts – and in particular to other speeches – to illuminate the pericope or defend some of its particular readings.

Importantly, however, and in distinction to some narrative approaches to this passage, the narratival perspective adopted in this study is used in conjunction with a focus on the analysis of the historical background alluded to by the pericope. Indeed, there has been a tendency in some narrative approaches to overemphasize the literary aspects of the narrative at the detriment of the

---

[107] Cf. Rowe 2009: 10–11: 'To speak of a *literary* project is already to say that over against the tendency to think of Acts' theology in bits and pieces we reject the idea that the passages treated in the coming chapters were read in isolation. As an increasing number of scholars are coming to affirm, to write a *story* is to give the hermeneutical direction, "read this as a narrative." Thus is this work interested in the cumulative or total effet of the passages treated in the body of the book.'

[108] Those repetitive elements of the speeches or the so-called 'Grundschema' have been analysed and discussed in many scholarly contributions. For a brief discussion of some approaches, see Soards 1994: 10–11. Soards (1994: 162–208) himself offers a detailed analysis of those repeated elements.

[109] Despite the assertion that the Areopagus speech differs significantly from the other 'missionary' speeches in Acts (e.g. Dibelius), many scholars have identified similarities of themes between Acts 17 and other parts in Acts. For example, Schubert (1968: 253–261) identifies precedents to the speech earlier in the narrative and discusses how those other passages illuminates the argument of the speech. For a more recent analysis of Acts 17 with an eye on the content of other speeches, see Soards 1994: 96–100.

[110] See especially Tannehill (1991: 401): 'The speeches are also complementary, for they supplement each other, one expanding a particular theme and providing supporting detail, another expanding a different theme.'

historical context presupposed by the narrative. In the case of the speeches, this has regularly taken the form of the assumption that the speeches are addressed to the readers of Acts, and need not to be understood as addressed to the audience of the speech in the narrative.[111]

Against such approaches, it is the fundamental starting hypothesis of this project that Luke has created a speech appropriate to its situation in Acts 17. There is widespread agreement in scholarship today that Luke's authorial hand stands behind the speeches in Acts.[112] That narrative verisimilitude was a concern in his work is suggested by several factors: the literary theories of narrative criticism itself, the widespread assessement that Acts belongs to the genre of historiography, and previous analyses of Luke's speeches in context. Indeed, the study of narratives in light of literary theories suggests that individual speeches need to be investigated within their narrative settings.[113] Futhermore, from the perspective of genre criticism, there is sufficient evidence that ancient historians argued that good historiography needed to include speeches appropriate to the audience and situation at hand.[114] The passages from Thucydides and Lucian which articulate this 'historiographical rule' have now become famous:

As to the speeches that were made by different men, either when they were about to begin the war or when they were already engaged therein, it has been difficult to recall with strict accuracy the words actually spoken, both for me as regards that which I myself heard, and for those who from various other sources have brought me reports. Therefore the speeches are given in the language in which, as it seemed to me (ὡς δ' ἂν ἐδόκουν μοι), the several speakers would express (τὰ δέοντα), on the subjects under consideration, the sentiments most befitting the occasion, though at the same time I have adhered as closely as possible to the general sense of what was actually said. (Thucydides 1.22.1 [LCL])

If a person has to be introduced to make a speech, above all let his language suit his person and his subject (μάλιστα μὲν ἐοικότα τῷ προσώπῳ καὶ τῷ πράγματι οἰκεῖα λεγέσθω), and

---

[111] To name only a few, this is the assumption of Schneider 1980: 97, Pervo 2008: 74, or Rowe 2009: 10. *Contra* Tannehill 1991: n. 4, p. 4 (see n.113 below).

[112] Scholars debate on whether and how Luke used sources for his narrative and his speeches, but not on the fact that his hand lies behind the speech in their actual form.

[113] Tannehill 1991: 400. Tannehill also emphasizes the role of the speeches within the plot of Acts' narrative. He notes: 'Isolating the common pattern from the narrative settings of the speeches encourages the idea that these speeches are really directed to a general audience, including the readers of Acts. However, the reading experience is truncated if we do not recognize that the individual speeches are actions within particular situations and produce particular effects. Alghough Acts as a whole may have significance for its readers, the speeches are not made directly to them. Readers experience a speech along with its situation and result in the narrative, which are part of the total reading experience and rightly affect one's understanding of a speech's significance.' (n.4, p. 401).

[114] The view that Acts belongs to the genre of historiography still remains the dominant position in scholarship. For recent summaries of the state of the question in scholarship, see Adams 2012; Phillips 2006.

next let these also be as clear as possible. It is then, however, that you can play the orator and show your eloquence. (Lucian, *How to Write History* 58 [LCL]).

The importance of this rule is corroborated by Dionysius of Halicarnassus' criticism of Thucydides precisely because on several occasions the speeches in his history do not sit well with the situation he describes.[115] Clearly, plausibility and verisimilitude seem to have been, in theory at least, an important criterion in ancient historiography, even if Dionysius' criticism shows that historians did not always succeed in producing such speeches in the eyes of their critics. What has been debated in scholarship, is the extent to which ancient historians respected this practice, and whether Luke always composed speeches appropriate and relevant to their narrative context. Thus, Eckhard Plümacher followed Dibelius and argued that the speeches in Acts, like those in Graeco-Roman historiography, are loosely fitted to their context and sometimes even conflict with the surrounding material.[116] For both exegetes, the Areopagus speech in Acts 17 was a case in point. Marion Soards, however, challenged this view and contended that the speeches in Hellenistic historiography, while they 'may be vague and unnecessarily lengthy,' nonetheless 'sill speak *around* the central concern that led to the delivery of the speech.'[117] Furthermore, Soards argued that Plümacher had underestimated the degree to which Luke has adapted the speeches to his characters.[118] He did, however, concur that the speeches in Acts often change the subject and seem to introduce material irrelevant to the situation.[119]

Despite those reserves, several scholars emphasize the care with which Luke has crafted speeches adapted to the speaker and the audience of the speech.[120] Marguerat goes as far as claiming that 'the Thucydidean rule is applied to the letter in Luke, who shows an impressive care for verisimilitude in the reconstruction of the oratory art.'[121] For those reasons, the starting hypothesis of this project is that Luke has crafted a speech which does justice to the verisimilitude of his narrative. Correspondingly, it will be necessary to also take into account more seriously the fact that the speech is addressing not only a Greek audience but also Epicurean and Stoic philosophers.

---

[115] *De Thucydide* 42–46; cf. Thucydides, *Peloponnesian War* 2.60–4.
[116] Plümacher 1972: 138–139.
[117] Soards 1994: 142. Emphasis his.
[118] Soards 1994: 142.
[119] Soards 1994: 142.
[120] E.g. Tannehill 1991; Marguerat 2004: 14, 17–19. On the adaptation of the basic scheme of preaching in Acts to the situation at hand, see also Rese 1984: 344.
[121] Marguerat 2004: 19.

1.3.3 A Re-Examination of the Teachings of Stoicism and Epicureanism

In light of Rowe's emphasis about the nature of ancient philosophy as complex traditions, this project also proceeds to a more thorough examination of Stoic and Epicurean teaching on the divine and piety. Indeed, although exegetes have long identified many parallels to Stoicism and even Epicureanism in the speech, to date no analysis of the speech has examined in details what Stoic and Epicurean philosophers taught about proper piety, or even divine images.[122]

Furthermore, the descriptions of the Stoic and Epicurean attitude towards traditional Greek religion or their theology in those discussions are regularly incomplete and even inaccurate. For example, most of the time Epicurean views on traditional religion and piety are simply overlooked in the analysis of this passage.[123] When they are discussed, usually minimally, commentaries often assume that Epicureans were wholly critical of Greek religion and/or materialistic in the modern sense of the term.[124] This is simply inaccurate. Similarly, in the case of Stoicism, even though exegetes regularly point out that the attitude of the Stoics towards traditional religion was usually more conservative and accommodating, it is still common in discussions on Acts 17 to focus on their criticism of divine images or temples. Those interpretations partly reflect the way scholarship has understood the attitude of Hellenistic philosophy towards ancient religion in the past century, namely as critical or accommodating but in tension with it. In recent decades, however, new and more nuanced paradigms have been advanced to understand the relationship between philosophy and religion in the ancient world.[125]

For those reasons, this project re-examines the teaching of Stoicism and Epicureanism on piety and traditional religion in the first century. The popularity of Stoicism in the early Roman empire is well attested, and some recent studies also suggest that Epicureanism was more widespread and well-known than has sometimes been assumed.[126] There are thus good reasons to believe that both Luke and his more educated readers would have been familiar with their basic teachings on this subject, and perhaps even with some of the nuances of their debates.

---

[122] Instead, studies have focused on their teaching on knowledge of the divine.

[123] Concerning the religious opinions of the Epicureans, Fitzmyer (1998: 604) simply notes that the Epicureans believed that 'the cosmos is the result of chance, and that there was no such thing as a provident god.'

[124] Johnson 1992: 313: 'Their commitment to a Democritean explanation of reality in terms of atomic particles was connected to a resolute rejection of religion.' Walaskay 1998: 165: 'The Epicureans were pragmatic atheists who taught that belief in the gods is not particularly useful, especially in light of life's inevitable sufferings. Even if the gods do exist, they obviously do not care much about human beings.'

[125] See, for example, Van Nuffelen 2011 or Opsomer 1996.

[126] Erler 2009; MacGillivray 2012. On the role of philosophy in the Imperial period more generally cf. Trapp 2014.

1.4 Outline and Structure of the Argument

As described earlier, methodologically, this study seeks to balance the narrative approach of many current studies of Acts 17 and to build upon Rowe's recent warning concerning the nature of ancient philosophy through an in-depth study of the historical context suggested by the immediate narrative framework of the speech in Acts 17.

The second chapter provides support for this approach through an analysis of the narrative framework of the speech and its very beginning (17:16–23). It argues that the diverse elements composing it neither support readings which emphasize the continuity of the speech with Greek philosophy, nor those who deny the philosophical atmosphere of the pericope. Rather the narrative itself suggests that the immediate context leading to the speech is *a debate with Epicurean and Stoic philosophers on the subject of divine images and appropriate worship or piety*. This context suggests that it is necessary to examine the teaching of those philosophical schools on those topics to understand the argument of the speech and its relation to Graeco-Roman philosophical teaching.

The third chapter sheds light on the Greek religious context of the pericope by focusing on one particular element of the *captatio* of the speech which has played a key role in assessing its subject and Luke's evaluation of Athenian religiosity in past scholarship: the characterisation of the Athenians as *deisidaimonesterous* (v.22). Highlighting the methodological problems of past studies on *deisidaimonia*, this chapter challenges the current scholarly consensus that the word means either pious/religious or superstitious. By offering the first synchronic semantic study of primary sources focusing on four contemporary authors (Diodorus Siculus, Strabo, Josephus and Plutarch), this chapter offers a new interpretation of the word which takes into account the particular grammar of ancient Graeco-roman religion, and demonstrates how this new understanding not only sheds light on the Lukan characterization of the Athenians, but also reframes the subject of the speech in Acts 17 as not just the nature of the divine as assumed in past scholarship, but the question of divine wrath against humanity and peace with the gods.

The fourth chapter focuses on the meaning and criticism of *deisidaimonia* among Stoic and Epicurean philosophers in early Post-Hellenistic times, and more broadly examines the teaching of those philosophical schools on the traditional cult, divine images, and proper human attitude towards the divine (i.e. what they called piety). Again, this chapter offers the first extensive synchronic study of the terminology and concept of *deisidaimonia* among those two philosophical schools – using primary sources such as Philodemus, Lucretius, Seneca, Epictetus, Cicero and Plutarch – and challenges the common scholarly assumption that the philosophical criticism of *deisidaimonia* focused on traditional religion, superstition or the veneration of images. Instead, it argues that the philosophers denounced *deisidaimonia* as an inappropriate and unnecessary fear of the gods, reflecting a misunderstanding about their nature as evil. This chapter also highlights that Stoic and Epicurean philosophers, far from being as critical as is often claimed, did actually integerate, reinterpret and sometimes even defend features of the traditional cult, including the use of divine images. In fact, both schools had not just excuses, but rationales for such practices. At the same time, they both argued that true piety is above all expressed by having correct notions about the gods as good and uninvolved in evil, and by imitating their nature. Those elements will have important consequences for understanding the specific line of argument of the speech and whether it constitutes a rapproachment with those philosophical schools.

The fifth chapter then re-examines the argument of the speech in Acts 17:22–31 verse by verse. Drawing on the results of the historical analysis of the previous chapters at several points, it suggests a new reading of the logic of the speech, and argues that its thrust is not the proclamation of the true God of the Old Testament, as the current and longstanding scholarly consensus affirms, but of the true image of this creator God, in the context of a debate about averting divine hostility and peace with the divine. This chapter thus demonstrates that the Christological climax which announces divine judgment through a resurrected man is not only closely connected with the rest of the speech, but actually constitutes its very climax.

As the conclusion, chapter six draws the results of the pervious chapters together and shows how they suggest new answers to the two longstanding questions of scholarship with respect to this pericope, namely the coherence of the speech and its relationship to Graeco-Roman philosophy. It also discusses the significance of those results for an assessment of the nature of the Christian message to the Gentiles in the book of Acts, and for an evaluation of Luke's attitude towards Graeco-Roman culture and his apologetic purposes in the book of Acts.

2. Setting Up the Debate – The Immediate Context and Beginning of the Speech (Acts 17:16–23)

The narrator devotes no less than six verses in setting up the stage for Paul's discourse (17:16–21), suggesting that he has crafted the context of the speech with particular care. While scholars have long noticed the sophistication of this introduction, they have not always taken it into account in their interpretation of the speech. In recent years, however, several studies privileging a narrative approach have re-emphasized the hermeneutical function of this part of the narrative to analyse this pericope and engaged in a detailed examination of its elements.[1]

This chapter re-examines the narrative introduction and the beginning of the speech (17:16–23) in order to establish its exact context and thereby provide a rationale for the approach taken in this project. It argues that both the interpretations which emphasize the speech's continuity with philosophical notions about the divine and those which deny the importance of the philosophical context of the pericope are problematic in light of this introduction. Indeed, three prominent elements in this narrative set-up need to be taken into account in its interpretation: the conflict and perception of newness brought about by the Christian message in Athens, the debate with Stoic and Epicurean philosophers which led to the speech, and the beginning of the speech which suggests that the question at stake is not only the nature of the divine, but more precisely the human relationship with the divine or more generally proper worship or piety. Based on those elements, this chapter suggests a new approach to the speech.

2.1 The Occasion of the Speech: Collision and Newness in Athens

The narrative context of the speech speaks against interpreting it as a discourse seeking to emphasize Christianity's shared conceptions of the divine with the Athenians or their philosophers. Indeed, according to the narrative, neither Paul, nor the Athenians or their philosophers perceived each other along favourable lines. Rather, the setting suggests a collision between the Athenians and Paul

---

[1] Rowe 2009; Rowe 2011; Jipp 2012.

because of his new teaching, and an examination of the apostle before the highest political instance in Athens.

2.1.1 Paul's Reaction to Athenian Worship (vv. 16–17)

The first indication of a conflict in Athens is provided by the reaction of the apostle when he contemplates the city.

> While Paul was waiting for them [i.e. Silas and Timothy] in Athens, his spirit was provoked (παρωξύνετο) within him as he saw that the city was full of idols. (v. 16)

Παρωξύνετο is translated by a wide range of expressions in the literature, including 'quite annoyed,'[2] 'quite disturbed,'[3] 'deeply distressed,'[4] and 'enraged.'[5] An analysis of the use of the word in a sample of contemporary Greek literature and in the LXX, however, suggests that the verb is not used to refer to emotions such as pain, distress, grief, trouble or pity.[6] Rather, it describes irritation, anger or provocation.[7] Verse 16 thus describes a Paul irritated or angry.[8] His negative reaction at a city 'luxuriant with idols,' to use Wycherley's now famous translation of κατείδωλος, corresponds to the narrative's negative stance towards idolatry so far in Acts (e.g.,14: 8–20), and fits the Jewish attitude towards idols.[9] The use of the word εἴδωλον itself suggests that the author embraces the Jewish derogatory view of idols, for the Greeks did not usually call their divine images εἴδωλον, but ἄγαλμα.[10] An εἴδωλον, for the Greeks, referred to a phantom, or any kind of unsubstantial form. It was used to describe an image reflected by a mirror, an image of mind, or the unsubstantiated

---

[2] Fitzmyer 1998: 599.
[3] Pervo 2008: 423.
[4] NRSV, Cf. NIV; Rowe 2008: 28; Gaventa 2003: 248.
[5] Haenchen 1971: 515. Schneider 1982: 232: 'zornerfüllt.'
[6] This is based on a study of the use of the word in Josephus's *Jewish Antiquities* 1–5 (11x), Diodorus Siculus (51x), Epictetus (1x) and the LXX (52x).
[7] See also LSJ, s.v. παροξύνω, which lists 'to urge, spur on, stimulate,' and 'to provoke, irritate.' In light of Luke's familiarity with the LXX, it is also interesting to note that out of the 52 occurrences of the verb παροξύνω in the LXX, it appears over 40 times in the context of a contention between human beings and God. Sinners 'anger' or 'scorn' the Lord, or the Lord is 'angered' by the wickedness or the idolatry of his people or humanity more generally.
[8] Marguerat 2015: 154: 'son esprit est au paroxysme de l'indgnation.'
[9] The word κατείδωλος is a *hapax legomenon* in the NT. Wycherley (1968) argues that it should be translated as 'luxuriant with idols' with the sense that Athens was a 'veritable forest of idols.' On the abundance of idols in Athens, cf. Livy 45.27.11 and Pausanias 1.17.1.
[10] εἰκών refers more generally to images, while ἄγαλμα refers specifically to statues of deities. Although εἴδωλον occasionally appears in the fifth century BCE to describe a statue (for example, the image of the dead ruler in Herodotus 6.58), it does not acquire a widespread usage as a term for cultic statues outside of the Jewish context. Cf. Stewart 2003: 25–8.

shadowy form of the dead in Hades. The use of κατείδωλος to describe Athens thus carries the usual Jewish negative connotations attached to idols.[11]

Paul's angry reaction at the view of the abundance of idols in Athens sets up the broader context of his discourse there. The conjunction οὖν in v. 17 indicates that his irritation influenced his decision to debate [διελέγετο] both at the synagogue with Jews and God-fearers, and every day on the marketplace with whomever happened to be there – a strategy which the apostle had never used before in the narrative. The mention of the σεβάσματα – i.e. the objects of awe or worship – Paul observed in Athens at the beginning of the speech (23), and the reference to idols in v. 29 confirms the importance that this first reaction has for the whole pericope.

2.1.2 The Athenians' Perception of Paul and His Message (v.18)

The Athenian perception of Paul and his message further suggests an atmosphere of conflict, or at best, a strong discontinuity between the Christian message and the Athenians' own teachings and philosophies.

τινὲς δὲ καὶ τῶν Ἐπικουρείων καὶ Στοϊκῶν φιλοσόφων συνέβαλλον αὐτῷ, καί τινες ἔλεγον· τί ἂν θέλοι ὁ σπερμολόγος οὗτος λέγειν; οἱ δέ· ξένων δαιμονίων δοκεῖ καταγγελεὺς εἶναι, ὅτι τὸν Ἰησοῦν καὶ τὴν ἀνάστασιν εὐηγγελίζετο. (18)

The philosophers' perception of Paul is divided. Some describe him as a *spermologos* and others as a 'messenger of foreign divinities.' The word σπερμολόγος literally means 'picking up seeds,' and refers to a type of bird which eats seeds. When used metaphorically to describe a person, the meaning of the word is more difficult to determine and it seems to have been used with different nuances.[12] At times it seems to simply refer to a 'good-for-nothing who wanders about the market and collects the scraps and debris scattered here and there.'[13] At other times, it designates a gossip or a babbler.[14] For example, Demosthenes (*Cor.* 18.127) denounces his accuser Aeschines who does not plead against him like the righteous Rhadamanthus or Minos, but like a *spermologos* and market-place loafer, who uses pompous words to accuse him. He is a calumniator and a poser who pretends to be cultivated but is destitute of education. Another example is provided by Dio Chrysostom (*Or.* 32.9) who denounces the Cynics who post themselves at street-corners, in alley-ways and

---

[11] *Contra* Rothschild (2014: 28, n.18) who translates κατείδωλον as 'chock-full of monuments' and writes: 'Although common in the LXX, the εἰδωλ-stem need not necessarily imply Jewish idols.'

[12] Spicq, s.v. 'σπερμολόγος,' 1994: 3.268.

[13] Spicq, s.v. 'σπερμολόγος,' 1994: 3.268. (cf. Dionysius of Halicarnassus, *Ant. rom.* 19.5).

[14] LSJ, s.v. σπερμολόγος III: 'one who picks up scraps of knowledge, an idle babbler, gossip.' In addition to the two examples that follow, cf. Plutarch, *Cohib. ira* 456D, *Alc.* 36; Athenaeus 8.344C.

at temple-gates and provide people with *spermologia* and other market-talk and thus lead to people's mockery of philosophers.

This last example provides the closest parallel to the context of Acts 17. As Dibelius rightly warned, we cannot be certain that the word has the nuance of 'catch-phrase hunter,'[15] but it is tempting to see in this characterization a foreshadowing of the allusions to the philosophical common-places which Paul uses in his speech. The passage would thus suggest that some of the philosophers perceived Paul to be using scraps of philosophical knowledge without having real knowledge of philosophy, and that he was felt to be some kind of poser, dilettante, or street-philosopher.[16] On all accounts, the term is clearly disparaging and shows the negative perception of Paul by at least part of the philosophers.[17]

Another group of philosophers, however, perceives Paul to be a 'herald of foreign divinities' (ξένων δαιμονίων δοκεῖ καταγγελεὺς εἶναι).[18] Luke explains the reason for this assessment: 'because he was announcing as good news Jesus and the resurrection' (ὅτι τὸν Ἰησοῦν καὶ τὴν ἀνάστασιν εὐηγγελίζετο). Since at least Chrysostom, many exegetes have interpreted this as a description of the Athenians' misunderstanding of Paul's message, whereby, hearing his preaching through polytheistic ears, they concluded that Paul is announcing two different divinities—one named Jesus and the other Resurrection.[19] The misunderstanding of the Athenians in this respect thus emphasizes the distorting effect of polytheism and idolatry in their perception of the Christian message. Additional support for this reading is drawn from sources which report that the worship of abstract concepts such as Victory, Love, or Order was common in Athens.[20]

Despite the popularity of this interpretation, however, this reading is unconvincing for both narrative and historical reasons. First, it is difficult to see how Paul's proclamation could lead to the conclusion that the resurrection is a divinity. Nothing in the speech which follows – nor anywhere in Acts – could explain such a mistake. Furthermore, this interpretation implies a very gross misunderstanding between a philosophically educated audience and the apostle.

---

[15] Dibelius 1939: 66–67.

[16] Cf. Schmid 1943: 82–83; Rowe 2011: 37; Marguerat 2015: 154.

[17] The demonstrative 'this' compounds the insult. So Gaventa 2003: 249; Barrett 2004: 830.

[18] In the mouth of the Athenians, δαιμονίων refers either to 'divinities' or more generally to some kind of inferior 'divine beings.' This is the only occurrence of the word in Acts. It is used 21 times in Luke, but always with the meaning of demon, i.e. evil spirit.

[19] Chrysostom, 9.286; Baur 1876: 192; Beurlier 1896: 344; Dibelius 1939: 67; Gärtner 1955: 48; Dunn 1996: 234; Rowe 2008: 28; Schnabel 2012: 726. Among unconvinced exegetes: Zahn 1921: 603; Jervell 1998: 44 ('kaum stichhaltig'); Barrett 2004: 831.

[20] Cf. Pausanias 1.17.1, Plutarch, *Cim.* 13.6.

Although not impossible, it does not constitute a very plausible narrative.[21] Finally, and above all, this interpretation does not make sense in light of the reaction of the Athenians when they hear about the resurrection in the speech. Indeed, they react by laughing or losing interest and adjourning the meeting (cf. v. 32). This confirms what exegetes frequently emphasize when commenting on this text: the Greeks did not believe in the resurrection and found it laughable. By all accounts then, at least on this point, Luke has created a very plausible narrative. In this light, it makes little sense that the Athenians would have asked Paul to expound his teaching in the first place if they suspected him to be announcing a divinity called Ἀνάστασις. The only way to justify this interpretation is by assuming that the Greeks did not know what ἀνάστασις meant or that they interpreted it differently, and thus ignored its connection with a bodily resurrection in Paul's preaching. But the word ἀνάστασις is used in Greek literature to refer to the phenomenon of a dead body coming back to life. The most famous passage comes from the mouth of Apollos in Aeschylus and is often quoted as evidence for the Greek lack of belief in the resurrection:

But when the dust hath drained the blood of man, once he is slain, there is no return to life (ἅπαξ θανόντος, οὔτις ἔστ' ἀνάστασις) (*Eum.* 647–48).

While this passage does indeed deny that an ἀνάστασις is possible, it also shows that the Greeks used the word to refer to *the return to life of a dead body*. The mention of the draining of blood makes the meaning unambiguous. This is not a reference to disembodied afterlife, but to the coming back to life of a body which has been drained from its blood. Closer to the date of Acts, Lucian uses the word when writing about Asclepius *raising* Tyndareus from the dead and the consequent wrath of Zeus against him (καὶ τὴν Τυνδάρεω ἀνάστασιν καὶ τὴν Διὸς ἐπὶ τούτῳ κατ' Ἀσκληπιοῦ ὀργήν, *Salt.* 45). This is again a clear reference to a coming back to a bodily existence in this world and shows that the Greeks were familiar with the concept of ἀνάστασις. In this light, the suggestion that the Athenians would have expressed interest in hearing a teaching on a new divinity called Resurrection is very unlikely. The personified concepts worshipped by the Athenians were phenomena about which they were concerned, and it is hard to see how a divinity called 'Resurrection' could fall into this category.

Another interpretation of Luke's narrative comment must therefore be provided to explain why the Athenians came to think that Paul was 'the proclaimer of foreign divinities' (ξένων δαιμονίων καταγγελεὺς). My suggestion is that the author signifies that the Athenians understood the good news of Jesus and

---

[21] So also Zahn (1921: 603–4 [n.52]): 'Wie aber ‚Philosophen' die sich noch ein wenig gesunden Menschenverstand bewahrt hatten und einiges Interesse für religiöse Fragen zeigten, durch die Verkündigung des Pl [i.e. Paulus] von der Auferstehung des Gekreuzigten und der zukünftigen Auferstehung der verstorbenen Frommen auf den Einfall geraten sein sollten, dass er den Kultus einer Göttin Anastasis einführen wolle, ist unverständlich.'

the resurrection (τὸν Ἰησοῦν καὶ τὴν ἀνάστασιν εὐηγγελίζετο) as the proclamation of new divinities because, from a Greek perspective, a resurrection into eternal life can easily be interpreted as a divinization or an affirmation of somebody's divinity. The possession of eternal life in particular is a divine prerogative.[22] Thus, Paul's proclamation of Jesus' resurrection and a resurrection of the dead (cf. v. 32: ἀνάστασιν νεκρῶν) most likely led the Athenians to the feeling that the apostle was announcing foreign gods. Another passage in Acts corroborates this interpretation. In Acts 28, just after having survived a terrible shipwreck, Paul is bitten by a viper on the island of Malta. When they see the creature hanging from his hand, the natives comment: 'This man must be a criminal for even though he has escaped from the sea, justice has not allowed him to live' (28:4).[23] Paul, however, does not drop dead as they were expecting, and the inhabitants of Malta begin to say that he is 'a god' (ἔλεγον αὐτὸν εἶναι θεόν). The conclusion of those Gentiles reflects the association of immortality with divine beings in Greek culture. Paul's incredible immunity to death, displayed by his survival to both the shipwreck and the viper's bite, can only point to one thing: he is a god. Along the same lines, Paul's preaching of the resurrection of human beings in Athens led to the conclusion that he was the messenger of foreign divinities.

Going back to the light this sheds on the setting leading to the speech, the perception of the Athenians of Paul as a 'messenger of foreign divinities' confirms the newness of Paul's message to them, just like their comment when they require him to speak before the Areopagus in v. 19-20: 'May we know what is this new teaching (καινὴ αὕτη ἡ [...] διδαχή) which you are presenting? For you bring strange things (ξενίζοντα) to our ears.'

In conclusion, Luke's description of the Athenians' verbal reaction to Paul's message suggests a mixed perception, some philosophers qualifying Paul as a scraper of philosophical knowledge, while others perceiving him to be the herald of foreign divinities. Those two reactions show that the Athenians perceived Paul's message to contain scraps of the familiar, and yet to be new. This is problematic for those who interpret the speech as teaching essentially Stoic doctrine. Furthermore, the description of Paul as a *spermologos* shows the disdain of part of the audience. The question which remains to be discussed is whether the Athenians' perception of Paul as announcing foreign divinities led them to put Paul on trial.

---

[22] See, for example, Cicero, *ND* 2.62, which speaks of benefactors who were deified such as Romulus, or Heracles: 'And these benefactors were duly deemed divine, as being both supremely good and immortal, because their souls survived and enjoyed eternal life.' [LCL]

[23] πάντως φονεύς ἐστιν ὁ ἄνθρωπος οὗτος ὃν διασωθέντα ἐκ τῆς θαλάσσης ἡ δίκη ζῆν οὐκ εἴασεν.

2.1.3 The Setting of the Speech (vv.19–21)

The exact setting of Paul's speech has been much debated and continues to divide interpreters. Broadly speaking, proposals follow three lines. Either Paul was taken out of the tumult of the market place – probably to the hill of Ares – to pursue his theological conversation or to make a presentation of his message before a larger cultured Athenian audience.[24] Alternatively, Paul was brought before the authorities of the Areopagus and put on trial for introducing new divinities.[25] Finally, some scholars have argued that Paul was led before the Areopagus council to examine a possible official sanction concerning the introduction of a new god in Athens,[26] or to examine his right to introduce a new teaching.[27] The issue is whether the scene is to be understood as a hostile and potentially dangerous situation for the apostle or an informal setting with little at stake.

The view adopted here is that Paul was led before the Areopagus to examine his teaching and possibly take legal action against him because he was proclaiming foreign divinities. There is little doubt that the Areopagus possessed the authority to judge and examine religious cases during the first century.[28] That the proclamation of new divinities could be suspicious and treated as a political threat in the first century in the Graeco-Roman world is equally attested.[29] Athens certainly had the reputation of inflicting trials for impiety, including precisely for this offence. Josephus lists five persons who were pursued by the Athenians for religious offences, including the priestess Ninus who was put to death precisely because she was accused of initiating people into the mysteries of foreign gods, and of course Socrates, who was well-known in the ancient world for having suffered a capital charge for a similar offence.[30] What is uncertain is whether Athens still adopted such a stringent attitude in the first century CE, for by then it had assimilated several foreign deities into its pantheon and the sources also praise the Athenians for their tolerance and piety

---

[24] Wendt 1913: 225; Zahn 1921: 608; Beyer 1949: 106; Bauernfeind 1980: 116; Schneider 1982: 236; Johnson 1992: 314; Jervell 1998: 444; Gaventa 2003: 249–250.

[25] Barnes 1969; Rowe 2009: 29–32; Jipp 2012: 569–575.

[26] Winter 1996:7 2; Schnabel 2014: 175.

[27] Dunn 1996: 234.

[28] Barnes 1969: 412–13.

[29] See the speech which Cassius Dio (52.36.1–2) puts in the mouth of Maecenas when he advises Augustus on the way to manage an empire.

[30] Josephus *Ag. Ap.* 2.262–268. The persons listed are: Socrates, Anaxagoras, Diagoras of Melos, Protagoras and Ninus. Concerning Ninus, he writes: 'They put Ninus the priestess to death, because someone accused her of initiating people into the mysteries of foreign gods; this was forbidden by their law, and the penalty decreed for any who introduced a foreign god was death.' (2.267, [LCL]) Little to nothing is known about this priestess. She might be the one mentioned by Demosthenes in *1 Boeot.* 19.281, which would situate her in the 4th c. BCE.

towards foreign gods.[31] Luke himself describes the Athenians as particularly keen on novelty rather than offended by it (v.21).

Beyond the historical question, however, the key issue is whether Luke wishes to convey that the speech was pronounced in the setting of a trial. In this respect, one of the most important arguments advanced in favour of the reading of a trial is the abundance of echoes to Socrates which the author has inserted in this pericope and especially the allusion to the charge which led the famous philosopher to be condemned to death for impiety in Athens. The participle ἐπιλαβόμενοι also could suggest that Paul was led to the Areopagus forcefully. At the same time, as is often noted, no charge is brought against Paul before the authorities, nor is any verdict given as is usually the case when Paul is on trial or accused because of his teaching (cf. 18:12–13; 24:2ff). Instead, Paul is asked to explain his 'new teaching.' Those latter elements seem to suggest that Paul is not on trial (yet?), but rather under examination.

In any case, it is unlikely that 'little is at stake'[32] and that what is taking place is an informal conversation. The presence of the Areopagus itself suggests a formal setting. A crucial point to interpret the atmosphere of this pericope is the interpretation of v. 21. Exegetes who claim that there is no threat to the apostle point to this verse as a key evidence that it is only curiosity which motivates the Athenians' move. But the author's aside in v. 21, which points out that 'all the Athenians and the foreign residents spent their time doing nothing but speaking and listening to something new,' is not introduced explicitly as an explanation grounding the interrogation of Paul by the Areopagus in Athenian curiosity (v.20). One would have expected a conjunction like γάρ if this were the case, and not δέ. The alternative is to interpret the comment as an authorial aside drawing attention to the irony of the situation at hand and highlighting the self-contradiction of the Athenians who are guilty of the criticism they level against Paul.[33] Indeed, while they describe Paul as a *spermologos*, they are the ones who spend their time propagating any kind of news (εἰς οὐδὲν ἕτερον ηὐκαίρουν ἢ λέγειν τι ἢ ἀκούειν τι καινότερον); while they claim that Paul announces foreign divinities (ξένων δαιμονίων), a new teaching (καινὴ διδαχή), and strange things (ξενίζοντα), Athens is filled with foreigners (ἐπιδημοῦντες ξένοι) and eager for anything new (τι καινότερον). It is difficult not to see a certain irony in those parallels.

A final conclusion on the setting of the speech remains difficult. The evidence points towards a contentious situation and a formal examination before an instance with judicial power, yet without a formal charge nor a verdict. Part of the reason for Luke's apparent lack of precision or ambiguity might lie in

---

[31] As far as we can tell, the persons listed by Josephus all lived in the 5–4th c. BC. On the Athenians' condemnation and adoption of foreign cults, cf. Garland 1992.

[32] *Contra* Gaventa 2003: 250.

[33] δέ could be read as a mild contrastive: 'But all the Athenians…'

the fact that, as Barnes has argued, examinations in the Roman world did not follow a uniform practice and informal process was the norm.[34] For those reasons it seems that what took place was an examination of Paul's teaching by the Areopagus, which would have, if necessary, taken measures against him.

Again, such a setting speaks against reading the speech's message as showing strong continuity with Greek philosophical teaching. Rather, it suggests that Paul's message was likely considered suspicious or at least worthy of a more formal discussion.

2.2 The Philosophical Context: Debating with Stoic and Epicurean Philosophers

If the immediate context of the speech describes a collision in Athens and that Paul's teaching was perceived as strange and new at best, and babbling philosophical catch-phrases and suspicious at worst, it also suggests that the apostle interacted with the philosophical context of the Athenians. As discussed in the introduction, several scholars downplay the importance of the philosophical context in the pericope in Athens. The narrator, however, not only makes clear that it is a debate with philosophers which led to the speech, but also depicts Paul as a philosopher grappling with issues which were precisely the crusade of the philosophers.

2.2.1 Debating With Stoic and Epicurean Philosophers

The most obvious sign of the philosophical atmosphere of the pericope is of course the mention that Paul interacted with Stoic and Epicurean philosophers on the marketplace in verses 18–19. What is not always observed, is that the narrative suggests a direct connection between this event and the discourse to the Areopagus.

And also, some Epicurean and Stoic philosophers were arguing (συνέβαλλον) with him, and some said: 'what does this *spermologos* want to say?' But others said: 'He seems to be the proclaimer of foreign gods,' for he was announcing the good news of Jesus and the resurrection. 19 And they took him and led him to the Areopagus and said: 'Can we know what is this new teaching which you are speaking about? For you bring strange things into our hearing. We therefore want to know what that might be.'

It is not absolutely certain that Luke wishes to convey that the assessments of *spermologos* and 'proclaimer of foreign divinities' are made by the philosophers and that they are the ones who take him before the Areopagus. But the accusation that Paul is a *spermologos* – a poser or third-rate street philosopher – would make particularly good sense on their part. It is unlikely that the speech

---

[34] Barnes 1969: 413.

was addressed only to philosophers, since the Areopagus must have included a broader audience. But the connection drawn between Paul's conversation with philosophers and them leading him before the Areopagus, as well as the many allusions to philosophical common places which have been identified in the speech, suggest that the conversation which Paul was having with the philosophers on the marketplace provides the background of his speech before the Areopagus.

The mention of Epicurean and Stoic philosophers raises the question as to why the author singles out those two philosophical schools, rather than just speaking of 'Greek philosophers' generally. Many scholars contend that the choice reflects the fact that the Epicurean and the Stoic schools were very popular or the most popular in the first century CE.[35] But there is little reason to suppose that the Academics were not equally popular. Another common explanation is that the mention of the Stoics prepares the way for the frequent connections the following speech makes with Stoicism.[36] Barrett also sees some allusions to Epicurean doctrine in the speech and thus explains the mention of Epicurean philosophers.[37] This explanation is on the right track.

Importantly, however, the philosophers are described as 'arguing' (συνέβαλλον) with Paul.[38] The word points to a debate. Despite their puzzlement about – or lack of respect for – Paul's new teaching, then, the philosophers were *willing* and *able* to interact and argue with Paul. Luke thus intimates that there was sufficient common ground and interest between the parties to engage in a serious conversation.

The connection the narrative makes between the debate with Epicurean and Stoic philosophers and the speech before the Areopagus, as well as the echoes to some of their doctrines in the speech demonstrates the importance of this background to interpret the discourse. In this light, a very plausible hypothesis is that author has the tenets of Stoicism and Epicureanism in mind as he is writing this pericope, and signals the importance of this background to understand the passage to his readers.[39] Two further elements of the passage strengthen this interpretation.

---

[35] E.g. Gärtner 1955: 47; Marguerat 2015: 154.
[36] Dibelius 1939: 66–67; Barrett 1974: 72.
[37] Barrett 2004: 829.
[38] Some exegetes translate the verb as 'conversing,' which is of course possible. In light of the philosophical context, however, the verb is better translated as 'arguing' because this was the mode of interaction between philosophers of different schools. Cf. Marguerat 2015: 154: 'συμβάλλω (18a) est le verbe de la joute oratoire.' Barrett 2004: 829: 'argued with him.'
[39] Cf. Barrett 1974: 72: 'It is suggested here that the two schools are named because Luke has their tenets in mind, and alluded to them in the speech he puts in Paul's mouth.'

2.2.2 The Socratic Allusions

Another interpretative clue provided by the immediate context of the speech are the allusions to Socrates and his trial in the narrative. Echoes were picked up early by Christian exegetes and modern scholars almost consensually acknowledged that there is an allusion to the great Greek philosopher in this passage.[40] Many sources testify that Socrates was remembered as a philosopher who spent his time in the agora conversing with philosophers and sophists.[41] The participle παρατυγχάνοντας in v.17 is particularly reminiscent of Socrates' habit of conversing with anyone willing to discuss with him: ὅτῳ ἄν ἀεὶ ἐντυγχάνω ὑμῶν (Plato, *Apol.* 29d). Some exegetes also see in the depiction of Paul 'reasoning' (διελέγετο, v.17a) in the agora a possible allusion to Socrates' well-known methodology of elenchus,[42] although the verb διαλέγομαι is frequent in Acts and its evocative power thus limited. The strongest allusion, of course, remains the 'charge' levelled against Paul, which is penned with a terminology highly reminiscent of the accusation which led to Socrates' death.

φησὶ γάρ με ποιητὴν εἶναι θεῶν, καὶ ὡς *καινοὺς* ποιοῦντα θεούς, τοὺς δ' ἀρχαίους οὐ νομίζοντα (Plato *Euthyphr.* 3b; cf. *Eutyphr.* 1c; 2c; *Apol.* 24bc, 28e–30e *passim*)

ἀδικεῖ Σωκράτης οὓς μὲν ἡ πόλις νομίζει θεοὺς οὐ νομίζων, ἕτερα δὲ καινὰ δαιμόνια εἰσφέρων· ἀδικεῖ δὲ καὶ τοὺς νέους διαφθείρων (Xenophon *Mem.*1.1.1; cf. 1.1.3 *passim*; *Apol.* 10-11)

τίνος γὰρ ἑτέρου χάριν Σωκράτης ἀπέθανεν; [...] ὅτι *καινοὺς* ὅρκους ὤμνυε καί τι *δαιμόνιον* αὐτῷ σημαίνειν ἔφασκε νὴ Δία παίζων [...] (Josephus *Ag. Ap.* 2.263)

ἀδικεῖ Σωκράτης, οὓς μὲν ἡ πόλις νομίζει θεοὺς οὐ νομίζων, ἕτερα δὲ καινὰ δαιμόνια εἰσηγούμενος· ἀδικεῖ δὲ καὶ τοὺς νέους διαφθείρων. (Diogenes Laertius 2.40)

ξένων δαιμονίων δοκεῖ καταγγελεὺς εἶναι [...] ἐπιλαβόμενοί τε αὐτοῦ ἐπὶ τὸν Ἄρειον πάγον ἤγαγον λέγοντες· δυνάμεθα γνῶναι τίς ἡ *καινὴ* αὕτη ἡ ὑπὸ σοῦ λαλουμένη διδαχη; ξενίζοντα γάρ *τινα εἰσφέρεις* εἰς τὰς ἀκοὰς ἡμῶν (Acts 17:18-20)[43]

What Luke wishes to convey through those allusions has been more debated.[44] But at the very least he pictures the apostle like a new Socrates, and makes him

---

[40] Justin (*II Ap.* 10.5–6) might be the first testimony to such an association among ancient readers. He argues that Socrates in his teaching urged the Athenians to know 'the unknown god' [ἄγωστος θεός]. (cf. Sandnes 1993: 20; Rowe 2011: 32 [n.3–4]). On the parallels between Paul and Socrates in this text, see for example Sandnes 1993, Marguerat 2015.

[41] Plato, *Apol.* 17c; Xenophon, *Mem.* 1.1.10; Diogenes Laertius, Lives 2.21; Dio Chrysostom, *Or.* 54.3.

[42] Laertius, *Lives* 2.20, 45, 122; Plato, *Apol.*19d, 33a, 38a; *Resp.* 454a.

[43] In addition to the parallels mentioned above, cf. also Justin *1 Apol.* 5.4; *2 Apol.* 10.5.

[44] Several exegetes argue that this characterization shows that Luke wants to depict Paul as a teacher of integrity and truth who was misunderstood by his contemporaries (e.g. Dunn 1992: 233; Marguerat 2015: 152), others underscore that the characterization underscores Paul's

enter the role of a philosopher by depicting him as debating in the agora with passers-by and with other philosophers. Some exegetes deny that Luke characterizes Paul like a philosopher on the ground that his message takes the form of a proclamation (cf. καταγγελεύς, καταγγέλλω) and not an argumentation.[45] But this introduces a dichotomy which Luke does not make since the philosophers in his narrative debate with the apostle, and reflects an anachronistic distinction between 'religion' and philosophy. Not only is our concept of 'religion' a recent invention which did not exist in the ancient world,[46] but the nature of ancient philosophy differed significantly from our notion of philosophy in the modern world.[47] In particular, it was characterized by an allegiance and commitment to an understanding of the world and life-style which makes it look strangely like what we categorize as religion today.[48] It was, in any case, the philosophers and not the priests who, in the Graeco-Roman world, provided most of the teaching which today falls in the category of theology, religion and ethics.[49] The different philosophical schools proposed explanations of the nature of the gods and their interaction in the world, the way one should live and behave towards them, and how to deal with evil or death. Hence, when he describes the different Jewish sects of the first century – the Essenes, the Sadducees and the Pharisees – Josephus calls them the 'three *philosophies* of old of the Jews' (*Ant.* 18.11).[50] In this context, the early Christian movement – which is indeed called a 'sect' (αἵρεσις) in Acts 24:14 – and the Greek philosophical schools would indeed have been 'rivals' in the Graeco-Roman world. This they were not in the sense that nascent Christianity would have been perceived as a real threat by any of Hellenistic schools, nor in the sense that it used a similar type of argumentation as the philosophers, but in the sense that Christianity

---

respectable status (Marguerat 2015: 152). Those proposals are not incompatible with the present analysis.

[45] Jervell 1998: 444.

[46] On this see the next chapter, especially section 3.1.2 and note 37.

[47] Sedley 1989: esp.102; Trapp 2014.

[48] Sedley 1989; Trapp 2014. As Trapp (49) writes: 'Rightly understood and taken seriously, philosophy was, as explained above, the art of life. From the philosophical point of view, therefore, real commitment to it ought to mean something more than an acknowledgment of a body of knowledge and doctrines, and appreciation of a corpus of fine writing; it ought to mean a continuing – indeed, lifelong – dedication to a personal project of self-improvement, a cumulative process of working on one's outlook, perceptions, and emotions, so as to approximate ever closer to the ideals of character-structure and relation to the world established by the great philosophers as right and fulfilling for thinking human beings […].'

[49] In his discussion of this subject, Van Kooten (2010: 395) comments that 'Platonism (and philosophy in general) was religion for the intellectual elite.'

[50] Cf. Josephus *War* 2.119–166.

provided an *alternative* explanation of the same topics treated by the philosophers and thereby called to a different embeded life.[51]

In addition to characterizing Paul as a 'philosopher,' the allusion to the charge brought against Socrates has often been interpreted as a sign that the apostle is on trial, or at least to underscore the seriousness or even ominousness of Paul's situation. The trial and death of Socrates was one of the most famous events in antiquity, and there is little doubt that Luke intends an allusion here.[52] As discussed above, it is difficult to be conclusive about the setting. But in light of the broader context of the pericope at hand, the allusion most likely also serves another obvious function which has been surprisingly overlooked in the literature: to evoke and underscore the seriousness of the subject debated at hand, i.e. piety. Socrates' trial was not only known as an unjust trial against one of the greatest philosophers, but it was the most famous trial against ἀσέβεια. As many ancient sources describe it, Socrates was charged with *impiety* because he brought new gods and did not worship those of the city. The characterization of Paul along the lines of a new Socrates then, and the allusion to his trial for impiety suggest that Luke presents the scene as a debate between Paul and the Athenian philosophers on proper piety. Another element which reinforces this interpretation is the fact that the figure of Socrates regularly appears in philosophical discussion about piety,[53] and that many philosophers considered him to be the paragon of piety.[54]

The Socratic allusions then reinforce the philosophical atmosphere of the pericope, but also cast it as a debate between the Christian representative and the philosophers about proper piety, or proper attitude towards the divine. This is confirmed by the beginning of the speech.

2.2.3 *The* Deisidaimonia *of the Athenians and Their Ignorant Worship*

The last element which suggests that Paul's conversation with the Greek philosophers forms the background of this pericope is his *Anknüpfungspunkt* with this audience at the very beginning of his speech, namely his mention of the altar to the unknown god as a proof that the Athenians are *deisidaimonesterous* (δεισιδαιμονεστέρους) (v.22).

---

[51] On the similarities between Hellenistic philosophies and early Christianity, see, for example, Stowers 2001; Van Kooten 2010.

[52] Dunn 1992: 233; Pervo (2008: 425) notes that anyone with a modest Greek education would hear an ominous development in the charge brought against Paul.

[53] E.g., Philodemus *Piet.* Col. 25, 701–720.

[54] Obbink 1996: 379. The Stoics, especially Epictetus, were particularly admirative of Socrates, and called themselves Socratics. The Epicureans, however, were generally critical of Socrates, including of his teaching on piety. On Socrates in Hellenistic philosophy, cf. Long 1988.

The highly debated meaning of *deisidaimonesterous* as well as its relation to the altar to an unknown god will be discussed in the next chapter. What is significant at this point and which several scholars have noticed is that *deisidaimonia* was precisely an object of criticism by Hellenistic philosophers. In particular, the Epicureans had made it one of the two central aims of their philosophy to eliminate *deisidaimonia*, together with the fear of death. Not only so, but Hellenistic philosophers denounced *deisidaimonia* as a form of perverted piety and the expression of *ignorance*, an assessment which the speech echoes by qualifying Athenian worship as 'ignorant' (ἀγνοοῦντες, v. 23).

By pointing to Athenian *deisidaimonia* and denouncing their ignorant worship at the beginning of his speech, Paul thus enters a well-trodden philosophical domain, and, as shall be seen in chapter 3, an area of debate among the philosophers.

In this context, those verses also shed important light on the subject of the speech. By and large interpreters have concluded from v. 23 that the purpose of the speech is to announce the nature of the true God, who is unknown to the Athenians. This exegesis of v. 23 will be examined in detail later. What can be pointed out now, however, is that the problem of the Athenians is not only their object of worship, but the *way* they worship, i.e. their piety. This is signaled by ἀγνοοῦντες which functions as an adverbial participle modifying εὐσεβεῖτε, and is confirmed by the structure of the speech, which is built around three negative sentences all commenting on the worship practices of the Athenians: 1. the God who made the world [...] does not dwell in temples made by human hands (v. 24), 2. nor is he served by human hands (v. 25), 3. Therefore, being the offspring of God, we must not think that the divine is like artefacts of gold, silver, and stone (v. 29).

Accordingly, the background conversation and subject of the speech should not only be understood as the nature of the divine, but also the nature of proper piety or worship, both of which were closely linked in ancient philosophical discussions.[55] Indeed, it is the nature of the gods which determines the way humanity must relate to them. Again then, allusions to *deisidaimonia* and ignorance at the beginning of the speech, both of which were used by Hellenistic philosophers to describe problematic piety, suggest the importance of the philosophical context in this pericope.

2.3 Conclusion

This chapter has shown that the narrative context invalidates interpretations of the speech which emphasize its continuity with Greek philosophy. Indeed, not only does Paul react with anger at the numerous idols displayed in Athens, but

---

[55] This will be detailed in chapter 3.

the philosophers perceived Paul to be either a babbler possibly using philosophical catch-phrases, or the proclaimer of foreign divinities. In any case, they all perceived his teaching as new and strange, and not as congenial. The setting of a formal examination of his teaching before the Areopagus most likely suggests that it was even suspicious to some. There is no reason to think that Luke intends the content of the speech before the Areopagus to be different from what the apostle discussed with people on the marketplace, and the reaction of the Athenians at the end of the speech (v. 32) confirms that the message is new, strange and for many, laughable.

At the same time, and importantly, the narrative and beginning of the speech raises serious questions for interpretations which deny or even downplay the importance of the philosophical background in this pericope. Not only does Luke picture the speech as the consequence of Paul's debate with Epicurean and Stoic philosophers, but he also pictures him as a new Socrates trading on the very specific philosophical turf of the Epicureans by tackling the *deisidaimonia* and ignorance of the Athenians.

Although those two assessments might seem contradictory and irreconcilable, they need not be, and it is at this point that past interpretations have missed a crucial hermeneutical clue given by those few verses. Indeed, instead of suggesting that the speech must be read as either seeking continuity with the philosophers or without any connection with Greek philosophy, the narrative context shows that the discourse in Athens must be understood within the context of a debate between Paul and Epicurean and Stoic philosophers.

More precisely, the analysis of the immediate narrative context points towards a specific subject of debate. On the one hand, the importance of the subject of idols for the whole pericope is highlighted by the direct connection the text makes between Paul's anger at Athens' idols and his debate on the market place and thus with the philosophers (cf. οὖν in v. 17), and by the reappearance of this subject at the beginning (cf. σεβάσματα in v. 23) and the end of the speech (v. 29). And on the other hand, the characterisation of Paul along the lines of Socrates and the allusion to the charge which led to his condemnation for ἀσέβεια, as well as the mention of the *deisidaimonia* and ignorant worship of the Athenians as the entry point of the whole speech (vv. 22-23), both suggest that the debate is connected with appropriate worship or piety more generally.

This setting of a debate has crucial methodological consequences. Indeed, instead of examining the parallels between the speech and philosophical teaching and comparing them in terms of continuities and discontinuities of motifs, a more appropriate approach will be to analyse how the speech's teaching on proper worship and idols differs from the teaching of those philosophical schools, and possibly how it addresses elements of the debate on this subject between Epicurean and Stoic philosophers.

2.3 Conclusion 47

Before turning to an examination of Stoic and Epicurean teaching on this question, however, another element of this introduction must be re-examined in more detail in the next chapter: the much-debated meaning of *deisidaimonia*.

3. Neither 'Piety,' nor 'Superstition' – Redefining *Deisidaimonia* in the Context of Graeco-Roman Religious Grammar (c. 100 BCE–120 C)

One of the longstanding interpretative questions of the pericope in Acts 17:16–34 is the meaning of δεισιδαιμονεστέρους at the beginning of the speech. It is a common assumption in scholarship that the noun from which this adjective is derived, δεισιδαιμονία, has two usages, one positive or neutral, meaning 're-ligion,' 'piety' or 'reverence,' and one negative, expressing 'superstition,' or 'excessive fear of the gods.'[1] Determining the nuance of the characterization of the Athenians as δεισιδαιμονεστέρους in Acts 17:22 has thus become an important clue to determine the narrative's attitude towards Greek religiosity: is Paul being praiseworthy or at least building upon something positive in the religious attitude of the Greeks despite their mistaken worship of idols, or is he dismissing Athenian piety outright as 'superstition'? The issue has long been debated in modern scholarship and there is little sign of a coming consensus on the question.[2] The arguments used on both sides of the debate highlight the difficulty of settling the issue.

On the one hand, many exegetes argue that the terminology should be translated by 'very religious' or 'very pious' because it is part of Paul's *captatio benevolentiae*, which – according to the recommendation of ancient rhetorical handbooks – aimed to elicit the goodwill of an audience and to raise its interest.[3] Athenian piety was well-known in the ancient world and it would thus

---

[1] See Foerster, 'δεισιδαίμων, δεισιδαιμονία,' in *TDNT*; Spic, 'δεισιδαίμων, δεισιδαιμονία,' in *TLNT*; LSJ s.v. δεισιδαιμονία: 'fear of the gods, religious feeling,' and, in a bad sense, 'superstition.' Versnel, in *OCD*, s.v. δεισιδαιμονία, describes it as 'scrupulousness in religious matters' when it is used positively, and 'excessive pietism and preoccupation with religion' when it is used in a derogatory way. So also Bowden 2008: 57; Moellering 1963: 47; Martin 2004: 18. Those two usages are assumed by most exegetes in their discussion of the terminology in Acts. E.g, Jervell 1989: 445: 'δεισιδαίμων kann sowohl negativ etwas Minderwertiges, etwa "abergläubisch", als auch anerkennend "gottesfürtig, religiös, fromm" bedeuten.'

[2] Already in 1929, Koet (24–25) writes that the meaning of the word is debated.

[3] Koet 1929: 25; Schneider 1982: 237–38; Conzelmann 1987: 140; Johnson 1992: 314; Klauck 2000: 81; Pervo 2008: 433; Rothschild 2014: 30–31; Holladay 2016: 342.

have been a deft way to open his discourse.⁴ In any case, it is unlikely that Paul would have begun his speech with an insult. Some interpreters also suggest that this positive description reflects the assessment that the Athenians are worshipping the true God albeit as an unknown god (cf. v. 23).⁵

On the other hand, scholars defend the pejorative meaning because v. 16 describes Paul as angry at the idolatry of the city, and the Athenians are said to worship 'in ignorance' – hardly a praiseworthy qualification.⁶ It is also argued that the speech echoes the philosophical criticism against 'superstition,' ignorance or curiosity being characteristics of *deisidaimonia* according to the philosophers.⁷ As for the argument that Paul's speech must begin with a captatio, it is pointed out that 'Paul's words are to be understood as a *captatio benevolentiae* only if we know that δεισ[ιδαιμονια] is intended *sensu bono*.'⁸

In light of the ambiguity of the evidence provided by the context, a third group of exegetes has suggested that the word is meant to be understood with two levels of meanings, and that Luke exploits the ambiguity of the word.⁹ Thus, in the narrative world, Paul's audience would have heard his characterisation positively, while Luke's readership, alerted by the description of Paul's anger in v. 16, would have perceived the irony and discerned the negative assessment of Athenian religiosity in the terminology. As Rowe puts it: '[…] in the story world, the Areopagus hears the former – the Paul of Acts does not blunder verbally so badly or so quickly – while the reader, who is positioned hermeneutically by vv. 16–21, also hears the latter. […] Through a deft use of dramatic irony, Luke unifies historical verisimilitude – and rhetorical skill – with theological judgment and, precisely, alerts the readers of Paul's speech to its multi-level discourse.'¹⁰ Despite its initial attractiveness, however, this last view is not unproblematic either. For even if Luke's implied reader is 'in the know' and suspects that *deisidaimonia* really should be understood as 'superstition' here, he still needs to make sense of Paul's intentionality in his use of the terminology in the narrative world of Acts. Some scholars thus explain that Paul plays on the ambiguity of the word and uses it either ironically or as part of his rhetorical strategy to gain the goodwill of his audience in order to communicate his message.¹¹ But Luke's implied audience might still wonder if it

---

⁴ Cf. Sophocles, *Oed. Col.* 260; Pausanias 1.17.1; Josephus, *Ap.*2.130.
⁵ Haenchen 1971: 520–21.
⁶ Jervell 1998: 445; Jipp 2012: 576.
⁷ Jipp 2012: 576–78; Gray 2005.
⁸ Barrett, 2004: 836.
⁹ Moellering 1963: 49; Given 1995: 364–5; Klauck 2000: 81–88; Rowe 2011: 40.
¹⁰ Rowe 2012: 40.
¹¹ So Moellering 1963: 49: 'It is therefore likely that he invests the term with a certain ambiguity so that his hearers will feel there are being commended for their religious scrupulosity, and yet he will be free to proceed to criticize their inadequacies and commend his own faith to them.'

is really plausible that the angry Paul of the narrative would begin his denunciation of idolatry and proclamation of coming judgment with praise about Athenian religiosity even for rhetorical purposes.[12]

As this brief overview shows, despite the longevity of the debate, none of the attempts to clarify the meaning of *deisidaimonia* in Acts 17 is without problem for the narrative realism of the pericope. Importantly, it is not only in Acts 17 that the current understanding of *deisidaimonia* has led to analytical difficulties. Indeed, scholars have long commented that some ancient authors seem to be guilty of self-contradiction or confusion in their use of this term. For example, Diodorus Siculus seems to be using *deisidaimonia* with different meanings and connotations. To explain this inconsistency, it has been argued that this reflects Diodorus' integration of varied sources in his work without taking care to harmonize them.[13] A similar well-known problem occurs with Plutarch's use of *deisidaimonia*: several behaviours and beliefs which are criticized by Plutarch as *deisidaimonia* in his treatise on the question – *De superstitione* – are endorsed in his work elsewhere.[14] This time, scholars have suggested different solutions to explain such discrepancies, the privileged one being that Plutarch's thinking on the question changed, and that he became more 'religious' and mystical when he became older.

The present chapter makes a new proposal to solve this enduring conundrum. It argues that the root of the problem lies in a longstanding misapprehension of the meaning of *deisidaimonia*. Indeed, *deisidaimonia* means neither 'piety, religion' nor 'superstition, excessive fear of the gods.' This chapter suggests that current misconceptions of the meaning of *deisidaimonia* are to a large extent the result of the use of anachronistic conceptual frameworks and categories to analyse ancient religious phenomena. More specifically, past analyses have not sufficiently taken into account the fact that the grammar of ancient religion differed significantly from modern religion, and have tended to read ancient philosophical criticism of religious phenomena through the prism of modern critical attitudes towards religion or superstition.

The present chapter presents an analysis of the use of *deisidaimonia* by ancient authors between the 1st c. BCE and the early 2nd c. CE which seeks to avoid such anachronisms and to present a definition of *deisidaimonia* within the grammar of ancient religious discourse during this period. It begins by highlighting some of the methodological weaknesses of past studies on the question and framing the approach taken by the present study. It is then followed by two sections analysing the use of *deisidaimonia* by ancient authors. Finally, the conclusion summarizes the results of the analyses and shows how they illuminate the meaning of *deisidaimonia* in Acts 17. As this chapter

---

[12] As Dibelius (1939: 176) points out, Luke would never have described Paul as a hypocrite.
[13] Koet 1929: 9; Martin 1997: 121; Martin 2004: 79–92.
[14] Moellering 1963; Brenk 1977; Martin 2004: 104.

demonstrates, a re-evaluation of the meaning of *deisidaimonia* which takes into account the grammar of Graeco-Roman religion both provides a new answer to the long-standing debate on the meaning of *deisidaimonia* in Acts 17, and sheds new light on what is at stake in the debate between Paul and the philosophers in Luke's pericope.

3.1 Methodological Concerns in the Study of *Deisidaimonia*

The present section suggests that past studies of *deisidaimonia* have suffered from two longstanding methodological weaknesses which have led to the current misapprehension of the meaning of this terminology. It then introduces the approach taken in this study.

3.1.1 The Lack of Semantic Study of the Terminology of Deisidaimonia

A crucial problem with current conclusions about the meaning of *deisidaimonia* is that they are not based on a semantic study of the terminology informed by modern linguistics. The only substantial study of the terminology of *deisidaimonia* remains Peter J. Koet's Δεισιδαιμονία: *A Contribution to the Knowledge of the* Religious *Terminology in Greek*, published in 1929. Koet was the first scholar to examine a high number of occurrences of *deisidaimonia* in their respective contexts. He studied the way *deisdaimonia* is used by a significant number of ancient authors ranging from Xenophon (c. 430–354 BCE) to Phavorinus (d. 1537 CE), and his work still represents the most detailed examination of the terminology in ancient literature.[15] Koet's aim, however, was not so much the semantic study of *deisidaimonia* as the verification of the common assumption that the terminology is used (almost) exclusively with negative connotations after Theophrastus (c. 372–c. 287 BCE). Koet demonstrated that the word continued to be used positively after Theophrastus until at least the third century CE even if the negative nuance becomes more prominent after him, and his conclusion has been widely endorsed by scholarship since him. Koet's approach, however, primarily consisted in 'classifying' the usages of *deisidaimonia* along positive and negative connotations. As far as the lexical meaning of *deisidaimonia* was concerned, however, Koet remained vague. In his appendix, he listed seven different meanings for the noun when

---

[15] Other discussions of the terminology include: Spicq, 'δεισιδαίμων, δεισιδαιμονία,' *TLNT* 1: 305–8; Moellering 1963: 42–52; Baroja 1974: 151–161; Martin 1997: 110–27; Gray 2004: 33–108; Bowden 2008: 56–71. See also Martin 2004 on the phenomenology of superstition. The meaning of the Latin word *superstitio* overlaps with *deisidaimonia* in some contexts. On *superstitio*, see: Otto 1909: 533–54; Benveniste 1969: 273–279; Calderone 1972; Janssen 1975: 135–89; 1979: 131–59; and especially Grodzynski 1974: 36–60.

it is used in a favourable sense, and no less than ten when it is used in a negative sense.[16]

Discussions of *deisidaimonia* after Koet either rely upon his conclusions, or tend to use the same approach, focusing on determining whether the word is used positively and means 'piety, religion' or negatively refers to 'superstition,' or, more broadly, to any religious outlook of which the author disapproves.[17] This approach, however, is unsatisfactory. What is needed is a study of the meaning or semantic range of *deisidaimonia* with the help of the tools of modern linguistics, a field which has undergone tremendous development since Koet's publication. At the most basic level, this means an examination of the syntagmatic and paradigmatic relations of *deisidaimonia*.[18] In terms of syntagmatic analysis this implies a study of the contexts and constructions in which the terminology is used. In addition to this syntagmatic analysis, *deisidaimonia* also needs to be analysed in its paradigmatic relations. In other words, what is needed is an assessment of the meaning of *deisidaimonia* over against words which share the same semantic domain. As Jost Trier put it in a classic formulation:

The value of a word is first known when we mark it off against the value of neighboring and opposite words. Only as part of the whole does the word have sense; for only in the field is there meaning.[19]

Determining the semantics of *deisidaimonia* thus necessitates an examination which delimitates its usage from other semantically closely related words, such as εὐσέβεια, θεοσέβεια or εὐλάβεια, and some of its opposites, such as ἀθεότης or ἀσεβεία. To my knowledge, however, no such study has been conducted. This is particularly problematic in light of the current scholarly consensus that *deisidaimonia* often means 'piety,' which implies that it is used as a synonym to εὐσέβεια or θεοσέβεια.

Finally, such a study will also need to consider each specific author's usage, and be careful in delimiting the timeframe of the analysis, privileging synchronistic study. Indeed, some past studies draw conclusions from authors which are chronologically too distant from each other.[20]

---

[16] Koet 1929: 104–105.

[17] See the lexical entries *s.v.* in LSJ, Spicq, or the usual debate about the meaning of *deisidaimonia* in Acts 17 as sketched above.

[18] Jobs 1994: 202: 'Modern linguistic theory teaches that the meaning of a given word is not located primarily in the word itself but is determined by the relationship the word has to other words in the context of a give occurrence (syntagmatic) and by the contrast it forms with other words which share its semantic domain (paradigmatic).'

[19] Trier 1931: 6 translated and quoted in Silva 1994: 161.

[20] For example, Moellering (1963: 57–58) draws conclusion on the pre-Christian use of the word based on Christian usage. But the word's meaning seems to have changed quite significantly in Christian literature.

3.1.2 The Assumption of Anachronistic Conceptual Frameworks in the Study of Ancient Religion and Philosophy

The second enduring and, in many ways, more fundamental problem in past studies of *deisidaimonia* is that they are conducted with modern, and thus anachronistic conceptual frameworks and models, rather than within the frameworks and grammars of antiquity. More precisely, those analyses import modern religious categories and especially 'post-Enlightenment' 'grammars' of religion to examine ancient 'religious' phenomena and ancient philosophical criticism. The grammar of ancient religion, however, differed significantly from the structure of modern monotheistic religion, and, despite some apparent similarities, ancient criticism in this field cannot be assumed to proceed along the same lines as the modern philosophical criticism of religion or superstition. By using anachronistic categories and models and attempting to fit ancient texts into them, studies both distort the data and fail to account for it in its entirety.

This problem is well illustrated by the persistence of the literature in using the word 'superstition' to translate *deisidaimonia* when it is used *malo sensu*. This is the case not only in most major dictionaries and lexica, but also in much literature on this topic.[21] For example, this is the way *deisidaimonia* is translated in Moellering's study *Plutarch on Superstition* (1963), or in Martin's two recent studies (1997, 2004). Certainly, several scholars warn that it is misleading or even mistaken to translate *deisidaimonia* as 'superstition' because it does not correspond to what is understood by this modern English terminology.[22] Bowden goes as far as arguing that it is a 'commonplace' 'that there is no exact equivalent of the word "superstition" in Greek.'[23] Despite this, the literature shows that it is still often assumed in scholarship that *at least in some cases*, *deisidaimonia* does correspond to what in English is designed as superstition.[24] It is easy to see how scholars could reach this conclusion when reading, for example, Theophrastus' portrait of the *Deisidaimōn* in his *Characters*.

> The Superstitious Man is the kind who washes his hands in three springs, sprinkles himself with water from a temple font, puts a laurel leaf in his mouth, and then is ready for the day's perambulations. If a weasel runs across his path he will not proceed on his journey until someone else has covered the ground or he has thrown three stones over the road. When he sees a snake in his house he invokes Sabazios if it is the red-brown one, and if it is the holy one he sets up a hero-shrine there and then. [...] He is apt to purify his house frequently,

---

[21] Moellering 1963; Martin 1997; Martin 2004. So also in commentaries and studies on Acts 17:22, such as Jervell 1989: 445; Rowe 2011: 39. Note, however, Haenchen 1971: 520, n.7: 'δεισιδαίμων is [...] by no means 'superstitious' – that is a modern concept! [...]'

[22] Cf. Moellering 1963: 42: 'To translate *deisidaimonia* as superstition is not only inadequate; it is misleading.' Koet 1929: 99: '...it is inexact to translate δεισιδαιμονία by 'superstition', as it very seldom means that, if we take this word in the modern sense.'

[23] Bowden 2008: 56.

[24] Koet (1929: 99) points out that *deisidaimonia* 'very seldom means' 'superstition,' thereby implying that sometimes it is an accurate translation.

claiming that it is haunted by Hekate. [...] He refuses to step on a tombstone or go near a dead body or a woman in childbirth, saying that he cannot afford to risk contamination. (Extracts from Theophrastus, *Char.* 16 [Diggle])

According to Theophrastus then, the behaviour of the Deisidaimōn is strikingly reminiscent of what would today be characterized as 'superstitious.'[25] Indeed, the online Oxford Dictionary gives the following two definitions of 'superstition.'

1. Excessively credulous belief in and reverence for the supernatural.
2. A widely held but irrational belief in supernatural influences, especially as leading to good or bad luck, or a practice based on such a belief.[26]

Despite the warning voiced by scholars against understanding *deisidaimonia* along the lines of the modern concept of 'superstition' then, in practice *deisidaimonia* is still generally translated as 'superstition' and studies still assume that its meaning is similar to the modern concept. This assumption is further illustrated by two other elements.

First, there is in the literature a continual tendency to identify *deisidaimonia* as referring to religious *practices or beliefs*, such as the worship of images, sacrifices or belief in oracles, myths or supernatural events. For example, Moellering writes:

How Polybius understands *desidaimonia* is apparent in his criticism of Timaeus whom he denounces for having his work filled with the supernatural: dreams, prodigies, fantastic stories, or to put it briefly: δεισιδαιμονίας ἀγγενοῦς καὶ τερατείας γυναικώδους ἐστὶ πλήρης. (Moellering 1963: 52)

Similar understandings of *deisidaimonia* as a term referring to specific religious practices and beliefs can be found in most studies on the subject.[27]

And second, as the quote from Moellering shows, *deisidaimonia* is regularly associated with *irrationality* and the *supernatural*, and set in opposition with the rational, a language reminiscent of the criticism of superstition or even religion more generally in modern times. Witness to this is also the tendency to describe ancient critics of *deisidaimonia* as 'enlightened.' Thus, speaking of Polybius' criticism of *deisidaimonia*, Koet calls him an 'enlightened historian' who is critical of all popular religion.[28] Moellering speaks of 'the enlightened

---

[25] Bowden 2008: 58–59. Cf. Gray 2004: 33–34: 'There is also much common ground between the mentality that generally passes for superstitiousness today in the West and δεισιδαιμονία or *superstitio* in ancient Greece or Rome. [...] The family resemblance with superstition is in fact quite impressive.'

[26] *Online Oxford Dictionary*, accessed at https://en.oxforddictionaries.com/definition/superstition (7.10.2017).

[27] Koet 1929: 70; Martin 1997: 114; Martin 2004: 94; Gray 2004: 34, 47.

[28] Koet 1929: 99.

rationalism' of Plutarch's critical treaties *De superstitione*, and describes Plutarch as 'repelled by the stupidities and irrationalities of superstition.'[29]

Certainly, scholars have warned against equating the criticism of *deisidaimonia* with the criticism of the supernatural or irrationality. It has often been pointed out, for example, that Plutarch is critical of *deisidaimonia* and yet not opposed to all what is supernatural in ancient religion.'[30] This has been emphasized by Martin in his recent work, where he warns against using anachronistic categories to analyse *deisidaimonia*. As he points out, it is inappropriate to associate *deisidaimonia* with belief in the supernatural and the irrational, the former because the ancients did not use the category of 'supernatural' and considered everything to be part of *physis,* and the latter because what is rational is largely subjective.[31]

As a result, some scholars, and particularly Martin in his recent studies, have attempted to find the 'logic' or the 'rationale' which made something worthy to be criticized as *deisidaimonia* by ancient authors.[32] A common conclusion has been that *deisidaimonia* is excessive piety, or excessive fear.[33] Another claim advanced in particular in discussions of Theophrastus is that he condemns certain practices as *deisidaimonia* because they are connected to private rather than public worship.[34] In his 1997 article, Martin emphasizes that philosophers criticized *deisidaimonia* because it broke upper-class social etiquette.[35]

The problem with those studies, however, is that, although they rightly reject the imposition of the anachronistic *category* of 'supernatural' to understand ancient discourse, they still assume that the *grammar* which underpins *deisidaimonia* and its criticism in antiquity follows the same logic or grammar which underpins the modern criticism of superstition or religion. In other words, they still assume that *deisidaimonia* – although not necessarily associated with the supernatural or irrationality like modern superstition – nonetheless refers to 'those forms of popular religion' with which their critics are out of sympathy.[36] This, however, reflects a *modern grammar* of superstition in which 'superstition' broadly refers to 'inappropriate religious behaviour.' It is thus still using an *anachronistic grammar* to analyse the data. What is needed, however, is not just a redefinition of *ancient* versus *modern* understandings of

---

[29] Moellering 1963: 103, 114.
[30] Koet 1929: 99; Moellering 1963: 52.
[31] Martin 1997: 113; cf. Martin 2004: 13–16.
[32] Martin 1997: 115; Gray 2004: 34.
[33] Moellering 1963: 53–54; Martin 1997: 119; Haenchen 1971: 520, n.7.
[34] Lane Fox 1997: 152.
[35] Martin 1997: 114. In his 2004 book, Martin gives many definitions of superstition, associating its criticism with the denounciation of excess, the 'other,' shameful behaviour, or the attribution of shameful behaviour to the gods. Cf. for example, 2004: 111.
[36] Koet 1929: 33.

superstition, as those studies presuppose, but a study which considers the possibility that the ancients *did not* criticize ancient religious behaviour or belief at all when they spoke of *deisidaimonia*.

The same remarks apply to the scholarly claims that *deisidaimonia* means 'piety' or 'religion' when it is used *sensu bono*. It is misleading to associate *deisidaimonia* with the modern categories of 'religion' and 'piety,' without carefully defining those categories within ancient religious grammar. Scholars have long noted that there is no Greek term equivalent to the English concept of 'religion.' Εὐσέβεια is the closest equivalent, but it only overlaps with the meaning of 'religion' in some contexts. The Greeks simply did not use this category.[37] It was not part of the *grammar* they used to speak about what we today call 'religious' phenomena. Therefore, to claim that *deisidaimonia* sometimes means 'religion' would need at the very least careful qualifications, and is in fact unlikely to be a useful category to describe this ancient phenomenology. Likewise, to comment that *deisidaimonia* means 'piety' is unhelpful without explaining precisely what the ancients meant by piety.

In its study of *deisidaimonia*, therefore, scholarship needs to take into account the different nature and grammar of ancient religion. To say—as is currently common in scholarship—that δεισιδαιμονία should be translated as either 'religion' or 'superstition' is unhelpful and misleading, for in antiquity people simply did not think in those categories. What is needed is an examination of *deisidaimonia* on the ancients' *own terms* and within the framework of their own conception of 'religion.' For this reason, the present chapter has retained the transliteration *deisidaimonia* to translate δεισιδαιμονία rather than using the misleading terminology of 'superstition' as most studies do.

3.1.3 Ancient Definitions of Deisidaimonia

To attempt an understanding of *deisidaimonia* on the ancients' own terms, this study uses as its starting point and preliminary hypothesis the ancient definition of *deisidaimonia*. The earliest definition available is provided by Theophrastus and could thus possibly go back to the 4th c. BCE. But it is often considered to be a later addition. Even if this is the case, however, it was added before Philodemus (1st c. BCE).[38]

---

[37] See Nongbri (2013: 4,7), who insists that the notion of religion is a recent invention which cannot be assumed to be a universal concept, and which is still mistakenly used by scholars of ancient Greece when they talk about 'ancient Greek religion.' Cf. Bremmer (1998: 12) who notes that the use of 'religion' in this context is 'an etic term' and does not reflect the perspective of the actor since 'the Greeks themselves did not have a word for "religion."'

[38] The line, like other introductory definitions in the *Characters*, is often considered to be a later addition, although this view is not without its opponents (cf. Lane Fox 1997: 164, n.140). Cf. Diggle 2004: 17–18.

Indeed, it would seem that *deisidaimonia* is cowardice towards the divine (δειλία πρὸς τὸ δαιμόνιον). (Theophrastus, *Char*.16.1 [MC])

No other definition is available before the timeframe of the present study, but several texts between the 1st c. BCE and the early 2nd c. CE corroborate the definition found in Theophrastus, defining *deisidaimonia* as the 'fear of the gods.'

Shame is fear of contempt; commotion is fear with noise urging on us; *deisidaimonia* is fear of the gods or the divine powers (φόβος θεῶν ἢ δαιμόνων) [...] (Arius Didymus [1st c. BCE], Epitome of Stoic Ethics 10χ, = SVF 3.408 [MC]) [39]

But *deisidaimonia*, as the appellation also indicates, is an emotional opinion and an assumption productive of a fear (δόξαν ἐμπαθῆ καὶ δέους ποιητικὴν ὑπόληψιν) which utterly humbles and crushes man, for he thinks that there are gods, but that they are causing pain and harmful. [. . .] Whence it follows that atheism is falsified reason, and *deisdaimonia* an emotion engendered by false reason (ἡ δὲ δεισιδαιμονία πάθος ἐκ λόγου ψευδοῦς ἐγγεγενημένον). (Plutarch, *Superst.* 165BC [MC])

Of all fears, the most impotent and helpless is *deisidaimonia* (Φόβων δὲ πάντων ἀπρακτότατος καὶ ἀπορώτατος ὁ τῆς δεισιδαιμονίας). (Plutarch, *Superst.* 165D [MC])

But the disposition (διάθεσις) toward god of the ignorant but not greatly wicked majority of people contains no doubt when they worship and pay reverence (τῷ σεβομένῳ καὶ τιμῶντι) an element of tremulous fear (μεμιγμένον τινὰ σφυγμὸν καὶ φόβον) – and this we call *deisidaimonia* (ᾗ καὶ δεισιδαιμονία κέκληται) (Plutarch, *Suav. viv.* 1101D9 [MC])

In addition, at least since the first century CE, δεισιδαιμονία is sometimes contrasted with εὐσέβεια.

Concerning this and the worship of the gods, what is done appropriately for their honour, the inherited customs and the complete tradition, take measures to lead the youth only into piety but not into *deisidaimonia* (εἰς τὸ εὐσεβεῖν ἀλλὰ μὴ εἰς τὸ δεισιδαιμονεῖν), teaching them to sacrifice, pray, kneel and to swear oaths according to custom and at appointed times according to fit measure (κατὰ τρόπον καὶ ἐν τοῖς ἐμβάλλουσι καιροῖς καθ' ἣν ἁρμόττει συμμετρίαν). (Cornutus [1st c. CE], *Theologiae Graecae Compendium* 35 [MC]) [40]

As this extract shows, piety and *deisidaimonia* are both connected with the worship of the gods, but they are distinct and contrasted with each other: the first is desirable and the second to be rejected.

At other times, δεισιδαιμονία is defined in relation to both εὐσέβεια and ἀθεότης or ἀσέβεια. In this case, δεισιδαιμονία and ἀθεότης/ἀσέβεια are the two extremes to be avoided—both being vices and perversions of piety—and εὐσέβεια is the mean, i.e. the virtue which should be strived for. Such statements are found, for example, in Plutarch and Philo, and, according to Stobaeus, in Aristotle and the Peripatetics.

---

[39] See also the Stoic definition of *deisidaimonia* as a kind of fear in *SVF* 3.394, 409, 411.

[40] According to Grodzynski (1974: 38, n.1), Cornutus is the first to contrast the two words.

For thus some who flee *deisidaimonia* fall into a harsh and opposite atheism (ἀθεότητα), thus overleaping piety (εὐσέβειαν) which lies in between. (Plutarch, *Superst.* 171F [MC])

The mean between temerity and cowardice is courage, [...] and between *deisidaimonia* and impiety (ἀσεβείας), piety (εὐσέβεια). (Philo, *Deus* 1:164 [MC])

Therefore, piety (εὐσέβειαν) is the art of serving the gods and the divinities, being situated between atheism (ἀθεότητος) and *deisidaimonia* (Stobaeus II, 147, 1–3 [MC]).

Such statements suggest that *deisidaimonia* could be described as an 'excess,' possibly an excess of fear or piety, something which is also suggested by Cornutus' passage above.

To conclude, when they define δεισιδαιμονία in the period which concerns us (1st c. BCE – early 2nd c. CE), ancient writers describe it as a 'fear of the divine,' and regularly contrast it with εὐσέβεια, sometimes even explicitly opposing them, εὐσέβεια referring to proper piety and δεισιδαιμονία to a perversion of it.[41] It is also noteworthy that while all the definitions examined are found in philosophers, they represent diverse philosophical traditions (Stoic, Peripatetic, Platonist and a Jewish writer) and are thus not specific to a particular philosophical circle.

3.1.4 Methodology of this Chapter

The ancient definitions of *deisidaimonia* examined above provide the starting hypothesis which will be tested in the present chapter. The next sections examine whether *deisidaimonia* always means 'fear of the gods' and whether it is always used distinctly from *eusebeia* between the first century BCE and the early second century CE. Indeed, although scholars regularly acknowledge the importance of the aspect of 'fear' connected with many occurrences of *deisidaimonia*, it is also often argued that the ancient definition of 'fear of the gods' does not fit all occurrences of *deisidaimonia*, or that it is not precise enough.[42]

This study therefore re-examines the evidence while taking care to avoid the methodological pitfalls highlighted earlier. To do so, it focuses on four authors and analyses their usage of *deisidaimonia* over against their use of *eusebeia* and *eulabeia,* two words belonging to the same semantic field. Those two words have been chosen because they are regularly mentioned in scholarly discussions of *deisidaimonia*, and, as said earlier, it is a common claim that

---

[41] A similar definition of *superstitio* and distinction between *superstitio* and *religio* or *pietas* is found in some Latin authors. E.g., Cicero calls *superstitio* an *inanis metus* (*ND* 1.117) and Varro writes: *Superstitioso dicat (scil. Varro) timeri deos, a religioso autem tantum vereri ut parentes, non ut hostes timeri* (ap. Augustine, *Civ. Dei*, VI, 9). Cf. also Cicero, *ND* 2.28.72; *Div.* 2.52.148–149; Seneca, *Clem.* 2.5.1.

[42] Gray 2004: 36; Martin 1997: 113; in 2004: 18–9, Martin argues that the definition is accurate if 'both halves of the terms are allowed a wide range of meaning.'

deisidaimonia sometimes means piety. A comparison of the use of *deisidaimonia* with that of *eusebeia* is thus urgently needed to highlight possible differences and similarity of usage between the two words. In addition, the present study also seeks to examine the meaning of those words *within the grammar of ancient religion*, and to avoid imposing anachronistic framework on the data.

Finally, a word about the choice of the four authors examined in this chapter is in order. All the authors examined wrote between the first century BCE and the early second century CE. However, because it has been claimed – in particular by Martin – that the philosophers understood *deisidaimonia* differently from other parts of the elite and common people, the first of the next two sections focuses on the usage of the terminology in three *non-philosophical* authors: Diodorus Siculus (90–30 BCE), Strabo (c. 64 BCE–c. 24 CE) and Jopsehus (37–100 CE).[43] While those three authors are all part of a Hellenistic educated elite and can hardly constitute evidence for the way common people understand the terminology, none of them has any philosophical commitment to the major Greek schools of their time, and their use of the terminology occurs mainly in narrative material rather than in reflections or comments about religious practices. They thus represent important evidence about how the terminology was understood and used outside of philosophical circles and debates, and will make it possible to verify if their use of the word really differs from that made by the philosophers. This will highlight whether the word in Acts 17 would have been perceived differently by an audience philosophically trained from an audience without philosophical background. The second section then examines the use of *deisidaimonia* in Plutarch, who has clear philosophical commitments, but also wrote a significant amount of narrative in his *Lives*. The next chapter will then focus more specifically on the discussion about *deisidaimonia* among Stoic and Epicurean philosophers.

As this limited selection of authors and terminology shows, the purpose of this chapter is not to provide an exhaustive study of *deisidaimonia* and its whole semantic field, even within the limited timeframe of the two centuries examined. Rather it seeks to provide the beginning of such a study through a new – and methodologically more rigorous – approach to the material, and thereby shed light on a longstanding conundrum in the exegesis of Acts 17. As will be shown, the results of this study – which of course must remain tentative and await further research – challenge several current assumptions on the subject of *deisidaimonia*.

---

[43] It is a central argument in Martin 2004 that the philosophers criticized *deisidaimonia*, whereas part of the rest of the elite and common people were unconvinced by their discourse and continued to use the terminology with positive connotations.

3.2 The Use of *Deisidaimonia* in Historians and Geographers

3.2.1 Diodorus Siculus (90–30 BCE)

a) Deisidaimonia

Diodorus Siculus uses δεισιδαιμονία 20 times, δεισιδαιμονέω 13 times and δεισιδαίμων four times in his *Bibliotheca*.[44] Although the assessment has been challenged, analysis nonetheless suggests that the meaning 'fear of the divine' fits well in each occurrence. For heuristic purposes, the contexts into which Diodorus uses the terminology can be classified into two groups.

First, *deisidaimonia* occurs when there is a concern of potential breaches of rituals or laws involving the gods, such as sacrileges, issues of ritual purity, or simply evil doing. Thus, *deisidaimonia* prevents people from committing sacrilege, such as stealing dedicated gold or offerings (5.27.4; 5.63.3), killing sacred animals (1.83.8), or breaking their sacred oaths (11.89.6; 11.89.8; 1.79.2). More generally, *deisidaimonia* spurs people to live a life pleasing to the gods and refrain from evil (1.70.8; 34/5.2.47), or fills them when they have done or about to do something sacrilegious (27.4.8; 27.4.5) or evil (20.43.1).

Second, *deisidaimonia* fills people when a particular event – especially an unusual event – leads them to think that the gods could be hostile towards them. Those events include phenomena in nature such as lightning, earthquakes, plague, war, military defeat, painful sicknesses, sudden death or other strange happenings (sea-monsters – 17.41.6; hermaphrodites – 32.12.3; 32.12.1). It also encompasses omen-like phenomena happening through human beings such as visions, ancient prophecies, or curses (17.41.8; 19.108.2; 15.54.4). Unsurprisingly then, people can be manipulated because of their *deisidaimonia*, either by priests (3.6.3; 36.13.2), oracles (15.54.4) or magicians (4.51.1).

What those two contexts have in common is that they are all susceptible to generate fear or anxiety about incurring the hostility of the gods. Often this hostility is perceived as divine punishment (1.70.8;1.83.8). Thus, in both types of situations, *deisidaimonia* may lead to attempts to propitiate the gods (15.54.4; 13.86.3), often through sacrifices (20.14.5; 34/5.10.1).

As has been pointed out by previous studies, there are, however, three cases which do not seem to fit this analysis because *deisidaimonia* is accompanied by happy expectations of help from the gods.[45] In the first instance, *deisidaimonia* occurs in the context of a military campaign, and is prompted by the apparition of a sea-monster:

As the construction of the Macedonians stretched to the range of emission of their missiles, a portent was sent from the gods to those being in danger. For from the sea a wave tossed an

---

[44] All searches in this chapter were conducted with *TLG*, except for Josephus, whose searches were conducted with Bibleworks' search engine.

[45] Cf. Martin 1997: 122.

incredibly great sea-monster upon their constructions, which fell upon the bank and did nothing evil, but leaning against a portion of its body for a long time, brought consternation [κατάπληξιν] to those watching, and swimming back into the sea, drew both sides into *deisidaimonia*. For each side was attempting to interpret [διέκρινον] the sign as Poseidon being about to help them, inclining by their judgments [ῥέποντες ταῖς γνώμαις] towards their own interest. (17.41.5–6 [MC])

Martin argues that here '*deisidaimonia* refers to the false belief that a freak occurrence is a good omen.'[46] But a case can be made that *deisidaimonia* also refers to fear in this context. Indeed, the strange event – interpreted as a sign from Poseidon – filled both sides with consternation (κατάπληξιν) and *deisidaimonia* as they were attempting to evaluate which side was to be the object of the help coming from the god, because the alternative was that they would be the enemies of the god![47] Διέκρινον is best interpreted as a conative imperfect here, meaning 'attempting to judge or evaluate,' and reflects the interpretative ambiguity of the sign. Thus, each side is trying to discern what the sign means and to interpret it as a sign of Poseidon's favour, the alternative being of course that it signals Poseidon's hostility – hence the mention of the fear of the gods (*deisidaimonia*) in this context. The fact that each side is inclined to interpret it towards its own interest, and thus optimistically, is not incompatible with a first reaction of anxiety or even a continuing nervousness despite the hope of being helped by the god. The situation of danger created by the context of war (κινδυνεύουσιν) and the incertitude concerning the interpretation of a portent which signals the intervention of a powerful divinity in the conflict, all suggest a context of anxiety, even if the sign is also generative of the hope of possibly being helped by the god. This interpretation seems corroborated by the next sentence in Diodorus, which reads: 'There were other strange happenings (σημεῖα παράδοξα) also, which could bring confusion and fear (διατροπὴν καὶ φόβον) among the people.'

The second instance occurs when Eumenes attempts to gain the cooperation of the other commanders after the death of Alexander. To secure their goodwill, Eumenes claims to have had a dream in which king Alexander appeared to him, and he suggests that they set up a throne for him where they hold their meetings and that they offer incense to Alexander every morning. Quickly Alexander is treated like a god, and Diodorus writes:

As their *deisidaimonia* for the king grew stronger [ἅμα δὲ καὶ τῆς κατὰ τὸν βασιλέα δεισιδαιμονίας ἐνισχυούσης], they were all filled with happy expectations, just as if some god were leading them. (18.61.3 [LCL slightly modified])

Martin writes: 'It is hard to say exactly what *deisidaimonia* is here except religious reverence for Alexander, which is certainly not considered inappropriate

---

[46] Martin 1997: 122 (italics original).
[47] See the similar association of κατάπληξις with danger and fear in Thucydides 7.42; 8.66.

by Diodorus.'⁴⁸ But again, the passage makes good sense with the nuance of fear, and a better translation would be '*fearful* reverence' in the context at hand. Indeed, Diodorus refers to the growth of the anxiety or nervousness not to offend the new god – i.e. Alexander – which accompanies the development of the new cult. This is not incompatible with the development of 'good hopes' which are created by the presence of the new god. Indeed, both go hand in hand (cf. ἅμα) in the context of Greek religion, where relationships with the gods are precisely characterized by this dual possibility: the hope of help if the gods are pleased, and the fear of harm if they are offended or simply in a bad mood. The new cult thus enabled Eumenes to rally all the commanders under the authority of the divinized Alexander whose divine leadership would command fearful reverence and create great hopes, and thereby establish Eumenes as 'a man worthy of the solicitude of the kings' (18.61.3).

In the last case Medea brings a terrifying statue of Artemis (τὴν θεὸν διεσκευασμένην καταπληκτικῶς) and uses her magical tricks to convince a city that Artemis in person has come into their midst to bring them good luck.

...Medea entered the palace, and she threw Pelias into such a state of *deisidaimonia* and, by her magic arts, led his daughters into such consternation/amazement [κατάπληξιν] that they believed that the goddess was actually there in person to bring prosperity to the house of the king. (4.51.3 [MC])

Again, the mention of the magical arts and amazement/consternation thereby created suggests that what people feel here is not just 'reverence' or 'piety,'⁴⁹ but the fearful reverence and awe which comes with the sense that a powerful god is present, a feeling compatible with the hope of being helped by the goddess if she is favourable. As in the previous example, this is a case where *deisidaimonia* is created for the sake of manipulation.

To conclude the analysis of those three cases, even though each time *deisidaimonia* occurs in a context where there are also good hopes, the nuance of fear and anxiety is still present. In each case, *deisidaimonia* is created by an unusual event which is interpreted as a manifestation of divine presence or will. This creates a sense of fear and unease, which is mixed with the hope of divine help. Although this mix of fear and hope might seem strange to modern readers, it is by no means in the context of Greek religion, where the sudden manifestation of a divine presence fills people with both the anxiety and the hope which come from the presence of a powerful being who can either be offended or help : indeed, such are the Greek gods.

Before comparing Diodorus' use of *deisidaimonia* with his use of *eusebeia*, three more remarks must be made at this point with respect to common understandings of the terminology. First, *deisidaimonia* never refers to particular

---

⁴⁸ Martin 1997: 122.
⁴⁹ Martin argues that the most common way Diodorus uses *deisidaimonia* is with the meaning of 'piety' or 'proper respect' (2004: 81).

religious practices or beliefs. Rather, it describes an emotion or attitude, namely the feeling of fear of the gods, and more particularly the *fear of being the object of divine hostility or wrath*. Second, although one of the contexts in which *deisidaimonia* appears is unusual phenomena which moderns might label 'supernatural' (visions, sea-monsters, eclipses), its usage is not limited to those situations. For example, doing evil can fill a person with *deisidaimonia*. Conversely, not all instances of 'supernatural' phenomena give rise to *deisidaimonia*. Finally, concerning the connotation of *deisidaimonia*, it is noteworthy that the terminology is always used descriptively: it is used to refer to the 'fear of the gods' or of the divine, and does not in and of itself connote an assessment of the religious practices or feelings of people, whether positive or negative. Thus, the terminology is never explicitly used to describe a virtue or a vice, for example. Only in a few cases, does the author comment on the 'validity' or 'usefulness' of the feeling, and interestingly, his assessment depends upon the circumstances at hand. Thus, Diodorus finds *deisidaimonia* inappropriate in the case of hermaphrodites – which he considers a natural phenomenon rather than a sign of divine displeasure (32.12.1). On the other hand, the historian finds *deisidaimonia* necessary to maintain morality in society at large, for very few people are virtuous because of their character, and most need the motivation which comes from the fear of divine retribution (34/5.2.47). In the great majority of cases, however, Diodorus does not comment and one is hard pressed to determine a pejorative or approving connotation. What is clear, is that there is no sign in his writings that he does not believe in the validity of traditional religious practices such as omen, prophecies and sacrifices to maintain a good relationship with the gods.[50] Indeed, the narrative he tells shows that sacrificing out of *deisidaimonia* – i.e. fear of divine hostility – can indeed avert bad things from happening, and the gods certainly do punish people (e.g., 14.77.4).

Because his assessment of *deisidaimonia* differs, Diodorus' use of this terminology has often been deemed inconsistent. It is said that he sometimes uses it with the nuance of 'piety, reverence' and at other times as 'excessively religious, superstitious.'[51] To explain those contradictions, scholars have pointed to the diverse sources used by the historian, arguing that he used them without much editing and thus incorporated different perspectives on *deisidaimonia*.[52] But understanding *deisidaimonia* as meaning 'fear of the gods' shows that his usage is perfectly consistent. *Deisidaimonia* always means 'fear of the divine' for Diodorus, whether it has the nuance of fear of divine hostility, fear of offending the gods or fearful reverence. Sometimes Diodorus comments on its

---

[50] Cf. Martin (1997: 123): 'As this and several other stories show, Diodorus himself takes things like omens, prophecies, and astrology quite seriously.'
[51] Koet 1929: 9.
[52] Koet 1929: 9; Martin 1997: 121; Martin 2004:79–80.

necessity, but in the majority of cases he does not. *Deisidaimonia* is simply a common phenomenon in Greek religion. Sometimes Diodorus finds it unwarranted, but most of the time, he seems to find it quite normal. He is aware that this fear of the gods can be used to manipulate, but even in those cases, he usually does not comment on the morality of the practice.

b) Eusebeia, theosebeia and eulabeia

Moving to Diodorus' usage of closely related words, the historian never uses θεοσέβεια or θεοσεβής, but he does use εὐσέβεια 48 times (+ εὐσεβής 17 times), and εὐλάβεια 9 times (never εὐλαβής). Εὐσέβεια is best translated by 'piety' or 'reverence.' Diodorus uses εὐσέβεια in three types of contexts.

Most frequently, εὐσέβεια refers to the *virtue* of piety. It is thus often used to characterize people positively, winning them the appreciation or admiration of both men and gods. It regularly occurs in lists of virtues or in coordination with other virtues such as δικαιοσύνη (1.2.2; 4.18.22; cf. 12.20.3), χρηστότης (1.65.2) or φιλανθρωπία (21.17.4). Just as proper human relationships should be characterized by 'righteousness,' εὐσέβεια describes the proper attitude of human beings towards the gods.[53] Εὐσέβεια makes one the friend of the gods and brings their favour or reward (5.7.7; 8.15.5), while the gods take vengeance upon the impious. The terminology can be used to characterize not only a person's attitude towards the gods, but her moral character generally. Implicit is of course that a person pious towards the gods must be virtuous and thus righteous towards men. Thus Diodorus often uses the adjective εὐσεβής substantively to refer to the 'pious' as opposed to the 'impious' or 'wicked' (8.15.2), and to talk about the fate of the deceased, who might be received in the company of the 'pious' (1.92.5) or endure the punishment of the 'wicked' (τῶν πονηρῶν, 1.93.3; τῶν ἀσέβων, 1.96.5).

Second, Diodorus sometimes uses εὐσέβεια with a meaning coming close to 'cult,' referring to the set of practices involved in the worship or reverence towards a particular deity (e.g. 4.8.5). Thus the Athenians were the first to honour Heracles as a god and the Greeks followed them in their reverence (εὐσέβεια) for the god (4.39.1). Finally, εὐσέβεια can refer to an attitude towards human beings (e.g. towards strangers – 4.46.4; towards parents – 4.52.2).

In conclusion, two elements stand out in Diodorus' use of εὐσέβεια in comparison to δεισιδαιμονία. First, εὐσέβεια is always positively connoted. Indeed, εὐσέβεια is a virtue and is thus a term of praise. And second, apart from two passages, εὐσέβεια does not occur in the context where there is a fear of divine punishment or a possibility to offend the deity. The first exception is in 12.57.4, where the Cercyraenans absolve suppliants who had fled to the altars of the

---

[53] The two are often linked: 'They who do not cherish piety towards the divinity show all the less concern to observe justice towards men.' (7.12.7)

gods 'out of their reverence of the gods' (διὰ τὴν πρὸς θεοὺς εὐσέβειαν), something which could be interpreted as a fear of incurring divine hostility if they had executed the suppliants. But the use of εὐσέβεια here probably gives a different nuance to the event in that it emphasizes that it is the piety of the Cercyraenans which motivated their action, rather than a fear from punishment from the deity. A similar case seems to be 33.5.2, where suppliants come to the Arcadians with branches of supplications and their city's idols, hoping to change their resolution by their piety towards the gods (θεῶν εὐσεβείᾳ).

Moving to Diodorus's use of εὐλάβεια, the terminology appears in contexts which partly overlap with δεισιδαιμονία, but it seems to imply an idea of 'restraint' rather than 'fear.' It is used in non-religious contexts where it refers to 'caution' or 'precaution' (8.12.8) or timidity, excessive caution (23.11.1). In religious situations, it occurs in similar contexts as *deisidaimonia* (sometimes the two words occur in the same paragraph: e.g., 13.12.6; 15.53.4), where there is a potential threat to be the object of divine hostility. In those cases, it is difficult to assess whether there is a different nuance between *deisidaimonia* or *eulabeia*, but *eulabeia*'s connotation of 'restraint' seems still present in that it is often used in contexts where something is *not* done or taking place out of precaution or caution towards the divinity. For example, in the story of Nicias, even those who are sceptical that an eclipse and an epidemic reflect divine disapproval are compelled to postpone the departure of the army 'out of caution towards the divine' (τὴν πρὸς τὸ θεῖον εὐλάβειαν, 13.12.6).

c) Conclusion

In conclusion of our analysis, the evidence suggests that Diodorus consistently uses *deisidaimonia* and *eusebeia* in different contexts and with different nuances. *Deisidaimonia* means 'fearful reverence towards the gods,' 'fear of hostility from the gods,' and refers to the anxiety or concern to avoid the hostility and harm of the divine. On the other hand, *eusebeia* means piety, worship or reverence without the nuance of fear. Finally, *eulabeia* means caution, precaution, but also appears in similar contexts as *deisidaimonia*, where there is a concern to not offend a divinity.

3.2.2 Strabo (c. 64 BCE–c. 24 CE)

Judgements about Strabo's use of *deisidaimonia* must remain more tentative as the geographer does not uses the terminology which interests us frequently : δεισιδαιμονία – 4x, δεισιδαίμων – 3x, εὐσέβεια/εὐσεβής – 8x, θεοσέβεια/θεοσεβής – 3x, εὐλάβεια/εὐλαβής – 0x. A good case can be made, however, that Strabo uses *deisidaimonia* with the nuance of 'fear of the gods' or 'fear of offending the gods' and *eusebeia* to refer to the positively connoted characteristic of piety or worship-reverence towards a deity.

a) Deisidaimonia

Looking first at the seven instances of δεισιδαιμονία and δεισιδαίμων, in three cases Strabo uses the terminology like Diodorus, in contexts where the breach of rituals or laws creates an anxiety of offending the gods and becoming the object of evil sent by them. Thus, like Diodorus, Strabo speaks of *deisidaimonia* preventing people from stealing gold in sacred lakes (4.1.13), and he also considers that *deisidaimonia* is useful to deter from evil (1.2.8). This latter passage is worth quoting in full, for it sheds helpful light on the relationship between *deisidaimonia*, *eusebeia* and myths and marvels:

> Most of those who live in the cities [...] are deterred from evil courses when, either through descriptions or through typical representations of objects unseen, they learn of divine punishments, terrors, and threats – or even when they merely believe that men have met with such experiences. For in dealing with a crowd of women, at least, or with any promiscuous mob, a philosopher cannot influence them by reason or exhort them to reverence [εὐσέβειαν], piety [ὁσιότητα] and faith [πίστιν]; nay, there is need of religious fear also [ἀλλὰ δεῖ καὶ διὰ δεισιδαιμονίας], and this cannot be aroused without myths and marvels [μυθοποιίας καὶ τερατείας]. For thunderbolts, aegis, trident, torches, snakes, thyrsus-lances, – arms of the gods—are myths, and so is the entire ancient theology. But the founder of states gave their sanction to these things as bugbears wherewith to scare the simple-minded. (1.2.8 [LCL])

This passage is particularly helpful for it illustrates the difference between εὐσέβεια and δεισιδαιμονία. As in Diodorus, εὐσέβεια is a positive behaviour (here associated with the other virtues of ὁσιότης and πίστις) towards which people are to be encouraged. *Deisidaimonia*, however, refers to the fear of the gods' retribution and plays a role as a deterrent from evil doing. The passage also sheds light on the relationship between myth and *deisidaimonia*: for Strabo *deisidaimonia* cannot be aroused without myths. Indeed, it is the mythological stories casting the gods as terrifying warriors and speaking of divine punishment which keep people in check morally, which is why politicians approve of those things as 'bugbears' aiming to scare away from evil doing. Thus, *deisidaimonia* is necessary as a deterrent from evil doing for the simple-minded – which includes women and common men.

The third case where *deisidaimonia* clearly refers to a fear is when Strabo speaks of the *deisidaimonia* which makes the gulf of Avernus a shadowy place (5.4.5). The word refers to the fear of the divine associated with the entrance of the underworld, and Strabo explains that legends report that the birds flying above the gulf fall into the water killed by the vapour arising from it, and only those who have propitiated the nether deities can sail above it.

In the other four occurrences of *deisidaimonia*, the context is not as clearly connected to divine punishment or hostility, but a good case can be made that the terminology can be appropriately translated by 'fear of the gods,' or 'fearful reverence.' In the first case, Strabo finds it implausible that people living without women would be particularly 'pious' [θεοσεβεῖς] because it is well-known that women are the main initiators of *deisidaimonia* [τῆς δεισιδαιμονίας ἀρχηγούς].

And of course to regard as 'both god-fearing [θεοσεβεῖς] and capnobatae' those who are without women is very much opposed to the common notions on that subject; for all agree in regarding the women as the chief founders of *deisidaimonia* [τῆς δεισιδαιμονίας ἀρχηγούς], and it is the women who provoke the men to more attentive worship of the gods [θεραπείας τῶν θεῶν], to festivals, and to supplications, and it is a rare thing for a man who lives by himself to be found addicted to these things.' (7.3.4 [LCL slightly modified])

Although LCL translates *deisidaimonia* by 'religion' and it might be tempting to render it by 'piety' as a synonym of the preceding θεοσεβεῖς, the fact that Strabo speaks about women here suggests that he uses *deisidaimonia* with the nuance of 'fear of the gods' rather than piety. Indeed, as 1.2.8 has shown, Strabo believes that women cannot be convinced into piety by reason alone but that they also need *deisidaimonia* (fear of divine punishment). He further singles out women as particularly prone to *deisidaimonia*. In light of this earlier assertion, it is unlikely that Strabo would characterize women as the chief founders of 'piety' in 7.3.4. Rather Strabo is pointing out that women being the most anxious about the gods and most nervous about not offending them, they are the ones who push men into taking more *care of the gods* (θεραπείας τῶν θεῶν). At the same time, this passage shows that *deisidaimonia* is closely intertwined with the cult of the gods and piety, and not necessarily incompatible with it.

In the second case, Strabo speaks about a 'substance mixed with wood and earth' 'which is used in large quantities as frankincense by the *deisidaimones*' [ᾧ πλείστῳ χρῶνται θυμιάματι οἱ δεισιδαίμονες] ([MC] 12.73). LCL translates δεισιδαίμονες as 'worshippers,' but the nuance of fear fits well here also in that Strabo is probably referring to the large quantities of frankincense used by those who are anxious to appease the divinity or protect themselves from negative divine action.

Finally, the last two occurrences appear in a passage discussing Jewish religion (16.2.37). Strabo describes the successors of Moses in this way:

His successors for some time abided by the same course, acting righteously and being truly pious [θεοσεβεῖς] towards god; but afterwards, in the first place, men fearful of god [δεισιδαιμόνων] were appointed to the priesthood, and then tyrannical people; and from the fear of god [δεισιδαιμονίας] arose abstinence from flesh (from which it is their custom to abstain even today), circumcisions, excisions and other observances of the kind.' (16.2.37 [MC])

In this passage, the worship characterized by *deisidaimonia* is contrasted with the true piety and righteousness which characterized the regime of Moses and his immediate successors, thereby assessing it negatively. Furthermore, it is identified as the cause which led to practices such as abstinence from flesh and circumcision, which Strabo contrasts with the worship advocated by Moses which was not oppressive or troublesome for the people (16.2.36). Again, the nuance of 'fear to conciliate the divine' fits the context: it is priests anxious about the divinity and about not offending it who introduced religious practices such as food taboos and circumcision.

While the contexts of those last four examples are not as explicitly associated with the fear of divine hostility as the two contexts identified in Diodorus, what they have in common is that they describe a situation in which an increase or abundance of religious practice is explained by *deisidaimonia*. This certainly fits the nuance of anxiety about the divine.

b) Eusebeia and theosebeia

This understanding of Strabo's usage is corroborated by an examination of his use of *eusebeia* and *theosebeia*, which shows that he uses them in contexts similar to those in which Diodorus uses of *eusebeia*. Strabo seems to use *theosebeia* like *eusebeia*, which appears again in three contexts. Like Diodorus, Strabo uses εὐσέβεια to refer to a desired character trait, coordinating it with other virtues (2x; cf. 1.2.8; 15.1.60), also using the adjective εὐσεβής in the context of a discussion of the abode of the pious in the afterlife (3.2.13). In addition, the terminology is also used with a nuance close to 'religious practices' (7.3.3). Finally, in two occurrences it refers to piety towards human beings (parents or a former commander – 6.2.3; 13.1.26).

Thus, like Diodorus, Strabo uses *eusebeia* in contexts different from those of deisaimonia. *Eusebeia* never occurs in situations involving the fear of divine hostility.

c) Conclusion

Although they must remain tentative in light of the few uses Strabo makes of the terminology, the following two remarks can be made about the geographer's use of *deisidaimonia*. First, all his uses make sense with the meaning 'fear of the gods,' or 'fearful reverence.' Indeed, like Diodorus, Strabo uses the terminology in contexts where there is a fear of offending the gods through sacrilege, evil doing, or breaching rituals connected to the gods, and also sometimes associates it with marvels. In this respect, Strabo importantly highlights the connection between *deisidaimonia* and myths and tradition. Belief in myth is not in itself an expression of *deisidaimonia*, but belief in myth fosters *deisidaimonia*, since the myths depict the gods in a way which fosters fear of them because they sometimes do evil to men, or because they can be offended. In addition, Strabo also uses *deisidaimonia* in association with the multiplication or abundance of religious practices. Here again, anxiety about the divine is the cause of such abundant practices.

Second, moving to the connotation of *deisidaimonia* in Strabo, only in one passage – the one discussing Jewish religion – does Strabo clearly assess *dei-*

sidaimonia negatively, contrasting the *deisidaimonia* of later priests with the proper piety (*theosebeis*) and righteousness advocated by Moses. While his discussion of myths shows that Strabo is sceptical towards them, there is no reason to believe that he rejects other traditional beliefs or practices, including those meant to appease the gods. Like Diodorus, Strabo is aware of the use of people's fear of divine punishment for political or social reasons, but again he sometimes sees this as necessary and useful for society. Finally, Strabo implies that women are more prone to *deisidaimonia*.

3.2.3 Josephus (37–100 CE)

a) Deisidaimonia

Δεισιδαιμονία occurs 15 times in Josephus, but because he recounts the same incidents several times, those 15 times actually only refer to 9 different situations. One of the particularities of his usage is that, out of those occurrences, 10 occur in the speech of foreigners. Although Josephus' usage is often cited as evidence that *deisidaimonia* frequently simply meant 'religion' in the ancient world, it is argued here that Josephus uses the terminology consistently with the nuance of 'fear of offending the gods.' The contexts in which he uses *deisidaimonia* are similar to those identified in Diodorus and Strabo in that they all reflect a concern not to offend a divinity, but with a particular nuance since they mainly occur in the context of Jewish and not Greek 'religion.'

Thus, like the preceding authors, Josephus uses *deisidaimonia* when particular events happen which can be interpreted as signs of divine displeasure. For example, Agatharchides mocked Stratonice for her *deisidaimonia*, because she obeyed a dream which forbade her to sail away and was thus caught and put to death (*Ag. Ap.* 1.208). Manasseh's *deisidaimonia* towards God after he was devastated by war and caught by the king of Babylon also falls in this category (*Ant.* 10.42). Josephus describes Manasseh's repentance of his sins following this divine punishment, and how he displayed much *deisidaimonia* towards God (πάσῃ χρῆσθαι περὶ αὐτὸν δεισιδαιμονίᾳ), consecrated the temple and purified the city. The context of divine punishment and repentance suggest that the nuance of *deisidaimonia* is different from simply 'reverence' (LCL) or 'religious life' (Whiston). Rather, it points to Manasseh's fear of offending the divinity again. As Josephus continues, by those actions Manasseh was 'seeking to make God propitious towards him for the rest of his life' (καὶ διατηρεῖν αὐτὸν εὐμενῆ παρ' ὅλον τὸν βίον) (*Ant.* 10.42). Josephus also uses *deisidaimonia* in the context of political manipulation. He thus describes how the *deisidaimonia* of Alexandra made it possible for the Pharisees to manipulate her so that she put their enemies to death (*War* 1.113). Although both Alexandra and the Pharisees were earlier characterized as pious (108, 110), the use of *deisidaimonia* in this context suggests that Alexandra was concerned to avert God's hostility by eliminating persons hostile to the 'pious' Pharisees.

The other instances of *deisidaimonia* in Josephus all occur in contexts where there is a concern about a sacrilege being committed, or a divine law being breached. Thus, three passages recount events where the Jews react violently because a sacrilege has been committed against God. In the first case, they react because Herod has introduced trophies – which were considered to be images – into their city. As a result, Herod tries to 'free them from their *deisidaimonia*' (τῆς δεισιδαιμονίας ἀφαιρούμενος) (*Ant.* 15.277). Similarly, in the second case, the Jews react to Pilate's introduction of standards in Jerusalem, preferring to die rather than to admit Caesar's images and transgress the law [ἢ τὸν νόμον παραβῆναι]. 'Astonished at the intensity of their *deisidaimonia*' (τὸ τῆς δεισιδαιμονίας ἄκρατον) Pilate commands the removal of the standards (*War* 2.174). In the third case, the Jews, drawn together by *deisidaimonia* (τῇ δεισιδαιμονίᾳ συνελκόμενοι), ask that a soldier who has torn the sacred book of the law into pieces and thrown it into the fire, be punished for such an affront to God and to his law (τὸν οὕτως εἰς τὸν θεὸν καὶ τὸν νόμον αὐτῶν ἐξυβρίσαντα, *War* 2.230). In each case, the Jews' *deisidaimonia* reflects their concern to remove or punish what they considered a serious offense against God.

Along the same line, three others times *deisidaimonia* is used in the context of the Jewish or Samaritan practice of keeping the laws associated with the Sabbath (*Ant.* 12.5; 12.6; 12.259). The first two occurrences are used in a passage where Agatharchides of Cnidus reproaches the Jews for having lost their freedom because of their 'unseasonable *deisidaimonia*.' Josephus writes:

> But Agatharchides of Cnidus, who wrote the acts of [Alexander's] successors, reproaches us for our *deisidaimonia*, as if we had lost our liberty because of it, saying: 'There is a nation, called the nation of the Jews, who possess a strong and great city named Jerusalem. And they took no care and let it fall into the hands of Ptolemy because they were unwilling to take arms, and thereby submitted to be under a hard master, on account of their untimely *deisidaimonia*.' (*Ant.* 12.5–6 [MC])

Deisidaimonia is best rendered by 'anxiety or concern not to offend the gods.'[54] A support for this translation is found in Plutarch's discussion of a similar event in his treatise *De superstitione* (169C). Plutarch lists the capture of Jerusalem because of the Jews' refusal to take up arms on the Sabbath as an example of the tragic effects engendered by *deisidaimonia* in critical situations. The context shows that he is effectively criticizing the 'cowardice' [cf. δειλίας] associated with *deisidaimonia*.[55] The second passage mentioning *deisidaimonia* in

---

[54] Note that Josephus refers to the same event in *Ag. Ap.*1.212, criticizing Agatharchides' mockery and pointing out that such a concern for the laws and piety (εὐσέβεια) should be praised.

[55] '...for God is brave hope, not cowardly excuse. But the Jews, because it was the Sabbath day, sat in their places immovable, while the enemy were planting ladders against the walls and

the context of Sabbath keeping in Josephus confirms this nuance. In this case, a Samaritan speaks about this custom.

> Our forefathers, because of certain droughts in the country and following a certain ancient *deisidaimonia* (παρακολουθήσαντες ἀρχαίᾳ τινὶ δεισιδαιμονίᾳ), made it a custom to observe that day which by the Jews is called the Sabbath. (*Ant* 12:259 [MC])

In light of the verb παρακολουθήσαντες – to follow, to keep – it is better to translate *deisidaimonia* as 'religious scruple' or 'practice born out of fear or concern to avert divine hostility' rather than 'fear of God.'[56] But the mention of the droughts makes it clear that keeping the Sabbath has an apotropaic function and aims to prevent the droughts which are the consequence of divine displeasure or punishment. There is no sign here that this *deisidaimonia* is criticized.

Finally, the last six occurrences of *deisidaimonia* in Josephus occur in the context of a Roman decree and are often pointed to as evidence that *deisidaimonia* can be translated by 'religion.' The first five times refer to the same instance, whereby a decree from the consul Lentulus exempts the Jews from military service on account of their *deisidaimonia* (δεισιδαιμονίας ἕνεκα, *Ant.* 14.228, 232, 234, 237, 240). The last occurrence appears in an edict from Claudius which permits the Jews to keep their ancient customs and enjoins them not to show contempt for the *deisidaimonia* of other nations, but to keep their own laws only (μὴ τὰς τῶν ἄλλων ἐθνῶν δεισιδαιμονίας ἐξουθενίζειν τοὺς ἰδίους δὲ νόμους φυλάσσειν, *Ant.* 19.290). The expression does not seem to carry negative connotations in any of those instances and has thus been seen as evidence that *deisidaimonia* can mean 'religion.'[57]

But even in those cases, what is at stake is clearly religious scruples, and not simply religious rites or piety.[58] Indeed, the reason for their exemption from military service is that it would prevent the Jews from following the law with respect to the Sabbath and food laws (*Ant.* 14.226). Moreover, the decrees use ἱερὰ Ἰουδαϊκὰ to refer to Jewish rites (*Ant.* 14.228, 237, 240). When the Jews are asked not to show contempt for the *deisidaimonia* of the other nations, therefore, they are asked not to show contempt for the religious scruples of other nations. At stake is the breaking of each nations religious laws aiming to prevent them from the wrath of their god.[59]

---

capturing the defences, and they did not get up, but remained there, fast bound in the toils of *deisidaimonia* as in one great net.' (LCL slightly modified)

[56] And not 'religious rite' or 'superstitious practice' (cf. Koet 1929: 23).

[57] Koet 1929: 23–24 and many others.

[58] Marcus [LCL] translates *deisidaimonia* by 'religious scruples' in *Ant.* 14.228, 232, 234, 237, 240.

[59] Even if *deisidaimonia* reflects a translation of the Latin *religio*, this point is still valid since *religio* can mean religious scruple.

In conclusion, Josephus's use of *deisidaimonia* presents strong parallels to Diodorus and Strabo's usage, but with some adjustments to the Jewish context of his narrative. Again, *deisidaimonia* appears after some events potentially indicating divine hostility or punishment (e.g., a dream, a plague and a military defeat). Likewise, *deisidaimonia* is exploited by religious figures to reach their political ends (the Pharisees). The particularity of Josephus's usage lies in the recasting of the second context which was identified – the fear to breach a religious law – into its Jewish mould. This anxiety thus becomes a fear of breaches or offenses against the Jewish law – such as bringing images in Jerusalem, burning the book of the law, breaking the Sabbath, or the non-respect of dietary laws.

Admittedly, this discussion of Josephus' use of *deisidaimonia* has consisted more in showing that the meaning 'religious scruple' or 'religious fear' fits each occurrence rather than showing that other translations such as 'religion' or 'piety' are not valid. This reading, however, is confirmed when Josephus' usage of *deisidaimonia* is compared with his use of *eusebeia/theosebeia* and *eulabeia*. Indeed, when there is no concern to avert divine offense, Josephus invariably uses *eusebeia*.

b) Eusebeia, theosebeia and eulabeia

Josephus uses the word εὐσέβεια over a hundred times in his writings.[60] As Diodorus and Strabo, however, he uses it differently from *deisidaimonia*, and it never occurs in contexts where there is a concern not to offend the divinity. The word is best rendered by 'piety' and appears in the three contexts already noted earlier in this study.

Thus, in the great majority of cases, εὐσέβεια refers to the virtue of piety. Again, it is regularly coordinated with other virtues, especially righteousness (*Ant.* 6.265; 8.121). Εὐσέβεια brings reward and fruit and makes one the friend of God (*Ant.* 5.116), but it is clear that the meaning of εὐσέβεια sometimes goes beyond a description of one's attitude to God and includes one's ethical behaviour towards human beings more broadly (e.g. *Ant.* 5.327). This is unsurprising in a Jewish context where proper attitude towards God includes keeping the commands of the law (*Ant.* 8.208). Correspondingly, εὐσέβεια is not only the antithesis of impiety but also of wickedness (cf. *Ant.* 6.127: πονηρίας).

Second, εὐσέβεια is used to refer to the set of cultic practices or religious attitudes related to a particular cult, such as the proper way to worship Yahweh (e.g. *Ant.* 4.31; *War* 7.430). In this case, it can be translated by 'worship' or 'cult,' and is sometimes coordinated with the word θρησκεία (*Ant.* 6.90). In some cases, it comes very close to the usage of 'religion' in English. For

---

[60] He also uses εὐσεβής 34x. He does not use θεοσέβεια, but uses θεοσεβής 6x, in contexts similar to those of εὐσεβής.

example, Josephus writes that 'the rewards of fighting are the freedom of your country, your laws and your religion' [ἐλευθερίας πατρίδος νόμων εὐσεβείας] (*Ant.* 12.304; cf. *Ant.* 13.243; *Ag. Ap.* 1.224). Finally, εὐσέβεια is also used to refer to piety towards other human beings, most specifically towards parents (*War* 1.630, 633) but also towards kings (*Ant.* 7.269).

Josephus uses εὐλάβεια five times, but it always means 'fear' and is used to refer to the fear of being the object of human violence, either as a form of retribution or punishment (*Ant.* 6.78, 11.239, 12.255, 12.278) or a form of slavery (e.g. monarchy – *War* 4.393). It is thus never used in the same contexts as *eusebeia* or *deisidaimonia*.

c) Conclusion

Three remarks on Josephus' usage can be made in conclusion. First, like Diodorus and Strabo, in the great majority of cases Josephus uses *deisidaimonia* and *eusebeia* in different contexts. *Deisidaimonia* occurs when there is anxiety about offending or having offended the gods, which in Josephus' corpus regularly occurs in relation to breaches of the Jewish law. On the other hand, *eusebeia* refers to the virtue of piety, a particular worship or cult, or piety towards human beings. Of course, as has been observed in other authors, some contexts would be suitable for either *deisidaimonia* or *eusebeia*, depending upon the nuance the author wishes to give to the event. This is particularly the case in the context of potential sacrilege, for example when a suppliant seeking refuge to an altar is hoping to be secure because of the king's piety (*Ant.* 8.13), or when Pilate does not touch any of the treasures of the temple on account of his piety (*Ant.* 14.72). In those cases, Josephus uses *eusebeia* because he wants to emphasize the virtue of the king and Pilate, rather than their concern not to offend the divinity and risk retribution.

Second, it is worth noting that this distinction is valid even in the mouth of foreigners or Roman official documents in Josephus' corpus. Indeed, it is sometimes argued that *deisidaimonia* is simply the way Greeks and Romans would have talked about the religion of other people. This, however, is inaccurate as far as Josephus is concerned. The Roman official documents quoted do not all use the word *deisidaimonia* when they talk about Jewish practices. Rather it is again the context at hand and whether there is a concern about divine hostility which determines whether the word used is *deisidaimonia* or *eusebeia*. Thus, as mentioned above, when the decree of Lentulus exempts the Jews from military service, it does so on account of their *deisidaimonia*, i.e. their religious scruples. But when Julius Antonius the proconsul sends a letter to the magistrates and people of Ephesus to transmit Caesar's directive that the Jews are permitted to follow their own laws and custom and to bring to Jerusalem the offerings which they make out of their free will and out of piety, he uses *eusebeia* (ἐκ τῆς ἰδίας προαιρέσεως εὐσεβείας ἕνεκα τῆς πρὸς τὸ θεῖον, *Ant.* 16.172).

Finally, *deisidaimonia* is the object of criticism only once, when Agatharchides of Cnidus reproaches the Jews for having lost their freedom because of their *deisidaimonia*. This, however, should not be explained away as reflecting Josephus' use of another source.[61] Rather, the word still means exactly the same as elsewhere, namely 'fear of the gods.'

3.3 The Use of *Deisidaimonia* in Plutarch of Chaeronea (c. 45 CE – Before 125)

The biographer and moral philosopher Plutarch of Chaeronea is treated in a different section from the other authors not only because he has clear philosophical commitments to Platonism, but also because he uses the terminology of *deisidaimonia* extensively – 127 times – in a notably varied corpus.[62] Plutarch's use of *deisidaimonia* and its relation with his religious thought, however, has been the object of much discussion in scholarship.

3.3.1 Plutarch's De Superstitione *and His Religious Thought*

Plutarch is the author of the only extant treatise on *deisidaimonia* which survives from antiquity.[63] His use of the terminology, however, is not limited to this work.[64] A TLG search on Plutarch's corpus retrieves 102 occurrences of δεισιδαιμονία and 25 occurrences of δεισιδαίμων. Among these, 25 occurrences of the noun and 21 occurrences of the adjective appear in his treatise on the subject, *De superstitione*. Plutarch's criticism of *deisidaimonia* in this treatise, however, has been a longstanding puzzle in scholarship.

Indeed, the religious views of this treatise have often seemed at odds with Plutarch's views elsewhere, for in his denunciation of *deisidaimonia* Plutarch seems to criticize and ridicule beliefs and behaviours which he endorses elsewhere in his writings, such as belief in post-mortem punishment, oracles, omen and dreams.[65] To explain such differences, scholars have sometimes appealed

---

[61] So Koet 1929: 66.

[62] On Plutarch's Platonism, see Russell 2001: 63–83; Dillon 2014.

[63] Smith 1975 is one of the rare scholars who rejects Plutarch's authorship of this treatise. For a recent edition and commentary, cf. Görgemanns 2003.

[64] On Plutarch's use of *deisidaimonia*, see Koet 1929: 68–83; Erbse 1952; Moellering 1963; Smith 1975: 1–35; Pérez Jiménez 1996: 195–225; Lozza 1996: 389–94; Baldassarri 1996: 373–387; Klauck 1997: 111–26; Gray 2004: 51–108; Martin 2004: 93–108; Bowden 2008: 56–71; Van Nuffelen 2011: 48–71 and 157–175.

[65] The main differences which are usually pointed out in the treatise are: the judgment that *deisidaimonia* is worse than atheism whereas elsewhere he argues the opposite; his affirmation that gods and demons are good, whereas elsewhere he endorses the existence of evil demons; his rejection of afterlife punishment, which he endorses elsewhere. They are listed in Mollering

to source criticism or to the rhetorical purpose of the treatise.⁶⁶ Most often, however, this discrepancy has been thought to reflect an evolution in Plutarch's thought, the moralist having moved from the 'rationalistic scepticism' of his youth to a more 'religious' and mystical outlook in his later years which coincided with his work as a priest in Delphi.⁶⁷ *De superstitione* is thus usually classified as a work of Plutarch's youth, whereas the *Lives* or *De Iside et Osiride* are later works.

While this view has gained the support of many scholars, it has not gone unchallenged. Morton Smith argued that the difference between *De superstitione* and Plutarch's other works is too great and challenged the assumption that Plutarch was the author of the treatise.⁶⁸ Taking the opposite view, Erbse and Brenk have contended that differences between *De superstitione* and other works have been exaggerated and emphasized the continuity between them. Erbse showed that many statements about *deisidaimonia* found in the treatise are paralleled in his other works, and that his understanding and criticism of *deisidaimonia* can be found throughout his writings.⁶⁹ Likewise, Brenk argued that 'mystical tendencies' or 'superstitions' are found throughout his corpus, and not just in later writings. He also contended that criticism of punishment in the afterlife can be found in later writings. More recently, Opsomer has rejected the evolutionary interpretation of Plutarch's thought on the ground that scepticism and religion often coexisted in the New Academy and were by no means opposed to each other, despite what has been assumed in much past scholarship.⁷⁰

Despite those contributions, however, it is still a common view that there are tensions between this treatise and the rest of Plutarch's work, and that such tensions are reflective either of an evolution in Plutarch's thinking, or of Plutarch's continuous grappling with conflicting loyalties between religion and philosophy.⁷¹ For example, Martin argues that Brenk underestimates the 'contradictions' in Plutarch, and contends that they reflect the influence of popular

---

1963: 106–147; Smith 1975: 3–4; Brenk 1977: 9–15. Gray (2004: 84) adds: 'Plutarch also ridicules a number of popular practices in the essay on superstition that, in other writings, he endorses. Throughout the *Lives* he reports without embarrassment numerous omens and dreams, and describes without condemnation various superstitious actions taken by his heroes.'

⁶⁶ For an overview of those different explanations, cf. Brenk 1977: 10–155. See Attridge 1978: 76, for an emphasis on the rhetorical nature of the treatise.

⁶⁷ Hirzel 1912: 8–10; Koet 1929: 79; Moellering 1963: 18–20; Babut 1969.

⁶⁸ Smith 1975.

⁶⁹ For example, the statement that *deisidaimonia* is as bad as atheism (*Is. Os.*11), or the example of the Jews refusing to fight on the Sabbath because of their *deisidaimonia* (*Mor.* 1051E).

⁷⁰ Opsomer 1996: 175–176.

⁷¹ Van Nuffelen 2011a: 48.

beliefs upon the philosopher and his difficulty in holding to strict philosophical 'orthodoxy.'[72]

This section suggests that the reconsideration of the meaning of *deisidaimonia* as advocated in this chapter significantly reduces the contradictions and tensions which have been identified in Plutarch's corpus. As in the previous section, it analyses the way Plutarch uses *deisidaimonia* and the related words *eusebeia* and *eulabeia* throughout his writings, while also paying particular attention whether this terminology is used differently in the treatise *De superstitione* and in his other works.

3.3.2 Plutarch's Use of Deisidaimonia, Eusebeia and Eulabeia

a) Deisidaimonia

As seen earlier, Plutarch defines *deisidaimonia* as a type of fear (*Superst.* 165D; *Suav. viv.* 1101D9) or 'an emotional opinion and an assumption productive of a fear' (δόξαν ἐμπαθῆ καὶ δέους ποιητικὴν ὑπόληψιν) (*Superst.* 165BC). Although some contexts provide little or no clue as to the semantics of *deisidaimonia*, the evidence suggests that Plutarch uses the terminology consistently with his own definition throughout his corpus. Indeed, in the great majority of cases, the biographer uses *deisidaimonia* in contexts in which – like in the authors examined so far – there is an anxiety about a possible negative or hostile divine intervention. Thus, the terminology appears in the same two types of circumstances identified in Diodorus, namely when there is a concern about having breached divine will or law and in association with events interpreted as signs of divine displeasure. In addition, the word occurs in a third new context: in ethical discussions. Importantly for our purposes, as can be seen by the examples provided in parentheses below, the terminology occurs in exactly the same contexts both in Plutarch's treatise *De superstitione* and in his other works.

First, *deisidaimonia* occurs when people are anxious about having breached a sacred law, or divine will. Thus, people are filled with *deisidaimonia* when there is a fear of committing sacrilege (*Rom.* 11.5.3; *Superst.* 169C) or of being tainted by pollution, a common example being the pollution coming from corpses (*Arat.* 53.2.3; *Superst.* 170B). It also results from improperly performed rituals (*Quaest. rom.* 277F4), or ill-omened days (*Cam.* 19.8.4). More broadly, *deisidaimonia* fills the person who has acted wickedly and is itself considered a divine punishment under the form of a tortured conscience and terrors (*Sera* 555A3; *Superst.*168C).

In the second category, *deisidaimonia* is associated with events interpreted as signs of divine displeasure or wrath, such as calamities like death, sickness, unfruitfulness, barrenness (e.g., *Rom* 24.2.1, *Superst.* 168BC) or strange

---

[72] Martin 2004: 107–108.

natural phenomena (e.g., rain of blood – *Rom* 24.2.1; eclipses – *Nic.* 23.1.4; *Superst.* 169A; premature or imperfect offspring – *Publ.* 21.2.1). Finally, people may also be filled with *deisidaimonia* because of apparitions or voices from the gods (*Num.* 8.3.9), dreams (*Superst.* 165EF), oracles or dreadful curses (*Crass.* 16.6.7). Unsurprisingly, then, in Plutarch as well, *deisidaimonia* is used to manipulate people (*Lys.* 25.2.4), or leads to measures taken for expiation such as sacrifices or festivals (*Sol.* 12.6.1).

In addition to those already familiar contexts, *deisidaimonia* occurs in a third set of passages in Plutarch's *Moralia*, namely in ethical discussions. In those cases, *deisidaimonia* appears most often in lists or discussion of vices or disorders (e.g. *Adol. poet. aud.* 34E6; *Rect. rat. aud.* 43D11). Those passages contain little contextual indication as to the actual meaning of the word, although it is clearly negatively connoted.

Moving to the connotation of *deisidaimonia*, like the other authors examined, Plutarch often uses *deisidaimonia* without authorial comment or explicit (positive or negative) connotation. The word is simply used descriptively, referring to the fear of hostile divine activity (e.g. *Apoph. lac.* 238D1). At the same time, it is also often clear that *deisidaimonia* is something negative for Plutarch. This is the case for the great majority of cases in the *Moralia*, but also in some cases in the *Lives*. This negative assessment is most obvious when *deisidaimonia* appears in lists of vices, or when Plutarch describes the deleterious effects of *deisidaimonia*.

b) *Eusebeia*

Turning to Plutarch's use of εὐσέβεια (30x) and εὐσεβής (11x), the pattern is similar to what has been observed in other authors, and again the three contexts associated with this terminology elsewhere reappear.[73] First, *eusebeia* is a virtue (*Comp. Lyc. Num.* 1.1.5). It brings rewards from the gods, even in the afterlife (*Cons. Apoll.* 120B4). It is frequently opposed to *deisidaimonia* (*Num.* 22.7.10; *Per.* 6.1), or said to lie between the two extremes vices of *deisidaimonia* and atheism (*Superst.* 171F5). Second, *eusebeia* refers to a specific set of worship practices, being used with the meaning of worship or cult (*Num.*14.2.9). As such it comes close to the meaning of 'religion' (cf. *Superst.* 166B7: τὸ θεῖον καὶ πάτριον ἀξίωμα τῆς εὐσεβείας – the divine and ancestral dignity of our religion). Finally, *eusebeia* can be manifested towards human beings (*Cons. Apoll.* 108F8).

---

[73] Plutarch only uses θεοσέβεια once in a fragment (Frag. 67.2) and θεοσβής once (*Rom.* 22.1) in a way similar to εὐσέβεια/εὐσεβής.

c) Eulabeia

Plutarch uses εὐλάβεια 82 times and εὐλαβής 16 times. In most cases, *eulabeia* seems to include an idea of 'restraint.' *Eulabeia* is used most often in non-religious contexts, but there are a few examples where the situation is connected with the gods.

In religious contexts, *eulabeia* often has the nuance of restraint or caution. Thus, people are to speak about the gods 'with *eulabeia*' because we do not know much about them (*Sera* 549E). People are also encouraged to believe in some stories, such as reports about moving statues (*Cam.* 6.6), with caution or with restraint. Sometimes, however, the nuance is more likely 'deference.' Thus, the Egyptians talk about their gods in some indirect ways because of their deference or restraint towards them (*Is. Os.* 354E). Numa legislates so that people stop their activities and show deference to the sacred procession (*Cor.* 25.2). Albinus takes his wife and children and lets the virgins and sacred objects sit on his wagon out of deference for the divinity (*Cam.* 21.3.1). In all those examples, there is still an idea of 'restraint' or 'self-restraint' in order to show deference to the divinity.

In a very few cases, however, the idea of restraint is difficult to discern and the nuance seems to be rather on 'cautiousness' in the sense of 'scrupulosity.' Thus, the Romans repeat their rituals several times if they are not performed appropriately because of their *eulabeia* (*Cor.* 25.3).

3.3.3 Plutarch's Use of Deisidaimonia in De superstitione and His Religious Thought

As highlighted by this analysis, in the great majority of cases *deisidaimonia* in Plutarch can be translated as 'fear of the gods' or 'anxiety not to offend the gods.' It thus refers to a disposition towards the gods, an emotion of fear or anxiety towards them, as Plutarch himself defines it. In a few cases, however, *deisidaimonia* is used to refer to the *practice* engendered by 'the fear of the gods,' whose purpose is to placate the divinities. This is the case for example in *Quaest. Rom.* 272B9, where Plutarch explains that in ancient days the barbarians used to throw Greeks into the river to kill them, but later Hercules put an end to their murder of strangers and taught them instead to throw figures into the river 'in imitation of their *deisidaimonia*' (τὴν δεισιδαιμονίαν ἀπομιμουμένους). Such occurrences, however, remain relatively rare.

Importantly, understanding *deisidaimonia* as 'fear of the gods or of divine hostility' and not, as many scholars have assumed, as a reference to certain practices and beliefs the philosopher is critical of, greatly diminishes the tensions which have been identified between Plutarch's *De superstitione* and his other works. Indeed, what Plutarch condemns and denounces in *De superstitione* is not so much specific behaviours or beliefs, but a fear which is caused by a wrong opinion about the gods and is debilitating for humans and impious towards the gods.[74] More precisely, as he explains in his treatise, *deisidaimonia* is a fear created by the mistaken belief that the gods harm human beings.

But *deisidaimonia*, as the appellation also indicates, is an emotional opinion and an assumption productive of a fear (δόξαν ἐμπαθῆ καὶ δέους ποιητικὴν ὑπόληψιν) which utterly humbles and crushes man, for he thinks that there are gods, but that they are causing pain and harmful (οἰόμενον μὲν εἶναι θεούς, εἶναι δὲ λυπηροὺς καὶ βλαβερούς) (*Superst.* 165BC [MC])

It was indeed a central belief among Platonists that the gods/god can only be good and benevolent, and therefore cannot harm.[75] For Plutarch, then, the fear of the gods (*deisidaimonia*) is based on a mistaken understanding of the gods' nature, and has disastrous consequences for humanity. To highlight the perverted effect of this fear upon human beings, the treatise describes at length the effects and practices to which it leads. But *De superstitione* does not aim to denounce, for example, belief in post-mortem judgment or in omens; rather, it shows how, *when a person has a wrong opinion about the gods and fears them*, such beliefs become terrifying and enslave human beings.[76] The criticism centres on the fear produced by such mistaken conception of the gods, mainly because it is based on a theological mistake – i.e. the belief that the gods are evil and harmful – but also because it makes human beings live in state of permanent 'terror' and leads to practices and beliefs which are exaggerated, unworthy of the gods and ridiculous or self-harming for human beings.

The question of the consistency or evolution of Plutarch's religious thought in his works cannot, of course, be solved only by the examination of his usage of *deisidaimonia*. But this analysis shows that his usage of *deisidaimonia* cannot be used to support a claim of inconsistency or evolution. Not only does Plutarch use *deisidaimonia* consistently through his corpus, but his criticism of *deisidaimonia* must be understood as centring on the fear of divine harm, and not on traditional cultic practices or beliefs as such.

---

[74] *Contra* Martin (2004: 94), who argues that in *Superst.* 'Plutarch mocks – no doubt with no small amount of exaggeration – many of the same sort of behavior: consulting witches, attempting to purify oneself by magic or bathing in the sea, squatting all day on the ground.'

[75] The theological underpinnings of the philosophers' criticism of *deisidaimonia* is discussed in detail in chapter four.

[76] Brenk (1977: 16) hints at this nuance in his study: 'The first impression one might get is that this is an all-out attack on the belief in the power of dreams and oneiromancy. However, it must be noted that Plutarch is always thinking in terms of the superstitious, and never explicitly attacks the belief in dreams on general philosophical principles. No mention is made of the validity of dreams coming to normal, tranquil mortals.'

3.4 Conclusion

3.4.1 The Use of Deisidaimonia Between the 1st c. BCE and the Early 2nd c. CE

Due to its limited focus on four authors, the conclusions of this chapter must remain tentative. But a consistent pattern can be discerned in the way the four authors examined in this chapter use *deisidaimonia*. Four remarks can be made here.

First, throughout the corpus examined, *deisidaimonia* almost always has the meaning given by ancient definitions, namely 'fear of the divine.' It thus refers in the great majority of cases to an *emotion* or a *disposition of fear* of incurring divine hostility or retribution. In a few instances, however, *deisidaimonia* refers by metonymy to the *action* which, motivated by anxiety, aims to avert this divine hostility. It thus describes an apotropaic activity. This usage, however, remains limited in our corpus.[77]

Second, and as a confirmation of this first point, *eusebeia* and *deisidaimonia* are not synonymous, and are used in different contexts in all the authors examined – with the exception of the few contexts in which either word and nuance would be possible. Thus, *deisidaimonia* occurs in contexts where there is an anxiety not to be the object of a divinity's hostility. It typically occurs when particular events, such as omen, special phenomena, or hostile circumstances could be interpreted as signs of divine displeasure. Or when human beings commit transgression which might lead to divine hostility, such as pollution, wicked deeds, sacrileges, or law infringement. In several cases, it comes thus very close to what we would call in modern English a 'bad or troubled conscience' or 'guilt.'[78] On the other hand, *eusebeia* is used to describe piety towards the gods, the cult of the gods, or piety towards human beings.

Third, moving to the issue of connotation, in an important number of instances, *deisidaimonia* is not obviously used pejoratively or positively. Rather, *deisidaimonia* is often used simply descriptively, to refer to the fearful or anxious attitude of people when there is a possibility to offend or have offended the gods. Furthermore, in the *corpora* at hand, the word is never used as a term of praise or to refer to a virtue. Rather, it is *eusebeia* and *eusebes* which describe the virtuous attitude towards the gods which leads to their favour. Sometimes, however, *deisidaimonia* is clearly negatively connoted, becoming the

---

[77] It is noteworthy that the noun δεισιδαιμονία occurs almost always in the singular in the texts analysed in this chapter. I have found only seven cases where it is in the plural form: Josephus, *Ant.* 19.290; Plutarch, *Aem.* 1.5; *Conj. praec.*140D8; *Superst.* 168F6; *An vit.* 500A; *Sera* 555A3; *Lat. viv.* 1128D8. This corroborates the conclusion that the word is used to refer to an emotion rather than to practices or beliefs.

[78] Moellering 1963: 75.

object of criticism, and a philosopher like Plutarch often identifies it as a vice, in fact as the opposite of piety.

Finally, it is noteworthy that in the authors examined, there is no notable difference in the use of *deisidaimonia* and *eusebeia* between non-philosophical or philosophical writings. Both Plutarch and the other authors examined use *deisidaimonia* as a reference to the fear or anxiety towards the gods' hostility and use it in similar contexts. The only significant difference lies in Plutarch's use of *deisidaimonia* in an additional context specific to his didactic works, namely where *deisidaimonia* is identified as a vice and impiety, and can be explained by his particular theology.[79] This finding will have to be further corroborated in the next chapter, which discusses the meaning of *deisidaimonia* in Stoic and Epicurean philosophers.

3.4.2 Deisidaimonia *and the Grammar of Graeco-Roman Religion*

As highlighted by this chapter, *deisidaimonia* is often used simply descriptively especially in narrative material. This can be explained by the nature of Greek religion. Indeed, unlike many modern religions, ancient religion was not characterized by belief in specific doctrines, but aimed to maintain the *pax deorum*, i.e. peace with the gods who could be either friends or enemies. As Davies writes:

Roman religion was profoundly unlike modern monotheistic religions, and brief accounts tend to mystify rather than explain. We tend to talk now of 'civic paganism' whereby citizens would participate in festivals that centered on gaining the gods' goodwill (the *pax deum*) through sacrifice and ritual. Failure to obtain the support of the gods before any venture would lead to disastrous results. If the gods were displeased, they would send signs (omens, prodigies) of their opposition (the *ira deum*), and they could usually be placated by appropriate sacrifice to restore the *pax deum*.[80]

It is within this particular grammar of ancient religion, that *deisidaimonia* as both common and yet undesirable makes sense. As Baroja writes concerning *superstitio*:

---

[79] Although this cannot be detailed here, those conclusions have been tested and prove valid also for the use of *deisidaimonia* and *eusebeia* in Polybius (c. 203–120 BCE) and Dio Chrysostom (c. 40 – c. 120 CE). Polybius uses δεισιδαιμονία or δεισιδαιμονέω four times, always with the meaning of 'fear of the gods,' 'religious scruples' (6.56.8; 12.24.5; 9.19.1; 10.2.9), and εὐσέβεια four times to refer to piety or reverence towards the gods (4.20.2; 5.10.6; 5.12.1; 16.12.9). Chrysostom uses δεισιδαιμονία only once with the meaning of religious fear or religious scruple (61.9); he uses εὐσέβεια and εὐσεβής five times with the meaning of piety or reverence towards the gods (12.48.5; 13.35.5; 31.146.7; 32.5.2; 75.5.3) and twice to refer to piety towards human beings (77/78.30.1; fragment 6). Philo, however, often seems to use *deisidaimonia* without the nuance of fear, to refer to perverted piety.

[80] Davies 2009: 168–9.

[...] notas que afectan a algo muy importante y difícil de comprender para una mente moderna, sea religiosa o sea laica. Me refiero a la idea de que entro los hombres y los dioses puede haber relaciones de amistad o de enemistad: la simpatía juega también entre ellos, como entre los cuerpos animados o inanimados, un papel decisivo.[81]

Deisidaimonia thus refers to the concern or fear – admittedly with different degrees of anxiety – of having made the gods enemies and thus incurring their hostility, wrath and retribution. This particular nature of Greek religion explains why Plutarch can say that the majority of people feel *deisidaimonia* towards the gods, and yet that those same people also experience hope and even joy in expecting help from them (*Suav. viv.* 1101DE). It also explains why ancient authors often do not comment on it. Indeed, *deisidaimonia* is a very common phenomenon in Graeco-Roman religion, in fact, it is very much an inherent and unavoidable component in a grammar where relationship with the gods is by definition characterized by enmity or friendship.[82]

Within this particular grammar, the question of whether *deisidaimonia* can sometimes refer to a 'good' fear of the gods makes little sense. Indeed, although *deisidaimonia* is a common phenomenon and plays a role in maintaining morality in society, it is obviously never desirable on a personal level and it is the very purpose of the cult to ensure that relationship with the gods is not characterized by enmity and *deisidaimonia*, but by friendship and peace.

Moving to the issue of a translation of *deisidaimonia* then, it is misleading to render it by 'piety' or 'religion,' for those words do not convey the notion of fear in modern English conceptualities. Even the word 'god-fearing' is inappropriate to render the adjective, for it often has strong ethical connotations and usually expresses 'respect' rather than 'fear' of god.[83] Likewise, the terminology of 'superstition' does not correspond to what is understood by *deisidaimonia*.

It is thus better to attempt to define *deisidaimonia* within the grammar and with the concepts and terminology which the ancients themselves used. The ancient did not speak about 'religion' and 'superstition,' but about *deisidaimonia, eusebeia* and *eulabeia* when they talked about religious attitudes and behaviours. This chapter has begun to sketch the role each of these terms played in this ancient grammar, highlighting that *deisidaimonia* and *eusebeia* were used in different contexts and differently, and that the ancients drew a clear distinction between them and came to oppose them directly. It is thus best

---

[81] Baroja 1975: 155.

[82] On the importance of the fear of the gods in Greek religion, see Festugière 1946: 71–82. He concludes: 'Ainsi la crainte des dieux, de leur colère à l'égard des vivants, de leur vengeance sur les morts, a-t-elle joué un grand rôle dans la religion des Grecs.' See also Grodzynski 1976: 44: 'La recherche de la *pax deorum* aboutit presque inévitablement à la superstition. Celle-ci est en somme la tare habituelle de la religion païenne.'

[83] EOD defines 'god-fearing' as: 'characterized by deep respect for God; deeply or earnestly religious.' Online edition, accessed 5.08.2017.

to translate *deisidaimonia* as fear of the gods' hostility or punishment, anxiety not to offend the gods, religious scruple, or, occasionally, action resulting from the fear of the gods' hostility and aiming to avert it. On the other hand, εὐσεβεία roughly corresponds to 'piety, cult, worship, religious practices or religion,' and εὐσεβής to 'pious, righteous.' As this study confirms, it is εὐσεβεία rather than δεισιδαιμονία which, in some contexts at least, comes closest to what is understood by 'religion' in modern English, if religion is understood in the modern sense of a particular ensemble of beliefs and practices.

3.4.3 Deisidaimonia *in Acts 17*

Going back to Acts 17, those results have several important consequences for the translation of δεισιδαιμονέστερους and for understanding the subject of the speech in Athens.

As the analysis in this chapter suggests, it is misleading to translate δεισιδαιμονέστερους as 'very pious' or 'very religious,' as most translations do. To convey the positive nuance of piety, Luke would have used εὐσεβής or θεοσεβής. Indeed, it is those latter adjectives which are used by other ancient authors when they emphasize the well-known piety of the Athenians. Thus, Josephus points out that 'all claim that the Athenians are the most pious (εὐσεβεστάτους) of the Greeks' (*Ag. Ap.* 2.130), an assessment found also in Sophocles (*Oed. col.* 260: θεοσεβεστάτας) and Pausanias (1.17.1: θεοὺς εὐσεβοῦσιν ἄλλων πλέον).

In light of this chapter's analysis then, δεισιδαιμονέστερους is best rendered by 'very anxious about averting the gods' hostility' or 'very concerned about keeping peace with the gods.' This meaning fits well with the context of Acts 17. Indeed, the Athenians are described as δεισιδαιμονεστέρους because (γάρ) they have even (καί) built 'an altar to an unknown god' (17:22-23). The existence of altars to unknown gods in Athens is attested in Pausanias. The most likely background of such altars is that they were built out of the concern not to overlook any god and to make sure that no god is offended.[84] They thus reflect an attempt either to atone for some sin or satisfy an angry divinity – or to prevent such a divine revenge by making sure that all divinities receive their share of honour. Furthermore, this fits well the description of the city of Athens as κατείδωλον – 'full of idols' (16). The construction of an altar even to an 'unknown god' in a city full of idols shows that the Athenians are indeed δεισιδαιμονεστέρους, namely they are very anxious about not being the object of divine hostility, going even to the extent of building an altar to an unknown god who could have been overlooked and thus offended.

Thus, in verse 22, Luke's Paul is not praising the Athenians for their piety, nor is he mocking them for their superstition. He is not either pointing to the

---

[84] Horst 1990: 1451; cf. Klauck 2000: 82–83; Dibelius 1939: 39–40; Marguerat 2015: 157.

altar to the unknown god as a sign of the Athenians' piety or religiosity, nor of their 'superstition,' but as a sign of their concern to maintain peace with the gods, and of their ignorance. It is this concern which provides the springboard and thus the framework of the speech. What Acts 17 aims to address then, is not just the question of the nature of the divine as is commonly thought, but also how the Athenians are to deal with it to avoid its hostility.

Importantly, then, the speech uses as its starting point a characterization which points to the Athenians' anxiety or concern to avert divine wrath and hostility and maintain peace with the gods. As several scholars have noted, however, the philosophers were among the major critics of *deisidaimonia* in the ancient world. The next chapter thus examines the philosophical discussion of *deisidaimonia*, and more broadly what they taught about the cult and how to maintain a proper relationship with the gods.

4. *Deisidaimonia,* Piety and the Gods in Debate – Polemics Between Epicurean and Stoic Philosophers Around the First Century CE

As several scholars commenting on Acts 17 have noted, *deisidaimonia* was a common object of criticism by the philosophers, especially the Epicureans, one of the two philosophical sects described as interacting with Paul in Acts 17:18.[1] Those comments, however, are usually made with the assumption that the philosophical criticism of *deisidaimonia* took the form of a denunciation of 'superstitious' religious beliefs or behaviours, such as the cult of statues.[2] They also seem to assume that the philosophers, whether Stoic, Epicurean or Platonic, criticized *deisidaimonia* along the same line.[3] As a consequence, the speech in Acts 17 has often been interpreted as converging, or at least seeking rapprochement, with the philosophical criticism of traditional religion and idolatry in particular.

The purpose of this chapter is to verify such assumptions about the Epicurean and Stoic criticism of *deisidaimonia*, and to examine more deeply what they taught about proper worship (piety) and divine images more specifically. More precisely, this chapter seeks to answer the following questions: what did Epicurean and Stoic philosophers denounce when they criticized *deisidaimonia* and why? Were they in agreement with each other on the question? What was their attitude towards traditional religion and divine images? And what did they teach about worship or piety? The present section thus continues the examination of *deisidaimonia* begun in the preceding chapter, but this time in the context of Epicurean and Stoic philosophy – the two schools debating with Paul in the narrative of Acts 17 – and in connection with their teaching about piety and attitude towards traditional worship.

By analysing this historical background, this chapter prepares the way for an examination of the relationship between the speech's message and the teachings of Stoic and Epicurean philosophy, and thus for the evaluation of the common claim that the speech represents a rapprochement with Graeco-Roman philosophy. Furthermore, this chapter also maps out the philosophical

---

[1] Barrett 1974: 74; Jipp 2012: 576–577.
[2] Barrett 1974: 74–75; Jipp 2012: 577, 580–81.
[3] Barrett 1974: 75; Jipp 2012: 576–577.

background conversation into which the speech of Acts 17 is purportedly speaking according to Luke. It is thus likely that it will also shed light on some of the specifics of the speech's argumentation.

Although there is a significant amount of literature on the attitude of ancient philosophical schools towards religion, there has been little detailed discussion of the philosophical criticism of *deisidaimonia* specifically.[4] Martin's book *Inventing Superstition* (2004) is one of the few contributions which treats this topic at greater length. Before him, Grodzynski's very influential study (1976) on the Latin term *superstitio* also devotes a few paragraphs to discussing the use of *superstitio* among Latin philosophers. And Plutarch's understanding of *deisidaimonia* has, of course, been the object of detailed study.[5] But both Martin and Grodzynski's works are diachronic studies covering several centuries, and therefore do not discuss in detail the passages involving the terminology of *deisidaimonia* or *superstitio* in philosophical works.

Furthermore, to my knowledge, apart from the particular case of Plutarch, no study has examined in detail how the criticism of *deisidaimonia* by Hellenistic philosophers – especially the Epicureans and the Stoics – related to their attitude towards traditional religion and their teaching on true piety. The assumption is still often that the criticism of *deisidaimonia* is the same as the criticism of popular religious practices and beliefs. This is an important methodological weakness of Martin's study. Indeed, Martin includes the discussion of authors who criticize popular beliefs and practices but never actually use the terminology of *deisidaimonia* or *superstitio*. This is even more problematic in light of Martin's neglect of the study of many contemporary authors who do use the terminology of *deisidaimonia* or *superstitio*. As Gordon puts it:

> M. has rightly refused to write an exclusively semantic study in the manner of Koets; but in reaction he has gone to the opposite extreme. There is for example no discussion of the use of *deisidaimōn/deisidaimonia/deisidaimonein* in Julio-Claudian Greek prose authors, in Josephus or the Second Sophistic (Lucian alone is mentioned—once). On the other hand, in view of M.'s initial problematic, what are we to make of the fact that Celsus, so far as we know, did not use the term at all in his attack on Christianity? As a result, the focus blurs: the imperial/Christian chapters—more than half the book—discuss not superstition but all manner of critique of 'popular belief'. Are these terms truly synonyms?[6]

By choosing not to focus on the use of the words *deisidaimonia* or *superstitio* in the literature and instead including other texts which simply criticize popular beliefs, Martin's study runs the risk of presenting a scholarly construct of 'superstition' in the ancient world, rather than what ancient philosophers understood as *deisidaimonia*.

---

[4] On the philosophical criticism of 'religion' in antiquity, see Decharme 1904; Attridge 1978; Babut 1974; Algra 2009.
[5] Most recently, see especially Van Nuffelen 2011a and 2011b. cf. also Gray 2004.
[6] Gordon 2006: 524.

The present chapter thus not only sheds light on the historical philosophical context alluded to by the narrative of Acts 17, but it also contributes to filling a gap in scholarship. It begins by examining each school's grammar of *deisidaimonia* – describing what they denounced as *deisidaimonia* and why, and what they taught as proper piety towards the divine. The conclusion then synthesizes those results with those of the last chapter and previous studies, and draws out consequences for the interpretation of Acts 17.

A final remark with respect to the sources used in this chapter is in order. Because of the time frame chosen (2nd c. BCE–early 2nd CE), it has been necessary to include Latin sources in the analysis. Indeed, especially in the case of the Stoics, because Epictetus (55–135 CE) does not use the word δεισιδαιμονία, nor treat the subject of the 'fear of the gods' otherwise, our main sources are Seneca (c. 4 BCE–65 CE) and Cicero (106–43 BCE). Likewise, although our main source for the Epicureans is Philodemus (c. 110–c.40/early 30s BCE), Lucretius (c. 95–55 BCE) also provides important evidence of the philosophical conversation during this period. In those cases, the analysis has focused on the terminology of *superstitio* or, in the case of Lucretius, on *religio*. Although it has been shown that the semantic range and connotations of *superstitio* and δεισιδαιμονία do not always overlap, several scholars note that Latin philosophers use *superstitio* or *religio* to refer to what the Greek philosophers described as δεισιδαιμονια.[7] It shall become clear that it is the case in the texts examined below.

4.1 Epicureans on *Deisidaimonia,* the Gods, and Piety

4.1.1 Deisidaimonia *and Piety in Epicurean Philosophy*

a) The Epicurean Critique of Deisidaimonia

The terminology of δεισιδαιμονία (or δεισιδαίμων and δεισιδαιμονέω) does not occur in Epicurus (341–270 BCE), and it occurs only once or possibly twice in Philodemus' extent works, in contexts which do not give much information about its meaning.[8] Plutarch, however, uses δεισιδαιμονία when he concedes that Epicurean doctrine is successful in 'eliminating a certain fear and *deisidaimonia*' (ὁ λόγος αὐτῶν φόβον ἀφαιρεῖ τινα καὶ δεισιδαιμονίαν – *Suav. viv.*

---

[7] Grodzynski 1976: 42; Gordon 2008: 74. Grodzynski notes that the Latin philosophers Varro, Lucretius, Cicero and Seneca understand *superstitio* like the Greek philosophers understand δεισιδαιμονία, namely with the meaning 'fear before the divine.' On the differences between *deisidaimonia* and *superstitio*, see Gray 2004: 36–51; Martin 2004: 125–139.

[8] Obbink 1996: 484. The occurrences in Philodemus are in *Piet.* Col. 40, 1135–6, and, if he is also the author of *P. Herc.* 1251, in col. 10, 12–15. *P. Herc.* 1251 is published as Philodemus' *On Choices and Avoidances* in Indelli and Tsouna-McKirahan 1995.

1100F). Likewise, in Cicero's *De natura deorum*, *superstitio* refers to what Epicurean doctrine strives to eliminate (1.117).[9] The terms δεισιδαιμονία and *superstitio* were thus used during our time frame to refer to what Epicurean doctrine strived above all to set humanity free from, namely 'the fear of the gods.'

As is well-known, the Epicureans defined the human *telos* as 'pleasure,' a state which, according to Epicurus, was characterized by 'the absence of pain in the body and trouble in the soul' (*Ep. Men.*). They identified the two most serious causes of disturbance to the soul as the fear of the gods and the fear of death.

In addition to all these we must recognize that the most powerful disturbance in human souls arises when they believe that these [the heavenly bodies] are blessed and immortal, and have at the same time intentions and actions and causes inconsistent with this. It also arises when they expect some everlasting evil either because of the myths or because they fear the very absence of sensation in death (as if that was something to us). (*Ep. Hdt.* 81 [MC])

For the Epicureans, fear of the gods is generated by wrong beliefs about them, and more specifically by attributing to them intentions and actions inconsistent with their blessedness and immortality. By this, they meant the belief that the gods are mindful of human affairs and interfere in the world. It is this mistaken notion of the gods as concerned with the world and active in it, which causes fear of the gods, since it opens up the possibility that the gods might harm.

More precisely, Epicurean literature identifies several important sources generative of fear and terror of the gods in human experience. As highlighted by *Ep. Hdt.* 81, one of them was the attribution of divine nature to celestial bodies or, more generally, the attribution of natural phenomena to divine causation. Epicurean philosophy thus emphasized the importance of the study of nature and especially the study of the causes of natural phenomena so as to show that they have nothing to do with the gods.[10] This lay at the heart of the project undertaken by Lucretius in *De rerum natura* (1.146–158).

Other important sources of fear of the gods identified by the Epicureans were dreams (Lucretius 1.104–106; Philodemus, *Dis*), or the utterances of priests [*vatum*] (Lucretius 1.102–111). Furthermore, and importantly, the Epicureans also identified a close connection between the fear of the gods and the fear of death.[11] On the one hand, the fear of death was enhanced by the fear of the gods' punishment after death. This is what is alluded to in *Ep. Hdt.* 81 above, which mentions the mythological stories speaking of divine punishment and retribution after death.[12] On the other hand, misunderstanding of the nature of death and the afterlife increased the fear of the gods during lifetime.

---

[9] Cf. *ND* 1.45.
[10] Cf. Plutarch, *Suav. viv.* 1092B.
[11] Cf. Warren 2009: 236–237.
[12] Cf. Plutarch *Suav. viv.* 1092AB.

Lucretius makes this association at the beginning of book 1, where he points out that mistaken understandings about the nature of the soul as surviving in the afterlife leaves humanity without any strength to defy *religio* – religious scruple – because of the fear of everlasting punishment (1.102–116).[13]

The contexts leading to the fear of the gods identified by the Epicureans are thus very similar to those which have been identified as leading to *deisidaimonia* in the previous chapter, including unexplained natural phenomena, oracles and dreams which might be interpreted as signs of divine hostility, and the sayings of the seers. Finally, it is also associated with afterlife punishment, and here again mythology plays a key role in reinforcing this fear.

For the Epicureans, the fear of the gods was not just a threat to attaining the human *telos* of pleasure, but it was an oppressive yoke with pervasive debilitating effects upon human beings and society, and the cause of many evils. Epicureans often use the image of slavery to talk about the fear of the gods and describe the suppression of this fear as freedom. Thus, Lucretius repeatedly speaks of man being crushed by *religio* – the term he uses instead of *superstitio* – and of Epicurus as the one who sets humanity free from this yoke.[14] Both Lucretius and Velleius, the Epicurean representative in Cicero's *De natura deorum*, call gods who interfer with human affairs taskmasters who hold humanity in slavery.

> For if those who have rightly learned that the gods lead a life free of care nonetheless all the time wonder how things can happen, especially in those events which are discerned above our head in the regions of ether, they revert back to the old scruples [*religiones*], and adopt severe masters [*acris dominos*], whom the poor wretched believe to be almighty, ignoring what can be and what cannot be, in short, how each thing has limited power and a deep-set boundary mark. (Lucretius 5.84–90 [MC])[15]

Furthermore, *deisidaimonia* leads to impious deeds and evils. Lucretius points to the sacrifice of Iphigenia as a typical impious consequence of an attempt to avert hostile gods (Artemis), 'so potent was *religio* in persuading to evil deeds' (*tantum religio potuit suadere malorum*) (1.80–101). The Epicurean author of

---

[13] Lucretius does not use *superstitio* but *religio*, in the sense of 'religious scruple,' to refer to what Epicurus strives to eliminate. This was the original sense of *religio* and is still well attested at that time, occuring, for example, in Cicero (*ND* 2.10) and Livius (9.29.10). Beveniste (1969: 270) defines it as follows: 'Au total la *religio* est une hésitation qui retient, un scruple qui empêche, et non un sentiment qui dirige vers un action, ou qui incite à pratiquer le culte.' See more fully Beveniste 1969: 269–270. The noun *superstitio* appears for the first time in the first century BCE in Cicero, where it is also contrasted with *religio*. The adjective *superstitiosus*, however, occurs for the first time over a century earlier in Plautus. (Cf. Janssen 1979: 135; Gray 2004: 37, n.11).

[14] Cf. 1.62–69.

[15] Cf. Lucretius 2.1090–92: 'If you hold fast to these convictions, nature is seen to be free at once and rid of proud masters (*superbis dominis*), herself doing all by herself of her own accord, without the help of the gods.' [LCL] Cf. *ND* 1.54.

P. Herc. 1251 speaks of the misfortunes brought upon cities because of the failure to take action due to the apprehension of acting against the will of the gods (διὰ ὑποψίας τοῦ μηδὲν παρὰ τὴν τῶν θεῶν ἐνεργεῖν βούλησιν – VIII).

For the Epicureans then, *deisidaimonia* is not just a psychological sickness among others, but it is *the* central problem of humanity, with its companion the fear of death. *Deisidaimonia* leads to a form of slavery and makes human beings take destructive decisions leading to the destruction of individuals, their cities and human society at large. Furthermore, the Epicureans believed that this disease was 'widespread and tenacious' among mankind.[16] It is thus not surprising that they use soteriological categories to speak about what Epicurus and Epicurean philosophy bring to mankind. By suppressing the fear of the gods, the Epicureans saw themselves not only as healing a widespread and debilitating desease, but also as delivering mankind from the yoke of angry taskmasters.

b) *The Nature of the Gods: Untouched by* Gratia *or* Ira

Because the Epicureans diagnosed the fear of the gods to be above all a cognitive fault of ignorance or misapprehension, they believed that its remedy laid in holding the right beliefs about the gods, and more broadly about the nature of all things. As Epicurus put it in *Ep. Men.* 123, to live the right life, one must 'exercise oneself' to hold right beliefs, and right beliefs about the gods are fundational.

> First, believe (νομίζων) that God is an immortal and blessed living being, as the common notion of a god [of mankind] indicates, bestowing upon him nothing which is foreign to his immortality or that does not agree with his blessedness. But believe about him all what can uphold his blessedness with his immortality. For there are gods; the knowledge of them is manifest; but they are not such as the multitude believe; for they do not uphold the notion which they form concerning them. (*Ep. Men.* 123; Diogenes Laertius 10.123 [MC])

Epicureans not only affirmed that the gods' existence was self-evident, but also that they were blessed and imperishable, as the common notion of god shared by all indicates. The problem was that most people held beliefs inconsistent with the gods' *blessedness and imperishability*, thus giving rise to anxiety about the gods. What this blessedness and imperishability entailed was encapsulated in the first of the *Kuriai Doxai* [*KΔ*] and often repeated in Epicurean literature.

> What is blessed and immortal neither has trouble itself nor does it bring trouble to another; hence it is exempt from the movements of wrath and favour, for all such movements happen in weakness. (*KΔ* 1; Diogenes Laertius 10.139 [MC, my emphasis]) Τὸ μακάριον καὶ ἄφθαρτον οὔτε αὐτὸ πράγματα ἔχει οὔτε ἄλλῳ παρέχει, ὥστε οὔτε ὀργαῖς οὔτε χάρισι συνέχεται· ἐν ἀσθενεῖ γὰρ πᾶν τὸ τοιοῦτον.

---

[16] Warren 2009: 237.

4.1 Epicureans on Deisidaimonia, the Gods and Piety

Upholding the blessedness and imperishability of the gods means above all to reject the popular belief that *the gods can be moved by favour or anger*, for this would imply weakness. This right belief about the gods is constantly repeated in Epicurean literature. The *locus classicus* expression of this idea in Lucretius is found at the beginning of book 1.[17]

For the very nature of divinity must of necessity enjoy immortal life with the greatest peace, far removed and separated from our affairs; for free from any pain, free from dangers, strong itself by its own resources, needing nothing from us (*nil indiga nostri*), it is neither bribed with rewards nor touched by wrath (*nec bene promeritis capitur neque tangitur ira*).[18] (1.44–48 [MC])

This passage is particularly interesting for our purposes for it echoes the affirmation in Acts 17:25 that God does not need anything. For the Epicureans, the gods are far removed from our affairs and wholly self-sufficient, because this is necessary for them to be perfectly peaceful – which is perfect happiness. This means that the gods do not need human service (*nil indiga nostri*), and that they are influenced neither by gains or rewards nor by wrath (*nec bene promeritis capitur neque tangitur ira*).[19] The same articulation of this fundamental belief is found in Velleius' mouth, just after he quotes Epicurus' first KΔ:

If we were seeking nothing else besides worshipping the gods piously and be free from the fear of the divine (*superstitio*), what has been said would suffice; for the excellent nature of the gods would receive the pious worship of men, since it is both eternal and supremely blessed (for whatever is preeminent receives a just veneration); and all fear of divine power or anger would have been driven away (since it is understood that anger and favour alike are removed [*et iram et gratiam segregari*] from blessed and immortal nature, and that these being eliminated, no fear threatens from the powers above [*a superis*]). (Cicero, *ND* 1.45 [MC])

Key in those definitions of the divine is that it is 'neither held by *gratia*, nor by *ira*.' In Epicurean philosophy then, the affirmation that the gods need nothing from human beings and are wholly self-sufficient and uninvolved in human affairs is an entailment of the fact that they cannot be influenced by wrath or favour because they are in a permanent state of ataraxia. The solution of the Epicureans to *deisidaimonia* thus lies in apprehending the true nature of the gods as not touched by wrath or favour, and thus uninvolved in human affairs.

Accordingly, it was capital for Epicurean philosophers to be able to demonstrate that the gods are uninvolved in the world and not, as many believed, active in it for better or for worse. Their arguments proceeded along two lines.[20]

---

[17] Cf. Bailey 1947: 2.603, who notes that this passage is an amplification of the first KΔ.
[18] According to Bailey (1974: 2.604), *promeritis* is a reference to the offerings which men make to the gods, as χάρισι in KΔ 1, and not, as often in Epicurus, 'gratitude.'
[19] See the same two lines in 2.646–651.
[20] Warren 2009: 239–240.

First, they argued that belief in divine intervention presupposed that the divine could be affected in its blessedness (e.g. through anxieties or anger), or that its blessedness was contingent upon other external factors (partiality – i.e. favours). But 'occupations, anxieties, angers and favours do not accord with bliss, but those things happen in weakness, fear and need of neighbours' (*Ep. Hdt.* 76–78). To believe in interventionist gods is therefore to deny the gods their majesty and what makes them gods – i.e. blessedness and immortality (cf. Lucr. *RN* 5.82–90).

The second line of argument against interventionist gods was to emphasize the faults and evils in the world, thus undermining the idea of a provident god.[21] According to Lactantius, Epicureans thus argued against the Stoic view of a benevolent and omnipotent god:

> Either god (i) wishes to prevent evils and cannot, or (ii) he can and does not want to, or (iii) he neither wants to nor can, or (iv) he both wants to and can. If (i), he is weak, which is impossible for god. If (ii), he is malevolent, which is equally alien to god. If (iii), he is malevolent and weak, so not a god. If (iv) – the only real possibility for a god – then where do evils come from? And why does he not prevent them? (Lactantius *On the anger of God* 13.19).[22]

The existence of evil and injustice thus provided the Epicureans with a strong argument against the providential gods of their philosophical rivals. This is well illustrated for example in Plutarch's *De sera*, which is an attempt to tackle the Epicurean argument against divine providence based on the delay of the divinity to punish the wicked.[23]

Epicureans thus affirmed the existence of the gods, in fact, of anthropomorphic gods, but strongly rejected divine providence and any kind of divine intervention in the world as incompatible with divine blessedness and immortality (and goodness). This belief set them up against other philosophical schools upholding providential views of god – especially the Stoics, but also the Platonists. In fact, because they defended the view of a providential god, the Stoics were accused by Epicureans of being defenders of and proponents of *superstitio*! The Epicurean argument is well illustrated by Velleius' attack against Balbus' school:

> Then, in this immensity of length, breadth and height, an infinite quantity of innumerable atoms flies around, which although separated by void, yet cohere together, and clinging to each other form unions which produce the forms and shapes of things which you cannot think are able to be produced without bellows and anvils; and so you have imposed upon our necks an eternal master, whom we are to fear day and night; for who does not fear a prying and busy (*plenum negotii*) god who foresees (*providentem*), considers (*cogitantem*), and notices everything, and thinks that everything is his concern? From this first came this fated

---

[21] Warren 2009: 240. E.g. Lucr. *RN* 5.195–324. See also Lactantius *Inst.* 3.17.7 (370 Us.).

[22] Translation in Warren 2009: 240, based on the Greek in Usener frag. 274.

[23] The treatise identifies this as the strongest argument against providence (548CD).

necessity of yours, which you call *heimarmenē*, so that you say that whatever happens is the result of an eternal truth and an unbroken continuation of causes. But what value must be assigned to a philosophy which, as old women – even ignorant old women – , thinks that everything happens by fate? Then follows your doctrine of *mantikē*, which is called divination in Latin, which would so steep us in *superstitio* (*superstitione*) that, if we were willing to listen to you, we would have to be devoted (*nobis essent colendi*) to southsayers, augurs, oracle-mongers, seers and interpreters of dreams. But Epicurus has delivered us from these terrors and has set us free, so that we do not fear those who, we know, neither create any trouble for themselves nor seek to cause any to others, and we worship that excellent and majestic nature piously and reverently. (Cicero, *ND* 1.55–56 [MC])

This passage shows how the Stoic view of the divine was thought to lead to the fear of the gods at all corners for the Epicureans. The first part of this text, which speaks of 'bellows and anvils,' mocks the doctrine of creation of the Stoics. The Stoics believed that the world was the creation of a provident and beneficent god. The Epicureans, on the other hand, believed that everything is the product of the collision of atoms. The doctrine of creation implies a divine interest in the world which, for the Epicureans, can only lead to the fear of the gods as prying masters. Next comes the Stoic doctrine of Fate, or their view that everything which happens in the world is necessary and in accordance with god's will, and although Velleius does not spell it out, it is easy to see how this can lead to the fear of the gods since nothing can be done to avoid misfortunes or nothing *should* be done since everything which happens is the will of the gods. Finally, closely connected is the Stoic doctrine of divination, which implies that the gods'will can and must be sought, thus filling people with fear and making them the devotees of augurs and seers.

c) *Epicureans on Traditional Religion and True Piety*

Although the Epicureans criticized the fear of the gods, they were, as far as we can tell, traditional and conservative in their attitude towards the cult.[24] This is attested by both Epicurean and non-Epicurean authors, and by the fact that Epicureans were apparently never tried for or even accused of impiety outside of philosophical debates.[25] The second section of Philodemus' *De pietate* (col. 3–36, 72–1022) devotes significant space to refute the charge of impiety by philosophical rivals by cataloguing instances where Epicurus and his early

---

[24] On Epicurus and traditional religion, see Obbink 1996: 1–23, Festugière 1946: 86–92, and Attridge 1978: 51–56. On Lucretius, see Summers 1995, who argues that Lucretius differs from Epicurus and Philodemus, by taking a more negative view of religion.

[25] The fact that ancient anti-Epicurean sources, while full of slander, say nothing of atheism and impiety support the view that early Epicureans were not accused on those accounts. See, for example, Diogenes Laertius' list of slanders against Epicurus in *Lives* 10.4–9. Likewise, Philodemus makes a point of emphasizing that Epicurus was never railed by his contemporaries in comedies nor prosecuted by the Athenians (*Piet.* Col. 53, 1505–32). See Obbink 1996: 13–14.

followers participated in cult and rituals. Specifically, the sources suggest that the Epicureans participated in most aspects of popular religion, including traditional festivals, sacrifices and prayers (e.g. Philod. *Piet.* col. 28, 796; col. 31, 879–82; col 64, 1850; col. 79, 2278; Plut., *Suav. viv.* 1102B), the adoration of statues (e.g. Philod. *Piet.* col. 32, 910–11; Cicero, *ND* 1.85[26]), or mystery initiation (Philod. *Piet.* col. 20, 558–9; col. 28, 808–10).[27] They did, however, criticize divination and prophecy, both of which were closely connected with belief in divine providence.[28]

While emphasizing that the gods do not need human worship, the Epicureans claimed that 'highest beings deserve honours' (Cicero, *ND* 1.45) and that it is 'natural' for human beings to worship and honour them.

> Let it suffice to say now that the divine needs no mark of honour, but that it is natural for us (ἡμῖν δὲ φυσικόν ἐστιν) to honour it, in particular by forming pious notions of it (ὁσίαις [ὑ]πολή[ψ]εσιν), and secondly by offering with each individual usage (i.e. as appropriate; or possibly: to each of the gods in turn) the traditional sacrifices. (Philod. *De mus*. col. 4.6 [Obbink])[29]

As suggested by this quotation, however, piety is above all expressed by having 'pious notions' about the gods, a view echoed by many other Hellenistic philosophers. From an Epicurean perspective, this meant to believe about them whatever upholds their blessedness and their immortality – namely that they are touched neither by *gratia* nor *ira*, and thus do not interfer in the world. As a consequence, Epicurus claims that 'not the one who suppresses the gods of the multitude is impious, but the one who attaches the opinions of the multitude to the gods' (*Ep. Men.* 123–124). Likewise, Philodemus writes:

> For pious is the person who preserves the immortality / and consummate blessedness of God together with all the things included by us; but impious is the person who banishes either where God is concerned. (*Piet.* Col. 39–40, 1127–46 [Obbink])

Furthermore, the Epicureans drew a close connection between this definition of the gods and their ethical *telos*, and this relationship is reflected in their understanding of piety as well. Indeed, to be pious is not only to have the right thinking about the gods, but also to be like them as far as possible. As Obbink puts it, 'piety is held to have a moral as well as a theological content, much along the lines of ὁμοίωσις θεῷ κατὰ δυνατόν "emulation of God's nature."'[30] This revision of the traditional definition of piety, which is already anticipated

---

[26] Cotta: 'I personally am acquainted with Epicureans who worship every paltry image, albeit I am aware that according to some people's view Epicurus really abolished the gods, but nominally retained them in order not to offend the people of Athens.'
[27] Obbink 1996: 10. See also the reference to Epicurus' piety in Diogenes Laertius 10.10.
[28] Attridge 1978: 52–55. Cf. Cic. *Div*.1.87.
[29] Obbink 1996: 391.
[30] Obbink 1996: 486.

in Plato's *Euthyphro* and echoed, for example, in Stoicism (see c)), is particularly well illustrated in Lucretius 5.1198–1203:[31]

> It is not piety (*pietas*) to be often seen with covered head, to be turned towards a stone and approaching every altar, nor to fall prostrate to the ground, and to stretch out hands before shrines of the gods, nor to sprinkle altars with much animal blood, nor to tie vows to vows, but rather to be able to uphold all things with a tranquil mind (*sed mage placata posse omnia mente tueri*). [MC]

There is probably a pun in this redefinition of piety as *placata mente tueri omnia posse*, in that the verb *placare* is also used with the meaning of 'placating' the gods. Rather than the different cultic activities which are often performed to 'placate' the gods, then, the pious person ought to be able to uphold everything with a 'placated' mind. Piety is thus redefined as 'to be able to survey all things with a tranquil mind,' which is an imitation of the gods, since the gods are in a state of perfect ἀταραξία. As showed later in Lucretius (6.73–78), this state of tranquility is itself produced by true worship, during which the worshipper's mind receives the *simulacra* of the gods.[32]

Piety, according to Epicurean philosophy, has thus not only a cultic aspect (participating in the civic cult) and a theological content (holding the right beliefs about god's nature) but also an ethical content, namely to emulate the gods as much as possible (ὁμοίωσις θεῷ κατὰ δυνατόν).[33] It is for this reason that the suppression of *deisidaimonia* – a fear which implies that the gods are harmful and do evil – is absolutely necessary. Indeed, only a right view of the gods as unharmful leads to proper ethical conduct and proper piety. For the Epicureans, then, emulation of the gods means to live a life without harming anybody, for the gods do not harm (Philodemus *Piet.* col 71, 2032–260). This abstinence from harming people is synonymous with justice. In fact, the definition of the 'righteous person' (ὁ δίκαιος, col 76, 2203) in the *De pietate* parallels the definition of the 'pious person.' As Philodemus points out, justice and piety are – for the Epicureans – virtually the same thing: σχεδὸν ταὐτ[ὸ φαίν]εται τὸ ὅσιο[ν καὶ δί]και[ον) (col. 78, 2263–5).

The pious person is thus the person who strives to emulate the gods as much as possible. Importantly, this godlikeness (ὁμοίωσις θεῷ) – i.e. the perfect happiness enjoyed by undisturbed gods called ἀταραξία – is also the human *telos*. It is also a state in which mortal human beings can enjoy a form of divine state – immortality – even though it is experienced in this life.[34] For this reason, the

---

[31] On the ideal of godlikeness or *homoiōsis theōi kata to dunaton* in Plato and his successors, see Sedley 1999.

[32] Cf. Bailey 1947: 3.1516. On the Epicurean redefinition of piety along ethical lines, see also Epicurus, *Ep. Men.* 123; Cicero, *ND* 1.116.

[33] On *homoiosis theōi* in Epicureanism, cf. Erler 2002; Warren 2011.

[34] On this see Warren 2011.

Epicureans sometimes called themselves godlike (cf. Plutarch *Suav. viv.* 1091BC; Lucretius 5.8).

4.1.2 Epicurean Theology in Debate: The 'Harms' of Gods Who Are Not Wrathful nor Favourable

It is in philosophical circles that Epicurean theology and more specifically their doctrine against *deisidaimonia* came under fire. The treatise *De pietate*, written in the first century BCE and usually attributed to Philodemus, represents a defence of Epicurean piety against several of those accusations.[35] Using the *De pietate*, as well as Cicero's *philosophica* and Plutarch's polemical works, this section begins by discussing the criticisms which philosophical opponents levelled against the Epicurean treatment of the fear of the gods (*deisidaimonia*), namely their claim that the gods are influenced neither by *gratia* nor *ira*, and do not interfere in the world. It then examines how the Epicureans responded to this criticism.

a) The Accusations of Philosophical Opponents

The accusations of philosophical rivals against the Epicureans doctrine of 'unwrathful' and 'unfavorable' gods proceeded along four lines.

Perhaps the most common accusation levelled against the Epicurean 'non-interventionist gods' was that it destroyed the very foundation of piety. By denying divine involvement with human affairs, the Epicureans eliminated the very basis for cultic practices such as sacrifices and prayers. In other words, because of this view, 'mysteries and festivals are regarded as foolishness, since those for whose sake they take place pay no attention to them' (Phil. *Piet*. col. 49, 1395–1402).[36] The Epicureans were thus accused of 'doing away with the whole notion of holiness (ὁσιότητα) together with the preservation of common traditions,' and of hurling people 'into insurpassable impiety' (Phil. *Piet*. col. 39-40, 1127-46). Cotta also expresses this criticism eloquently by appealing to the common accepted definition of piety as 'justice towards the gods':[37]

> Furthermore, what piety do you owe to one from whom you have received nothing? Or how can you owe anything at all to one who has done you no service? For piety is justice towards the gods; but what claim of justice is there between us and them, if god and man have no fellowship? Holiness is the science of worshipping the gods; but I do not understand on what account the gods should be worshipped if no good is received or hoped for from them. (Cicero, *ND* 1.116–117 [MC])

---

[35] The authorship of the treatise is not totally certain. Obbink 1996: 88–99.

[36] Quotations from *Piet*. are from Obbink's translation (1996).

[37] For this definition of piety, see for example: Sextus Empiricus, *Adv. Phys.* 1.124: ἡ ὁσιότης, δικαιοσύνη τις οὖσα πρὸς θεούς.

There is no basis for worshipping the gods if they are not responsible for our good, and if there is no hope to receive anything from them. At this point, Cotta criticizes the Epicurean solution to *superstitio*, denouncing it as destructive not only of *superstitio*, but of all *religio*.

As for the freedom from 'superstition' (*superstitione*), which is the usual boast of your school, that is easy to attain when you have taken away all the power of the gods; unless perhaps you think that Diagoras or Theodorus, who denied that there are any gods altogether, could be afraid of the gods (*superstitiosos esse*). As for me, I don't think it was possible even for Protagoras, for whom it was not clear whether the gods exist or whether they do not. For the doctrines (*sententiae*) of all those men suppress not only 'superstition' (*superstitionem*), in which there is a vain fear of the gods (*in qua inest timor inanis deorum*), but also religion (*religionem*), which is preserved by the pious cult of the gods (*quae deorum cultu pio continetur*). (Cicero, *ND* 1.117 [MC])

Here and in the following lines, Cotta dangerously compares the Epicureans with the famous atheists of antiquity, pointing out that they also suppress *superstitio*, but at the same time destroy all religion.[38] This quote shows that the Epicurean solution to *deisidaimonia* did not convince its rivals. Indeed, Epicurean theology seemed to eliminate not only the necessity of piety but also the possibility of any kind of relationship with the gods. Because of this, the Epicureans were accused of engaging in religious practices hypocritically, and partly for this reason, some philosophers suggested that Epicurus was really a closet atheist, engaging in popular practices only out of fear of encountering the displeasure of the common people (Plut. *Suav. viv.* 1102BC).

A second accusation was that the Epicureans had also eliminated the greatest characteristic of divine excellence: goodness and benevolence. This criticism, closely associated with the accusation of abolishing all religion, was voiced frequently by both Academic and Stoic philosophers.[39] For example, at the end of book 1 of the *De natura deorum*, Cotta says:

Epicurus, however, when he took away from the immortal gods both their power to bring aid (*opem*) and their kindness (*gratiam*), uprooted completely religion from the heart of men. For although he affirms that the nature of god is the noblest and the most excellent (*optimam et praestantissimam*), yet he also denies that there is kindness (*gratiam*) in god, [that is to say] he takes away what is most characteristic (*maxime proprium*) of the noblest and most excellent (*optimae praestantissimaeque*) nature. For what is better or more excellent than kindness and beneficence (*bonitate et beneficentia*)? (*ND* 1.121 [MC])

---

[38] The ancient understanding of 'atheism' was broader than the outright 'denial of the existence of the gods.' Ancient discussions of 'atheists' tend to include agnostics (e.g., Protagoras), and those whose views were taken to imply that there are no gods (e.g. Epicurus). Cf. *P. Herc.* 1428 col.14.32–15.8. On this subject, cf. Obbink 1996: 1–2.

[39] According to Plutarch, the Stoics frequently attacked Epicurean theology based on the notion that the gods are 'beneficent and humane' (εὐεργετικοὺς καὶ φιλανθρώπους) (Plutarch, *Stoic. rep.* 1051DE; cf. 1052B).

There is a clear allusion here to the Epicurean definition of the gods as neither moved by *ira* nor by *gratia*. For both the Academics and the Stoics, however, suppressing the attribute of goodness from the gods was tantamount to denying their excellence, and thus there very existence as gods, since the gods are, by definition, the most excellent beings which exist. For Cotta, divine excellence must be manifested in *gratia*. Continuing his refutation of the Epicurean understanding of the gods and in particular their claim that *gratia* and *ira* are signs of weaknesses, Cotta points to the Stoics, who used the paradigm of friendship to explain how 'benefits' can be exchanged with the gods, even though they do not need anything (*ND* 1.122). Indeed, even though the gods are in need of nothing which human beings can give them, this need not imply their lack of care for human beings and the impossibility of a relationship between men and gods. The relationship between true friends is not based on a utilitarian, mercenary basis – i.e. the *do ut des* principle – but on disinterested love and common love for the good. Likewise, the gods care for human beings because of their own excellence, which is most supremely expressed in their goodness and beneficence, and because 'there is natural affection between the good.' In Cotta's (and the Stoics') view, not only are the gods friends with each other, but it is possible for human beings to be friend with the gods. This friendship is based on common affection for the good and for virtue, and it is the virtuous man (i.e. the wise) who is the friend of the gods.

The third criticism against the Epicurean suppression of divine providence was that it is potentially damaging to mankind and the state, because it threatens the moral fabric of society. Philodemus hints at this type of charge in his treatise (*Piet.* col. 46–47, 1306–1344). Indeed, to deny that the gods punish the wicked and reward the good threatens to eliminate what preserves social cohesion, reducing human society to a society of beasts. Plutarch raises this issue in his treatise against Colotes, one of Epicurus' disciples.

> Then when will our life be that of a beast, savage and unsociable? When the laws are taken away, but the arguments of those who urge to pleasure remain, when the providence of the gods is not believed in, and when people hold as wise those who spit on the good, if no pleasure attends it, and who mock and scoff at words such as these:
>
> 'An eye there is of Justice, that sees all,' and 'For God standing near, looks from nigh at hand,' and: 'God, even as the old account relates, holding the beginning, middle and end of the universe, accomplishes his purposes rightly, walking according to his nature; Justice follows him, punishing those who fall short of divine law.'[40] (*Adv. Col.* 1124E–1125A [MC])[41]

There is no sign that Epicurus or the Epicureans were ever troubled politically for advancing views threatening mankind or society, as Philodemus emphasizes in his defence. Philodemus does, however, devote a significant part of his

---

[40] Plato, *Leg.* 4.715 E–716A.
[41] On Plutarch's critique of Epicureanism, cf. Hershell 1992b.

4.1 Epicureans on Deisidaimonia, the Gods and Piety

treatise on piety to this issue of harms and benefits from the gods and to defending the view that Epicurean theology is no socially harmful and preserves justice better than the poets and the views of philosophical opponents (see below). Obviously, among philosophical rivals, the 'unharmful' gods of the Epicureans were denounced as harmful to human society, religion, and mankind in general.

In the same vein, a last criticism deserves mention. By denying divine providence the Epicureans were also accused of depriving the pious of their good hopes to be the beneficiaries of divine salvation, reward and vindication. This is an important point in Plutarch's *Non posse suaviter vivi secundum Epicurum*, a treatise where the Platonist endeavours to demonstrate that Epicurus' philosophy – far from enabling people from attaining the Epicurean ethical goal of pleasure – actually makes a pleasant life impossible. Indeed, Plutarch points out that while the Epicureans might be able to suppress in some measure the fear of the gods (*deisidaimonia*), at the same time, they also suppress any hope of receiving something good from the gods (1100F). This might be the simple hope to have one's prayer heard at a festival, the hope of receiving help from the gods in a dangerous situation like a strom at sea, or the greatest hope of all, i.e. the reward of immortality for one's just and good life (1105C). At this point, Plutarch has moved to criticize more specifically the denial of an afterlife by the Epicureans. But the use of the language of reward of the just and punishment of the wicked shows its close connection with divine providence.

What then do we think about the good (τῶν ἀγαθῶν) and those who have lived holy and righteous lives (βεβιωκότων ὁσίως καὶ δικαίως), who look forward to nothing evil in that other world, but to what is most excellent and divine (τὰ κάλλιστα καὶ θειότατα)? For first, as athletes do not receive the crown while there are contesting, but when the contest is over and they have obtained the victory, thus those who believe that the awards of victory (τὰ νικητήρια) of life await the good after life, are inspired wonderfully to virtue under the expectation of those hopes, which includes to see those who in their wealth and power are now committing outrages (τοὺς ὑβρίζοντας) and foolishly (ἀνοήτως) laugh at the higher powers (τῶν κρειττόνων) receiving the judgment they deserve (ἀξίαν δίκην). (*Suav. viv.* 1105C–1106A [MC])

Although Plutarch's argument is influenced by his aim of denouncing Epicurean self-contradictions, it is clear that his Platonic concerns about the goodness of god – which includes his righteous treatment of humanity – and the transcendence of death motivate his argument. Philodemus also alludes to the charge that Epicureans 'deprive good and just men of the fine expectations which they have of the gods,' in *De pietate* (col. 49–50, 1412–1425), confirming that this was a common criticism of their theology.

b) The Epicurean Counter-Arguments

A significant part of Philodemus' *De pietate* specifically addresses the philosophical accusations connected to the Epicurean denial of providence. Of the six sections of the treatise, the third (col. 36–59) addresses the accusation that Epicureans leave no rationale for piety and dwells at length on the Epicurean doctrine of harms and benefits from the gods. The fourth section (col. 60–86) then discusses the origin of atheism and justice, and argues that the Epicurean doctrine, unlike the doctrines of the poets or other philosophers, does not threaten social justice, but provides a more solid basis for it. Those two counter-arguments are briefly discussed in this section.

The Epicurean Doctrine of Harms and Benefits From the Gods

Against the accusation that their theology destroyed piety altogether, the Epicureans pointed to a redefinition of the popular view that the gods transmit 'harms and benefits' to human beings.

> But I by contrast do not think that this manner on account of these things impiously does away with the whole notion of holiness together with the preservation of common traditions, and that, as those who are said to be *deisidaimones* think (ὡ[ς] δ' οἱ λεγόμεν[οι δει]σιδαίμονες), it hurls us into unsurpassable impiety. For pious ([ὅσιος]) is the person who preserves the immortality and consummate blessedness of God together with all the things included by us; but impious (ἀ]σεβὴς δὲ) is the person who banishes either where God is concerned. And the person who sees also that the good and ill sent us by God come without any unhealthy anger or benevolence, declares that God has no need of human things . . .
> (Philodemus, *Piet.* col. 39–40, 1127–55 [Obbink slightly modified])

After affirming that piety is to have opinions about the gods which preserve their immortality and blessedness, Philodemus adds another detail: the pious person also rightly conceives that god provides goods and ills (τῶν ἀγαθῶν καὶ τῶν κακῶν) but without being affected by weakening anger and favour (χωρὶς ὀργῆς καὶ χάριτος ἀσθενούσης) which would suggest that they need us. Thus, while they denied that human beings can, by their cultic practices, influence the gods towards anger or favour, the Epicureans nonetheless held that the gods have beneficent and harmful influences upon human beings. This, however, the gods did without interfering in the world, by giving 'harms and benefits' to the good and to the wicked through their notions of the gods. The conceptions people have of the gods affects them, either under the form of harm or benefit. The passage of Philodemus above recalls the later part of Epicurus' *Ep. Men.* 123.

> For the utterances of the multitude concerning the gods are not preconceptions, but false assumptions; hence it is that the greatest harms happen to the wicked and the greatest benefits happen to the good from the gods (ἔνθεν αἱ μέγισται βλάβαι τε τοῖς κακοῖς ἐκ θεῶν ἐπάγονται καὶ ὠφέλειαι τοῖς ἀγαθοῖς). For they always accept those who are similar to their own virtues as one's own, but consider as alien what is not of their kind (ταῖς γὰρ ἰδίαις οἰκειούμενοι διὰ

παντὸς ἀρεταῖς τοὺς ὁμοίους ἀποδέχονται, πᾶν τὸ μὴ τοιοῦτον ὡς ἀλλότριον νομίζοντες). (*Ep. Men.* 123 [MC])[42]

As Obbink notes, the causal role traditionally attributed to the gods in conferring harms and benefits to humanity is here redefined along the notion of ὁμοίωσις θεῷ, or divine emulation. Thus, although divine intervention in the world is ruled out by its incompatibility with the gods' own blessedness, the gods do have a real, albeit indirect, influence on human beings, inasmuch as one's own view of the gods affects one's own διάθεσις or psychosomatic constitution for better of for worse. Thus, as Obbink puts it, 'the wise, who preserves a correct conception of the gods, derive a sense of immense calm and religious awe from perceiving and imitating their nature.'[43] On the other hand, the one who has mistaken notions of the gods as being moved by anger or favour is himself affected by those false notions. At the same time, the notions people have of the gods is dependant upon their own 'moral' condition. As the last sentence from *Ep. Men.* 123 quoted above shows, the wise have conceptions of the gods as virtuous because of their own virtue. Festugière paraphrases this sentence as follows: the wise 'have familiarized themselves with the true nature of the gods through their own excellence and thus easily receive in their mind gods which are like themselves, rejecting all what is not such as foreign to divine nature.'[44]

This doctrine of 'harms and benefits' from the gods plays a crucial role in Epicurean theology, and the third part of Philodemus's treatise is entirely devoted to it. It provides not only a rationale for engaging in the cult, but an incentive for it. Indeed, when one engages in cultic practices with the correct notion of the gods, one strengthens those correct notions in oneself, and thus gains a greater peace of mind. For example, the wise form their correct notions of the divine especially during festivals (*Piet.* col. 27, 765–73). Cultic practices thus had to be performed with a right view of the gods – and above all – without opinions about the gods which would create disturbance (cf. *Piet.* col. 31, 873–898).

When the wise engages in rituals with a correct view of the gods then, reaching a perfect state of ἀταραξία, he becomes like god in so far as it is possible for mortal nature. This explains why Epicureans did not just 'tolerate' participation in traditional religious practices, but actively encouraged it as something beneficial. Participation in the cult strengthened one's view of the gods, thus enabling one to be benefited by them by becoming like them. On the other hand, evil men are harmed by their own defective conceptions of the gods, suffering

---

[42] For a discussion of this passage: Festugière 1946: 48–50, Long-Sedley 1987: 2.145, Obbink 1996: 459–64.
[43] Obbink 1996: 9–10.
[44] Festugière 1946: 85.

from the fears of post mortem-punishment (*Piet.* col. 77, 2233–41; cf. Lucretius *NR* 6.68–78). [45]

There is thus a sense in which the Epicureans spoke of the gods as the 'cause' or 'source' of retribution and salvation for humanity (αἰτία νεμέσεως καὶ σωτηρία ἀνθρώποις in *Piet.* col. 37, 1045–9). Recasting the traditional beliefs that the gods harm and benefit humanity along psychological lines thus also enabled the Epicureans to show that their doctrine fitted common conceptions of the gods, after those had been purified.[46]

The Gods of the Poets and Other Philosophers as Harmful for Justice

As mentioned above, the philosophical opponents of the Epicureans criticized their theology for being harmful, or at least not beneficial, to mankind. They denounced their view of the gods as uninvolved in human affairs as a potential threat to social justice.

Against this accusation, Philodemus argued that the Epicurean doctrine of harms and benefits from the gods provides a much stronger religious basis for social justice than the accounts of the poets or the doctrines of their philosophical rivals. This argument takes up a very large part in the latter part of his treatise on piety, which is very much preoccupied with the question of justice and theodicy.

He thus begins by demonstrating that, according to the Epicurean view, a divine justice is constantly at work in that the unjust and wicked suffer punishment in the form of mental anguish because they believe in gods like themselves – i.e. who will hurt them in this life and in the next (col. 76–77). On the other hand, the righteous who do not harm anybody are benefited by their views of unharmful gods in that they derive an incredible peace and sense of security. There is thus a very direct incentive to being righteous, since it is beneficial. As Philodemus emphasizes, for the Epicureans, then, piety and justice are virtually the same thing (*Piet.* col. 78, 2263–5).

The view of the gods propagated by the poets and other philosophers, however, not only does not ensure social justice and piety, but actually encourages injustice and impiety. Unlike what is commonly affirmed, Philodemus contends that it is not useful to encourage belief in the myths to preserve social justice. The claim that the gods punish the wicked – made both by the poets and other philosophers – is hardly a deterrent of wickedness and injustice in

---

[45] Obbink 1996: 395: 'The choice between types of gods, and hence of harm or benefit, is to some extent beyond an individual's control: it is determined by the kind of person one is: since we have affinity for our own virtues, we all individually of necessity choose gods like ourselves (*Ep. Men.* 124). But obviously Epicurus thinks that it is possible through reasoning to sort out our ideas about divinity, conceptually improve if not exchange one's gods, and so maximize benefits.'

[46] Obbink 1996: 10–11.

society, for it is obvious that the gods do not enact such a retribution on the wicked, at least not in the crass sense advocated by the myths (col. 80, 2313-20). In the latter part of his treatise, Philodemus discusses in detail the poets and the different philosophical schools, underscoring their failure to provide a deterrent for injustice. His exposition climaxes with the Stoics, whose view he denounces as not only failing to promote justice, but actually *encouraging* injustice. Indeed, if people who blaspheme the traditional gods are not punished by those gods for their wickedness, nobody will ever refrain from injustice out of fear of gods who are as insensible as the Stoics' aethers and breezes (*P Herc.* 1428 col. 13-15).[47] Philodemus concludes his argument against the Stoics by returning their accusation against them, reproaching them for 'turning human life into that of beasts.'

4.1.3 Summary: The Epicureans on Deisidaimonia *and Proper Piety*

As this overview shows, the Epicurean critic of *deisidaimonia* did not correspond to the criticism of traditional religion, as is often assumed in discussions of Acts 17. Rather, the Epicureans criticized the fear of divine hostility and wrath, because they found it 'irrational,' i.e. built on a false understanding of the nature of the gods as interfering in human affairs. For them, the strict self-sufficiency of the gods and the presence of imperfections and evil in the world implied that the gods do not interfere in it. There is thus no need to fear the gods. But the Epicureans were not against the use of divine representations and much less against the traditional cult. They did, however, claim that ultimately proper worship is expressed through imitation of the gods, i.e. to be moved neither by wrath or *gratia*. As Philodemus put it, to be pious and to be just was virtually the same thing. In fact, proper worship was the way by which one could 'benefit' from the gods, namely psychologically. By worshipping the gods along traditional lines but with a right view of them, and by imitating them, the worshipper gains true peace of mind and gains a form of immortality. And alternatively, improper worship – worship without the right view of the gods and thus without a proper emulation of them – led to 'damages' from the gods – mainly fear and a troubled conscience expecting punishment from the gods in this life and the other.

---

[47] Obbink 1996: 496, cf. Henrichs 1974a: 25.

4.2 The Stoics on *Deisidaimonia*, the Gods, and Piety

4.2.1 *Deisidaimonia* and Piety in Stoic Philosophy

a) The Stoic Criticism of Deisidaimonia

The criticism of the fear of the gods or *deisidaimonia* did not have for the Stoics the central role it had in Epicurean philosophy. Epictetus, for example, does not use the terminology of δεισιδαιμονία at all, and does not discuss the fear of the gods in the sources which have come down to us.[48] The Stoics did, however, denounce it, and we know of two treatises entirely devoted to that subject. According to Athenaeus (*Deipn.* 8), Antipater of Tarsus (died c. 130 BCE) wrote a Περὶ Δεισιδαιμονίας which has not come down to us. The second treatise is Seneca's *De superstitione*, of which some fragments were incorporated in Augustine's *De Civitate dei*. Because the fragments do not mention the word *superstitio* and are extracted out of their original context, this section relies primarily on the criticism found in Seneca's other writings and in the mouth of Balbus in Cicero's *ND*, before examining the fragments incorporated in Augustine.

Turning first to Cicero's *ND*, as discussed earlier, in the first book *superstitio* refers to what Epicureanism strives above all to eliminate, namely the fear of the gods. Later, Cotta identifies *superstitio* as containing a 'vain or groundless fear of the gods' (*timor inanis deorum*) and distinguishes it from *religio* which 'consists in the pious worship of the gods' (*deorum cultu pio continetur*) (1.117).[49] A similar distinction between *superstitio* and *religio* is expressed by the Stoic spokesman Balbus in the second book.

> For not only the philosophers but also our ancestors have distinguished *superstitio* from religion. For those who were praying and sacrificing during entire days so that their children might outlive (*superstites essent*) them, were called 'superstitious' (*superstitiosi sunt appellati*), and the word later acquired a wider application. On the other hand, those who reconsider carefully and so to speak reread all what concerns the cult of the gods, those indeed were called 'religious' (*religiosi*) from *religere* (to reread), like elegant from *eligere* (to select), 'diligent' from *diligere* (to value), 'intelligent' from *intellegere* (to understand); for in all these words there is the same strength as picking out (*legendi*) that there is in 'religious.' Thus 'superstitious' (*superstitioso*) and 'religious' (*religioso*) came to be terms of censure (*vitii*) and approval (*laudis*) respectively. (*ND* 2.71–72 [MC])

Although several scholars concur that *superstitio* most likely does come from *superstes* or *superstites*, the validity of Cicero's etymological explanation of

---

[48] A TLG search retrieves four occurences of δεισιδαιμονία attributed to Chrysippus, each time identifying it as a kind of fear among other vices (cf. *Fragmenta moralia* 394.16; 408.4; 409.16; 411.8).

[49] Cotta: [...] *non modo superstitionem tollunt in qua inest timor inanis deorum, sed etiam religionem quae deorum cultu pio continetur.*

4.2. The Stoics on deisidaimonia, the Gods and Piety

superstitio has often been rejected.[50] Indeed, it is not clear how people praying all day that their children might outlive them would lead to them being called pejoratively '*superstitiosi.*' After all, the desire that one's children outlive oneself is a very legitimate and common desire in antiquity. Thus, Janssen suggested that this practice was criticized because it showed an excessive interest for personal concerns, at the detriment of the concern of public affairs, which is what true religion was supposed to concern itself for.[51] This explanation, however, does not fit with the way *superstitio* is understood or criticized elsewhere in the *ND*: nowhere is *superstitio* criticized because it is obsessed with personal piety. Rather, as this chapter has begun to argue, in *ND superstitio* refers to a groundless fear of the gods.

Despite the reluctance of scholars to accept his explanation, this meaning does, in fact, make good sense of Cicero's etymological argument. Indeed, the text does not suggest that people were called '*superstitiosi*' because they desired that their children outlive them. As Janssen has amply demonstrated in his study, that children outlive their parents – at least once they had survived the first few precarious years of their young life – was not only every parent's desire, but the normal *ordo naturae*.[52] In this context, it was certainly not a bad or impious desire to wish that one's children live longer than oneself. Rather, what led to those parents being called '*superstitiosi*' is that they were 'praying and sacrificing entire days' to ensure that what is normal would happen, a persistence which shows that they were overly scared that the gods would allow or perhaps even cause the children to die prematurely.[53] The attitude of the *superstitiosi* thus betrays an inordinate fear of the gods, and possibly a serious lack of belief in their goodness. It is this abnormal fear which led people to call them *superstitiosi*, namely 'the survivors.'[54]

Balbus uses *superstitio* two other times, both in the context of the false beliefs and crazy errors which have been generated by the myths.

> Do you see therefore how from a true and useful natural philosophy the account has evolved into imaginary and counterfeit gods? This has generated false beliefs, unruly errors and *superstitiones* hardly above old wives' tales [*falsas opiniones erroresque turbulentos et superstitiones paene aniles*]. And indeed, we know the forms of the gods, their age, dress and equipment, and also their ancestry, marriages and relationships, and all is converted into the

---

[50] Otto (1909: 550) rejects it as *kindisch*; Beveniste 1969, who discusses many theories about the origin of *superstitio*, does not discuss Cicero's explanation. Other ancient authors have provided other etymological explanations of *superstitio*, but they cannot be discussed here.

[51] Janssen 1975: 173; 1979: 142.

[52] Janssen 1975: 161–163.

[53] On the 'superstitious' persons' belief that the gods might avenge themselves against them by killing their children, cf. Plutarch, *Superst.* 170A.

[54] I am not hereby endorsing the validity of Cicero's explanation of the origin of *superstitio*, but only explaining the logic of the origin he suggests. To my knowledge, the explanation I am advancing here has not been proposed in scholarship.

likeness of human frailty [*omniaque traducta ad similitudinem inbecillitatis humanae*]. For they are given to perturbed feelings: indeed, we learn of their being in love, afflicted, angry; and as the myths tell us, they even engage in wars and battles, and not only when the gods support different sides when two armies are opposed to each other, as in Homer, but they even fought wars of their own as with the Titans and the Giants. Such things are rapported and believed most foolishly and are full of nonsense and the greatest depravity. But though despising and repudiating these myths, we shall nevertheless be able to understand the divine permeating nature and several elements, Ceres permeating earth, Neptune the sea, and others, who and of what they are like; and it is our duty to revere and worship these gods under the names which tradition has bestowed upon them. (Cicero, *ND* 2.70–71 [MC])

The Stoics did not generally reject the myths but insisted on the necessity to interpret them allegorically within the framework of Stoic philosophy.[55] This is what is alluded to in the last sentence. What the passage criticizes is a literal interpretation of the myths whereby the gods are anthropomorphized and are attributed 'perturbed feelings' and depraved actions like men. The context thus suggests that *superstitiones* (i.e. vain fears of the gods – or perhaps religious scruples, or practices or beliefs inspired by them) are generated when the gods are believed to have feelings such as love, affliction and anger, and to engage in battles and depraved actions. The second passage confirms this reading.

Another account also, even scientific, has been the source of a great multitude of deities, who dressed up in human form (*specie humana*) have supplied the poets with legends, while filling up the life of men with every kind of *superstitio* (*superstitione omni*). And this topic treated by Zeno was later explained more fully by Cleanthes and Chrysippus. For while the ancient belief had spread through Greece that, Caelus (i.e. Uranus) having been mutilated by his son Saturne, Saturn himself had bound Caelus, a scientific account not unreasonable (*non inelegans*) is contained in those impious tales (*impias fabulas*). [...] But Jupiter himself— that is the helping father, whom with a change of inflexion we call Jove from juvare 'to help', is called by the poets 'father of gods and men,' and by our ancestors 'the best and greatest', and indeed 'best,' that is 'most beneficent,' comes before 'the greatest' because to benefit to all (*prodesse omnibus*) is greater and certainly more beloved than to have great wealth [...] (Cicero, *ND* 2. 63–64 [MC])

Again, it is the depiction of the gods as immoral beings in the myths – again a result of anthropomorphism – which is criticized, and which earlier Stoics (Zeno, Cleanthes and Chrysippus) corrected by providing allegorical interpretation. In both passages then, Balbus points out that tales depicting the gods as immoral and evil – and thus potentially hostile and harmful – has given rise to *superstitiones* (i.e. vain fears of the gods or possibly, by metonymy again, apotropaic practices). This, however, is mistaken since, as Balbus emphasizes, 'Jupiter' – as indicated by the etymology of his name – is the 'helping' father. Indeed, the greatest being is a *beneficent* being. Here lies the heart of the Stoic

---

[55] See, however, Seneca's critic of allegorical interpretation of mythical gods at the beginning of his *De beneficiis* (Sen. *Ben.* 1.3.2–4.6). On Seneca and Cornutus' attitude towards poetry and the allegorical interpretation of myth, cf. Setaioli 2004: 341–367.

4.2. The Stoics on deisidaimonia, the Gods and Piety

criticism of *superstitio*: the gods are beneficent and good and do not harm. *Superstitio* then is the fear produced by the belief that the gods are evil and harm.

The same idea is found in Seneca's treatment of the topic. The word *superstitio* occurs nine times in his extent works, many times in contexts which we have already encountered elsewhere.[56] Thus in *Thyestes* 678, Seneca speaks of the *superstitio inferum*, i.e. the fear (of the gods) associated with the underworld. Again in the context of the fear of death, Seneca writes that Nature enjoins men to leave the world as they came into it, namely 'without desires, fears, *superstitio* (*sine superstitione*), treachery and other curses' (*Ep.* 22.15). He also links *superstitio* with the fear generated by eclipses which make 'cities cry out and each person make a din in accordance with inane *superstitio*' (*Nat.* 7.1.2.78). Finally, as several authors did in the case of the Jews, he also mentions abstinence from animal food in certain foreign cults as a proof of *superstitio* (*Ep.* 121.4.2).

One of the most useful passages to understand Seneca's treatment of *superstitio* is *Ep.* 123:

Poverty is an evil to nobody unless he rebels against it. Death is not an evil: you ask how so? Death alone is the equal right of mankind. *Superstitio* is a crazy error; it fears those whom it ought to love; it dishonors those whom it worships. For what difference is there between you denying the gods or you defaming them?' (*Superstitio error insanus est: amandos timet, quos colit violat. Quid enim interest utrum deos neges an infames*?) (Seneca, *Ep.* 123.16 [MC])

Superstitio is the error whereby one fears the gods rather than loving them. This is not only foolish, for the gods are good and not to be feared; but it is also impious, for it implies that the gods are evil or wrathful.[57] For Seneca, this is not different from denying their existence. As the wider context shows, the passage aims to correct understandings about evil along Stoic lines, redefining poverty and death as indifferents rather than evils. The criticism of *superstitio* is thus also to be understood as a correction of the mistaken notion that the gods are evil or harmful. Seneca's argument here is similar to Plutarch's criticism in *De superstitione*, where he explains that *deisidaimonia* is 'an assumption productive of fear which utterly humbles and crushes a man, for he thinks that there are gods, but that they are the cause of pain and injury' (Plut. *Superst.* 165B [LCL]). Plutarch likewise denounces *deisidaimonia* as impiety because it assumes that the gods are evil and cruel (*Superst.* 169F–170A).

---

[56] The search was run with PHI and does not include the fragments of the treatise on the subject.

[57] Cf. Setaioli 2007: 353, 349. Seneca also highlights the difference between religion and *superstitio* along those lines in *Clem.* 2.5.1.

It is probably a similar argument which runs in the background of Seneca's criticism of *superstitio* in his lost work *De superstitione*.[58] Several of those fragments are regularly used as evidence of the philosopher's criticism of traditional religion or cultic statues, not least in discussions of Acts 17. But the absence of the context of those excerpts integrated in Augustine's polemic makes their meaning in Seneca's original argument very difficult to ascertain. Augustine himself begins by claiming that Seneca was more unambiguous about his criticism of civic religion than Varro (*Civ.* 6.10.1),[59] but he also points out that Seneca continued to follow traditional religion and enjoined others to do so albeit out of obedience to the laws and traditions, rather than because they are welcomed by the gods (*Civ.* 6.10.6–7).[60] This suggests that his treatise was probably not a wholesale rejection of cultic images and all religious traditions. In light of the preceding discussion of the criticism of '*superstitio*' in Seneca and other authors, it is noteworthy that several of those fragments reflect a concern about practices and divine representations which imply or suggest that the gods are terrifying, harmful, wrathful or immoral. For example, in his discussion of statues, Seneca writes:

> They consecrate the sacred, immortal, indestructible deities in materials totally tawdry and lifeless. They clothe them in the appearances of men and beasts and fishes; some indeed depict them as both male and female entwined in divergent bodies. They call them deities, but if they came alive and suddenly confronted them, they would be regarded as monstrosities. (*Superst. ap.* Aug. *Civ.* 6.10.2 [Walsh])

Seneca denounces not just the materiality and anthropomorphism of statues, but specifically their terrifying aspects and the fact that these are called deities. In another fragment, he criticizes those who mutilate and hurt themselves as an offering to the gods or to avert their wrath, denouncing those practices as even worse than what is inflicted by tyrants.

> One man [...] slices off his genitals, and another slashes his arms. Since these are the means by which they deserve to have the gods look kindly on them, for what behaviour do they fear their wrath? If this is the kind of worship the gods seek, they should not be worshipped by any kind whatsoever. (*Civ.* 6.10.3 [Walsh])

---

[58] Those fragments are mainly contained in Augustine's *De Civitate Dei*, book 6.10. Walsh 2014 is followed for the English and Latin text here.

[59] '[...] For in the book which he composed against superstitions, he condemned the civic theology of the city at much greater length and with much greater emphasis than Varro had censuered that of the theatre and of myth.' (*Civ.* 6.10.1 [Walsh]).

[60] 'What he says is: "The wise man will preserve all these rites on the ground that they are prescribed by laws rather than welcomed by the gods." [...] "As for all that undistinguished horde of gods garnered over many years by lenthy superstition (*superstitio*), we will worship them," he says, "but we shall keep in mind that their worship is related more to custom than to actuality." ' (*Civ.* 6.10.6 [Walsh]).

4.2. The Stoics on deisidaimonia, the Gods and Piety

He also denounces services to the gods, and in particular those which imply their immorality, such as women on the Capitol claiming to wait for their lover Jupiter, and mocks the poet describing a jealous Juno.

> Then a little later he remarks: 'Yet though these men offer pointless service to god, that service is neither squalid nor obscene. Some women sit on the Capitol believing that Jupiter is their lover. They are undeterred even when Juno eyes them very angrily, if you care to believe the poets.' (Augustine, *Civ.* 6.10.5 [Walsh])

Again, the interpretation of those fragments is ultimately uncertain. But they would be consistent with Seneca's criticism of *superstitio* as the fear of wrathful or harmful gods which need to be placated.[61]

Like Balbus, then, Seneca associates *superstitio* with the fear generated by the belief in harmful gods, a belief which is nourished by literal interpretation of the poets, anthropomorphic or terrifying divine representations, and natural phenomena interpreted as signals of divine displeasure (e.g. eclipses). It is also associated with the fear of death and afterlife punishment, and gives rise to deviant religious practices – such as abstention from certain foods, self-harm or trying to please the gods through all kinds of services. What is perhaps distinctive in Balbus and Seneca's criticism of *superstitio* is that it is regularly associated with an *anthropomorphic* representation of the gods both in myths and statues, and thus the association of passions, weaknesses and needs to the gods. The phenomenon of *superstitio*, however, is the same as what was denounced in the writings of the Epicureans, and like them, the Stoics believed it to be a perversion of piety, and something to be eliminated. Their solution, however, differed from the Epicurean one because they rejected their understanding of the nature of the gods.

b) The Nature of the Gods: Provident Benefactors of the Human Race

Like the Epicureans, the Stoics saw *deisidaimonia* as rooted in ignorance about the nature of the gods, and its solution in knowledge of their true nature. Unlike the Epicureans, however, the Stoics stressed that progress away from *deisidaimonia* necessitated the realization that god *is beneficent and cares for humanity*. This is emphasized by Seneca:

> Although one hears what limit (or what manner: *quem modum*) he must keep in sacrifices, and how far he sould recoil from troublesome *superstitionibus* (*quam procul resilire a molestis superstitionibus*), he will never make sufficient progress, unless he conceives a right

---

[61] Attridge (1978: 68) argues that the heart of Seneca's criticism of *superstitio* is 'the emotional condition which is fostered by the religious practices which he castigates.' He points out that this emotionalism was 'incompatible with the Stoic ideal of the sage who has freed himself from passion.' Attridge is certainly right that Seneca denounces *superstitio* as *furor*, madness; but the heart of his criticism is that *superstitio* displays a misapprehension of the true nature of the gods as good and beneficent towards mankind. The next section confirms this reading.

idea of god, regarding him as possessing all things (*omnia habentem*), allotting all things (*omnia tribuentem*), and bestowing them freely (*beneficum gratis*). And what reason have the gods for doing deeds of kindness (*Quae causa est dis bene faciendi*)? It is their nature. One errs if he thinks that they are unwilling to harm; they cannot. They cannot receive nor are able to inflict injury; for doing harm and to suffer harm are connected. This greatest and most beautiful nature of all has not even made threatening those whom it has removed from danger. (*Ep.* 95.49 [MC])

In this context, *superstitionibus* most probably refers to practices meant to avert the wrath of the gods. Progress against *superstitio* necessitates the right idea of god as 'possessing all things, alloting all things, and bestowing them freely,' namely in understanding that god is good and what he does is good. The Stoics argued that god's providential and beneficent nature is part of the human preconceptions about god.[62] As mentioned earlier, it is precisely for denying this divine excellence manifested in goodness and providence that the Stoics criticized the Epicurean solution to *deisidaimonia*.[63]

To strengthen and defend their belief in a provident and beneficent god, the Stoics used cosmological and teleological arguments emphasizing the good design of the cosmos – its beauty and purposefulness, and especially the propitiousness of the world for *human* life, the beneficiary of divine goodness by excellence (see esp. Cic. *ND* 2).[64] Crucially, however, and this distinguished them from the Platonists, the Stoics saw god as immanent and identical with Nature. God, also called the *Logos* (rationality) or Nature, permeates the whole world and ensures its rationality and orderliness. Therefore, they also identified god with fate and providence. Importantly for the problem of *deisidaimonia*, this immanence of the divine ensures that the world is the best as it can possibly be. God as fate determines everything and his providence ensures the goodness of the cosmos. Providence does not only secure that 'the world as a whole is a beautiful and well-organized' animal (Cicero, *ND* 2.58, and 71–153), but it also 'extends to the position of man: the world is said to be there for the sake of gods and men (Cicero *ND* 2.154–167).'[65]

If the Stoic god is good and beneficent, it needs to be stressed that the Stoics identified the good as virtue or perfect rationality. Above all then, god's beneficence and providence towards men is expressed in that he has given them the greatest gift of all – reason (*ND* 2.147). Thanks to this rationality, this *logos* within themselves, human beings are able to 'tune' themselves with the *logos* which permeates the cosmos and thus 'live according to nature,' which is the

---

[62] Chrysippus *ap.* Plut. *Stoic. rep.* 1051E. On Stoic theology, see Mansfeld 1999; Algra 2003.

[63] Plut. *Stoic. Rep.* 1051DE.

[64] 'Many further illustrations could be given of this wise and careful providence of nature, to illustrate the lavishness and splendour of the gifts bestowed by the gods on men.' (*ND* 2.140 [LCL])

[65] Algra 2003: 170.

Stoic *telos*. This life according to nature is equivalent to the virtuous life, and enables humanity to become like god himself, fully rational, virtuous and good. Virtue then, according to the Stoics, is the only good, and vice the only evil. The rest – including health, wealth and even life itself – is redefined as indifferent because it is not 'up to us' (Sen. *Ben.* 1.6.2; Epict. *Ench.* 31.2). God is good, not only because he has created a good world – orderly and tailored for humanity – but because he has given humanity the greatest gift of all, rationality, which is what he needs to withstand everything which happens in life.[66] There is thus no need to fear 'this god who possesses all things, allots all things, and gives them freely.'

c) The Stoics on Traditional Religion and True Piety

The evidence is limited, and some Stoics were probably more critical of tradition than others, but the sources suggest that the Stoics generally engaged in traditional cultic practices, including the worship of the statues of the gods in temples.[67] For example, Cicero's Balbus and Epictetus enjoin people to worship the gods according to tradition.

It is our duty to revere and worship these gods [Ceres, Neptune and others—MvH] under the names which custom has bestowed upon them. (Balbus in Cicero, *ND* 2.71)

It is always appropriate to make libations, and sacrifices, and to give of the firstfruits after the manner of our fathers, and to do all this with purity, and not in slovenly or careless fashion, nor, in a niggardly way, nor yet beyond our means. (Epictetus, *Ench.* 31.5)

Balbus mentions divination and omen as evidence both for the existence of the gods and for their care for mankind, even if, like medical diagnostics, they can be misinterpreted (Cic. *ND* 2.12, 163). Epictetus assumes the appropriateness of traditional cultic practices in his work, such as the interpretation of omen (*Diss.* 3.1.37; frag. 32), making sacrifices or the Mysteries of Eleusis (*Diss.* 3.21.12–16), and lists reverence to god as part of the duties of mankind (*Diss.* 3.2.4; 3.7.26).[68] Seneca is often singled out as more critical than other Stoics towards traditional religion.[69] But as we have seen above, despite his criticism, he enjoined to follow traditions even if it is more out of custom than because it represents worship pleasing to the gods. Certainly, this is hardly a happy

---

[66] On this topic, cf. Algra 2007b: 40–41.

[67] On the attitude of the Stoics to traditional religion, see Babut 1974 (he identifies a continual tension between criticism and conservatism), Pià 2011, Algra 2003: 168–170, 2007a, 2009, Attridge 1978: 66–69. For Seneca's attitude, see also André 1983, Manning 1996, Setaioli 2007, Merckel 2012.

[68] On Epictetus and Stoic theology, cf. Algra 2007b: 32–55; Long 2002: 156.

[69] For Seneca as more critical, or at least more elaborate and explicit in his criticism towards popular religion, cf. e.g. Attridge 1978: 67; Manning 1996; Algra 2009: 240.

endorsement, but it suggests that Seneca did not find following such traditions incompatible with his philosophical commitments.[70]

Because they believed in a god which permeates everything, the Stoics could revere a plural manifestation of the divinity 'under the names which tradition has bestowed upon them' (Cicero, *ND* 2.70–71). At the same time, they insisted on the necessity to interpret the myths allegorically and firmly rejected their literal interpretation. Their acceptance of tradition was thus qualified. But because they believed that human beings have preconceptions of the gods, the Stoics also argued that old beliefs or traditions contain elements of truth.[71] They were thus able to assign a positive role to the myths and traditions if they were interpreted philosophically and provide a philosophical basis for their 'qualified' integration into the 'religion' of the philosopher. The Stoics' attitude towards the tradition is thus better described by words such as reinterpretation, adaptation, or 'appropriation,' rather than total rejection or acceptance.[72]

As for the veneration of statues, the fragments from Seneca's treatise against *superstitio* certainly denounces lifeless and horrible divine representations (Cf. *Superst. ap.* Aug. *Civ.* 6.10.2 quoted in a)), as well as the services to the statues which are interpreted as service to the gods.

> One servant informs Jupiter of the names of his worshippers, another announces the hours: one is his bather, another his anointer [...] There are women who are hairdressers for Juna and Minerva: while standing far away from the temple as well as from the image they move the fingers as if they were dressing the hair, there are others who hold a mirror. (*Superst. ap* Aug. *Civ. Dei* 6.10.4)

But it is hard to know if the philosopher was totally opposed to any representation of the gods in statues or any such ritual as means to express piety.[73] Certainly, because of the pantheistic nature of Stoicism, god could not be confined to a particular shape, and Stoic texts regularly denounce the problems created by anthropomorphic divine representations, *superstitio* being an important one. At the same time, the fact that divine rationality is similar to human rationality seems to have provided some support for anthropomorphic

---

[70] Modern scholars usually find him inconsistent (Attridge 1978: 69; Algra 2009: 240–41).

[71] Cf. Algra 2009: 228–232; Algra 2003: 169. He concludes (169–70): 'It would be wrong to view these varying Stoic conceptions of god as the result of incoherent and unconnected concessions to the tradition. In fact, the Stoics took great pains to account for the juxtaposition of what we might call pantheistic and polytheistic elements in their theology, by 'appropriating' and reinterpreting some aspects of traditional polytheism, while clearly rejecting others.'

[72] Algra (2009: 234) notes that 'appropriation' (συνοικειοῦν) is the term used by Philodemus to describe Chrysippus' practice (cf. Philodemus, *Piet. ap. P. Herc.* 1428, col. 4.16–26), and Cicero uses *accommodare* in the same connection (*ND* 1.41).

[73] On this passage, Algra (2009: 240) comments: 'If Seneca is here critical of an overly anthropomorphic conception of god and of the childish rituals to which it gives rise, he does not believe that a Stoic could straightforwardly advocate their rejection.' On Seneca and images, cf. also Clerc 1915: 104ff.

4.2. The Stoics on deisidaimonia, the Gods and Piety

representations of the gods. Thus, although god cannot be 'conceived anthropomorphically in any physical sense [...] he does resemble humans in so far as his [...] rationality and its various qualities are concerned.'[74] This is how Dio Chrysostom, an author influenced by Stoicism, defends the anthropomorphic statue of Zeus created by Pheidias: only the human shape can convey Zeus' intelligence and rationality, as well as his attributes – beauty, majesty, benevolence (*Or.* 12.59, 76–77). Furthermore, Chrysostom underscores the *didactic* function of this divine representation, not only singling out the role that material visible representations of the gods play in strengthening humanity's conception of the deity (*Or.* 12.44), but also stressing its need of such statues to connect to the god and worship him (*Or.* 12.60).[75] Along similar didactic lines, Epictetus points to the proud and steady look of Pheidias' Zeus to encourage his student to become like him, steady and unperturbed (*Diss.* 2.8.15–7).

The testimony of philosophical opponents confirms this general picture. Thus, famously, Plutarch criticizes the Stoic involvement in traditional cult as one of their self-contradictions.

> Moreover, it is a doctrine of Zeno's not to build temples of the gods, because a temple not worth much is also not sacred and no work of builders or mechanics is worth much. The Stoics, while applauding this as correct, attend the mysteries in temples, go up to the Acropolis, do reverence to statues, and place wreaths upon the shrines, though these are works of builders and mechanics. Yet they think that the Epicureans are confuted by the fact that they sacrifice to the gods, whereas they are themselves worse confuted by sacrificing at altars and temples which they hold do not exist and should not be built. (Plutarch, *Stoic. rep.* 1034B–C [LCL])

In the literature on the Areopagus speech, this passage is often mentioned as a proof that the Stoics rejected temples, or that they were acting in self-contradiction or in tension with their own teaching when involved in the cult. But if anything, this passage suggests that the Stoics *did* go to temples in Plutarch's time. Furthermore, Plutarch is here providing his own interpretation of a passage from Zeno, which he took to mean that temples should be forbidden.[76] Zeno's comment, however, appears in his *Politeia*, where he describes a utopian 'city of sages,' and where, according to other sources, he thought there should be no temples or statues of the gods. His reasons for this are clarified in another source mentioning this passage, Clement of Alexandria:

> There will be no need at all to build sanctuaries. For a sanctuary that is not worth much at all should not be regarded as sacred. But the work of craftsmen and mechanics is not worth much and not sacred. (Clement, *Strom.* 5.12.76; SVF 1.264)

---

[74] Algra 2009: 144.

[75] This didactic function – especially for the benefit of non-philosophers – might well explain the apparent 'inconsistency' of some Stoic philosophers with respect to some traditions.

[76] For a discussion of this passage, see Algra 2009: 238–239. My discussion relies on him.

As this passage shows, Zeno's statement needs not imply that temples or statues are always inappropriate, but rather, that they would be unnecessary in a city of wise men. Algra comments that this is presumably due to the fact that wise men worship the gods by other means.[77] The passage thus does not constitute evidence against Stoic involvement in the cult. Certainly, the Stoics considered the cosmos or man's breast, to be the only appropriate temple for god.[78] But this does not seem to have translated into a systematic rejection of temples or traditional means of worship.

At the same time, as this passage shows, the Stoics also redefined conventional piety along philosophical lines. Like other philosophers, they claimed that piety is first of all to have the right opinion about the gods, and to imitate them. This redefinition of conventional piety is particularly well illustrated in the passage of Seneca already partly quoted above.

It is common to instruct as to how the gods should be worshipped. But let us forbid anyone to light lamps on the Sabbath, since the gods do not need light and neither do men take pleasure in soot. Let us forbid to engage in morning salutations and to throng to the doors of temples; human desire for flattery is bribed by those services (*humana ambitio istis officiis capitur*), [but] the one who worships god is the one who knows him (*deum colit qui novit*). Let us forbid bringing towels and flesh-scrapers to Jupiter, and provide mirrors to Juno; god seeks no servants (*non quaerit ministros deus*). Why not? He himself does service to mankind, everywhere and to all he is at hand to help. Although one hears what limit (or what manner: *quem modum*) he must keep in sacrifices, and how far he sould recoil from troublesome *superstitionibus* (*quam procul resilire a molestis superstitionibus*), he will never make sufficient progress, unless he conceives a right idea of god, regarding him as possessing all things (*omnia habentem*), allotting all things (*omnia tribuentem*), and bestowing them freely (*beneficum gratis*). And what reason have the gods for doing deeds of kindness (*Quae causa est dis bene faciendi*)? It is their nature. One errs if he thinks that they are unwilling to harm; they cannot. They cannot receive nor are able to inflict injury; for doing harm and to suffer harm are connected. This greatest and most beautiful nature of all has rendered incapable of inflicting ill those whom it has removed from danger.

The first way to worship the gods is to believe in them; then to give them back their majesty, to give them back their goodness (*reddere bonitatem*), without which there is no majesty. To know that they preside over the universe, control all things by their power, and that they manage the guardianship of the human race, even though they are sometimes unmindful of the individuals. They neither give nor have evil; but they do chasten and restrain certain persons, and inflict penalties, and they sometimes punish by what has the appearance of good. You wish to win over (*propitiare*) the gods? Then be a good person. Whoever imitates them, is worshipping them sufficiently. (Seneca, *Ep.* 95.49–50 [MC])

---

[77] Algra 2009: 239: 'We may perhaps connect this text with the doxographic testimony in Epiphanius (*Adv. Her.* 3.2.9 = *SVF* 1.146) which tells us that Zeno said we shouldn't build sanctuaries, but that we should instead have the divine solely in our mind (ἐν μόνῳ τῷ νῷ), and with the repeated claim of such later Stoics as Seneca and Epictetus that the only proper way to honour the gods is by our own spiritual attitude, i.e. by imitating them through becoming virtuous.'

[78] The Stoics believed the cosmos to be the city of gods and men (Cicero, *ND* 2.62).

Again, this text is often interpreted as a rejection of traditional means of worship.[79] But this is not the emphasis.[80] Rather, this passage presents a redefinition of the relationship between men and gods using the common language and paradigm of benefaction in the ancient world, and therefore reinterpreting the '*do ut des*' principle of Graeco-Roman religion.

The first part of the extract insists that practices such as lighting lamps on the Sabbath or morning salutations should be forbidden. The reason given is that the gods *do not need those services*. At this point Seneca comments that it is human ambitions which are held (*capitur*) by such services (*officiis*). This is an allusion to the relationship between benefactors and their clients, as is confirmed by the mention of morning salutations typical of this relationship. Seneca goes on forbidding bringing towels, flesh-scrapers and mirrors to the gods, because, again, god needs no servants, but he does service to mankind and he is always ready to help. What Seneca challenges here, is not traditional worship, at least not *in toto*, but that the god-man relationship functions like the benefactor and client system between human beings. Relationship with the gods in antiquity was indeed understood along the *do-ut-des* benefaction relationship which also defined human relationships. This relationship was based on reciprocity. Seneca denounces the view that services to the gods will win over the gods and bring their friendship and gifts or avert their anger and harm. This, he insists, is mistaken, for the gods do not need anything and do not harm.

Rather than rejecting the reciprocity and benefaction paradigm to explain how human beings are to relate to the gods, however, Seneca redefines it.[81] He thus explains the *do-ut-des* paradigm between humanity and god as a friendship of the good. Thus, rather than giving services to the gods in return for their services to mankind, men are to 'give the gods back their goodness' (*reddere bonitatem*). To be friend with the gods, one needs to become of one mind with the gods – to attune one's *logos* with the cosmic *logos* – and become like them, virtuous and fully rational. Hence Seneca's explanation that to worship the gods, one needs to know god and be a good man, imitating them. There is thus a reciprocity of relationship between god and men, but it is similar to the relationship between the wise, in that both god and the wise man benefit each other through their virtue and rationality.[82] This passage thus redefines the traditional understanding of the exchange of *beneficia*. The friendship which humanity can have with the gods is a friendship sealed by the common love of the good,

---

[79] E.g. Houte 2010: 219; Klauck 2000: 84; Jipp 2012: 580.

[80] The fact that Seneca speaks of the necessity of knowing the proper measure/or manner of sacrifice (*quem modum servare in sacrificiis debeat*) itself implies that there is a proper measure for sacrifice, rather than the belief that sacrifices are totally inappropriate.

[81] Note the language of benefaction used to describe the gods: [...] *omnia habentem, omnia tribuentem, beneficum gratis. Quae causa est dis bene faciendi? Natura.*

[82] Algra 2007b: 41–42. Seneca is clear that God gives benefits to all, including to the ungrateful and evil (*Ben.* 4.28.1–4), but the greatest benefits are for the virtuous.

virtue. Through virtue, humanity becomes like the gods and enjoys friendship with them, showing itself to be its true pupil, imitator and offspring. Thus, the good man need not to fear to be hurt by them.

But let such matters be kept for their fitting time – all the more so, indeed, because you do not lack faith in Providence, but complain of it. I shall reconcile you with the gods, who are ever best to those who are best. For Nature never permits good to be injured by good; between good men and the gods there exists a friendship brought about by virtue.

Friendship, do I say? Nay, rather there is a tie of relationship and a likeness, since, in truth, a good man differs from God in the element of time only; he is God's pupil, his imitator, and true offspring, whom is all-glorious parent, being no mild taskmaster of virtues, rears, as strict fathers do, with much severity. (Sen. *Prov.* 1.4–6 [LCL])

This explains why only good men can make pleasing sacrifices to the gods, since the sacrifices themselves are not considered 'good,' but only the virtue of the worshippers.

Good men, therefore, are pleasing to the gods with an offering of meal and gruel; the bad, on the other hand, do not escape impiety although they dye the altars with streams of blood. (Sen. *Ben.* 1.6.3 [LCL])

Like the Epicureans, then, the Stoics redefined piety as the knowledge of god and his imitation (ὁμοίωσις θεῷ). Crucial to piety then, is to understand that the gods are good:

In piety towards the gods, I would have you know, the chief element is this, to have right opinions about them – as existing and as administering the universe well and justly – and to have set yourself to obey them and to submit to everything that happens, and to follow it voluntarily, in the belief that it is being fulfilled by the highest intelligence. For if you act this way, you will never blame the gods, nor find fault with them for neglecting you. But this result cannot be secured in any other way than by withdrawing your idea of the good and the evil from the things which are not under our control, and in those alone. [...] Wherefore, whoever is careful to exercise desire and aversion as he should, is at the same time careful about piety. (Epictetus, *Ench.* 31.1–4 [LCL]).

Epictetus' description of what piety entails shows that to be pious, one has to have a right notion about the gods – namely that they are provident, good and just. But to reach that conclusion in light of the apparent neglect of the gods in daily experience, one must also have a correct understanding of the true good – i.e. virtue. Only so will the Stoic sage stop blaiming the gods for being negligent, evil or harmful, and thus be truly pious. True piety is thus the opposite of *deisidaimonia*. It rejects the association of the gods with harm and evil, affirms their goodness and emulates them, thereby reaching a true friendship with the gods.

4.2.2 Stoic Theology in Debate: The Problems of Stoic Providence

Like the Epicurean response to *deisidaimonia*, the Stoic solution did not satisfy their philosophical opponents. Indeed, the Stoic claim that the gods are beneficent and provident was criticized by both the Epicureans and the Academics.[83] For the Stoics' rivals, their view of providence was highly problematic. This section discusses four of their criticisms.

a) Fate, Divination and a Universe Full of Gods as Conducive to Deisidaimonia

As already mentioned, the Epicureans argued that the Stoic view of God was conducive to the fear of the gods – to *deisidaimonia*.[84] A creator god involved in the world who notices and cares about everything is terrifying – 'a prying master' (Cicero, *ND* 1.55–56). Furthermore, the doctrine of necessity of the Stoics and their belief that the gods communicate with men through divination enslaves human beings to seers and oracle-mongers, in the fear of not offending the gods (*ibid*).

Similar arguments were made by the Academics, who denounced the doctrine of fate (Cicero, *Div*. 2.19) and practice of divination of the Stoics as full of *superstitio* (Cicero, *Div*. 2.83–85). Martin argues that Cicero denounces the *false* beliefs of the Stoics about the gods.[85] But the focus of the criticism seems to be the way the Stoic doctrines of fate and divination lead to a constant concern about the gods' will and thus to an aboundance of 'superstitious' practices, i.e. practices meant to conciliate the gods and avert their anger. As he explains:

For while on the watch for these 'oracles' of yours could you be so free and calm of mind that you would have reason and not *superstitio* to guide your course? (*Div*. 2.83 [LCL])

The problem with the Stoic view of god is that this god directs and permeates everything, and thus people are led to 'interpret' everything as signs from the gods and to be constantly concerned about them.[86] Along the same line, the Academics denounced the propensity of the Stoics to identify gods with everything (the sea, the earth, etc.) as an 'infinite cause for *superstitio*' (*ND* 3.52).[87]

---

[83] Plutarch and Cicero's writings provide a good insight into the polemic. On Plutarch and Stoicism, see Opsomer 2014; Hershbell 1992b; Babut 1969. On the validity of Plutarch's critique and accusation against Stoicism, see Babut 2004.

[84] See b).

[85] Martin 2004: 128.

[86] The Academics were not against divination, nor against providence, but against the Stoic understanding of providence, which was based on an identification of the world as it is with an all-permeating divine Rationality. Indeed, such a belief had the disastrous consequences, not only of mixing the divine with matter, but above all of associating the divine will with everything which happens in the world, including evil (more on this below).

[87] *Nec illa infinita ratio superstitionis probabitur.*

b) Counter-Evidence: Evil and Injustice in the World

The strongest argument against a good and provident god was of course the presence of much evil and injustice in the world. This argument is best illustrated by Cotta's plaidoyer in the third book of the *ND*.

Challenging the Stoic assertion that the gift of reason constitutes the greatest gift and shows divine beneficence towards mankind, Cotta argues that reason is just as much used for wicked deeds as for good. In fact, malicious deeds can only be perpetrated through reason. Reason is thus as much responsible for the vices and disasters which plague mankind than anyting good. To the Stoic answer that the gods are not to be responsible for the bad use of reason of mankind, Cotta argues that, unlike men who sometimes make gifts which are used badly but couldn't have anticipated it, the Stoic god cannot claim not to know that human beings will put reason to bad use since he foresees all things (*ND* 3.78). In other words, if god had wanted to make a gift to mankind through reason, he should have given him *virtuous* reason.

The second argument invoked by Cotta is the all-too-common injustice whereby the wicked prosper and the good men come to grief. Cotta goes on giving examples of good men touched by misfortunes and wicked and cruel men prospering. He comments that if the gods do really care for men, their verdict suggests that they do not distinguish between good and bad men. Injustice thus stands as a witness against the gods (*ND* 3.82–83). Cotta continues by listing examples of sacrilegious people who plundered temples and mocked cultic statues and were never punished by the gods for their impiety or their injustice.

Cotta then briefly addresses some of the Stoic responses to those accusations. To the Stoic argument that the gods, like human rulers, cannot take notice of everything, Cotta argues that the gods cannot have the excuse of ignorance which human kings have (*ND* 3.90). To the Stoic argument that divine retribution is sometimes exercised upon the children of the wicked, Cotta complains that this cannot be proper justice: no state would tolerate a lawgiver who sentences the son or grandson for the sins of his fathers (*ND* 3.90). Finally, to the Stoic claim that the gods do not care for individuals but only for the whole, Cotta replies that the evidence shows that the gods show no more concern for cities, tribes or nations, indeed the human race as a whole (*ND* 3.93).

c) The Stoic God as Cause of Evil and Excuse for Wickedness

Plutarch's argument against Stoic providence in his treaties takes a different form from Cotta's critique in *ND*. Rather than offering counter-evidence against the affirmation that god is beneficent and provident, he denounces the contradictions and problems of Stoic theology on its own terms. Basically, the great problem of Stoic theology is that it makes god responsible for evil.

Thus, Plutarch points to the willingness of the Stoics to attribute evils such as wars to god, while they claim those gods to be beneficient as one of their contradictions. Plutarch's argument targets the claim that wars were sometimes necessary because of an excess of population. The Stoics indeed claimed that some evil in the world is necessary. Plutarch, however, complains that a good god should have prevented overpopulation in the first place rather than destroying human beings (*Stoic. rep.* 1049A–D). Furthermore, attributing wars to god makes him responsible for human vices, since wars are caused by human lust or greed. Here again he sees a contradiction in that the Stoics affirm that god is not responsible for shameful things (1049D–E). For Plutarch, Chrysippus makes the gods responsible for human vices rather than human beings themselves because everything happens 'not merely of necessity or according to destiny but also in conformity with god's reason and with the best nature' (1049F–1050D [LCL]).

Despite this, the Stoics say that the gods chastise evil. This however, is a contradiction because the gods would thus chastise what they are themselves responsible for, or an evil which is useful in the greater scheme of things (1050D–1051A). Plutarch denounces at length and with much sarcasm the Stoic view that vice and evil are necessary to the universe, or that when evil happens to virtuous men, it is because providence entrusts some things to base spirits, just like some charges are neglected in larger households.

d) The Triviality of the Benefits of the Stoic God

Finally, Plutarch attacks another self-contradiction of Stoic theology by pointing out that if the only 'good' in the world is virtue, and everything else is indifferent to the wise, then the Stoic god does not really give 'meaningful' benefits to mankind or the wise. Indeed, things such as wealth or health are not really goods according to the Stoics, but trivialities. There is thus no meaningful gift exchange happening between the wise and god if virtue is the only good, for virtue is precisely what god does not give to humanity, but what it has to strive for (*Stoic. rep.*1048).

e) Conclusions

Not all the accusations mentioned above were legitimate. For example, Plutarch overlooks that the Stoics were compatibilists and held to a sophisticated view in which moral responsibility was compatible with the fact that vice plays a role in the overall structure of the universe.[88] Furthermore, the Stoics provided answers to those criticisms, in particular to the question of evil, by

---

[88] Opsomer 2014: 93. On Stoic compatibilism, see Bobzien 1998.

developing several lines of arguments in their theodicy.[89] What those accusations show, however, is that while their diagnosis and criticism of *deisidaimonia* was similar to that of the Epicureans and the Platonists, the theology the Stoics offered as a solution to it was accused, ironically, of threatening the goodness of god and his benefits, and being conducive to *deisidaimonia*.

4.2.3 Summary: The Stoics on Deisidaimonia *and Proper Piety*

This analysis suggests that the Stoics also understood *deisidaimonia* to refer to the fear of the divine, and not to traditional religion generally or the worship of divine images, as has regularly been assumed in discussions of Acts 17. A contextual examination of the texts which have regularly been appealed to as parallels to the criticism of idolatry in the speech in Athens shows that they cannot be invoked to support the view that the Stoics rejected divine representations or the cult more generally.

Admittedly, and importantly, some Stoic texts show a connection between divine representations and the development of *deisidaimonia*: the representation of the gods under terrifying traits or sometimes simply with human traits encouraged the belief that they were evil or could at least seek revenge. But the criticism of *deisidaimonia* focused on a wrong attitude towards the divine which could be encouraged by divine representations, not divine representations in toto. Like the Epicureans, the Stoics denounced *deisidaimonia* because it was based on a false knowledge of the gods, who, according to the Stoics, are fundamentally good. There is thus no need to fear them. The Stoics did hold that the gods punish the wicked, but this was understood as a form of healing rather than a form of evil.

As for proper worship or piety, the Stoics generally advocated worship along the lines of tradition. But like the Epicureans, they emphasized that true piety constitutes above all of having a right view of the gods and imitating them, namely being good. Again, then, it is imitation of the divine which brings blessedness from the gods, while wickedness brings punishment according to the Stoics. But in any cases, fear is inappropriate.

4.3 Conclusions

As discussed in the introduction of this chapter, scholars have noticed that the word which Luke puts into the mouth of Paul to characterize the Athenians – *deisidaimonesterous* – was the object of criticism by the philosophers of his time. Usually, however, exegetes have assumed that this criticism could

---

[89] On the Stoic treatment of evil, cf. Long 1968; Kerferd 1977–1978; Frede 2002; Algra 2003; Liebersohn 2012; Opsomer 2014.

4.3 Conclusions

broadly be equated with the criticism of traditional religion, or more specifically of idolatry. As has been shown, this assumption is also found in some other scholarly discussions of *deisidaimonia* – most recently in Martin's contribution to this subject. In light of such claims or assumptions, the aim of this chapter was to identify what the Epicureans and the Stoics understood by the terminology of *deisidaimonia* (or *superstitio*) in early Post-Hellenistic times[90], why they criticized it, and how this related to their attitude towards traditional religion and piety. This conclusion synthesizes those results in light of previous research, and shows how this context sheds new light to interpret Acts 17.

4.3.1 The Philosophical Criticism of Deisidaimonia in Early Post-Hellenistic Times

a) The Meaning of Deisidaimonia

First, Epicurean and Stoic philosophers use *deisidaimonia*/*superstitio* with the meaning 'fear of the gods,' or occasionally, by metonymy, to refer to practices and beliefs which either reflect such fears – i.e. apotropaic activities meant to avert divine hostility – or are conducive to such fears – e.g. some tales or traditions implying harmful, evil or immoral gods. As in the last chapter then, the criticism of *deisidaimonia* does not focus on particular cultic practices or beliefs per se, but on an emotion and the actions and beliefs which are the result – or generative – of this fear.

As this chapter has shown, Epicureans and Stoics also associate *deisidaimonia* with the same contexts and situations as Plutarch, Diodorus, Strabo and Josephus: events or phenomena which might suggest divine hostility (eclipses, thunderbolt, sickness, dreams, etc.), or infringement of cultic or 'moral' law (breaking an oath, stilling sacred gold, wickedness or injustice, etc.).

Importantly, then, both philosophical and non-philosophical authors refer to the same phenomenon when they use *deisidaimonia*. It is thus misleading to say, as Martin does, that the philosophers – or even the intellectual elite – 'invented' *deisidaimonia*.[91] As argued in the previous chapter, *deisidaimonia* was a logical entailment of the nature of Graeco-roman religion, and the cult – which aimed to ensure the *pax deorum* – was the normal way to deal with such fears. The philosophers did not invent it nor were they the only ones who noticed it: it was there all along, intrinsically bound to a worldview in which the world is full of more or less powerful gods who can be friends or enemies. And while only the Epicureans argued that *deisidaimonia* is one of the two roots of all the problems of humanity, the Stoics and Plutarch found it widespread and wrote against it. Thus, for Plutarch, *deisidaimonia* is a feeling which most

---

[90] According to Van Nuffelen (2011: 1), the 'Post-Hellenistic period' ranges from the first century BCE to the second century CE.
[91] Martin 2004: 226.

people experiment towards the gods, especially when they participate in religious festivals (*Suav. viv.* 1101DE). This feeling of fear, however, is in the majority of people mixed with good hopes to be helped by the gods and joy to be in their presence, and this, for Plutarch at least, balances its negative effect. The Platonist is clear, however, that only the few wise do not experience *deisidaimonia* and that this is the ideal to which one should aspire. What the philosophers did, therefore, is attempt to provide a philosophical solution to eliminate it so that people could reach the *telos* of *eudaimonia* and have peace with the gods.

Going back to Acts 17, this means first that both philosophers and non-philosophers in Athens would have understood the characterisation of '*deisidaimonesterous*' in the speech along the same lines. More importantly, this analysis suggests that to discuss *deisidaimonia* and the relationship of humanity with the gods with the philosophers – or indeed with anybody – is to enter the subject not only of the nature of the gods, but also of their hostility, their wrath and the question of divine retribution – including post mortem retribution. And in fact, both Stoics and Epicureans believed in a form of divine retribution. It further means discussing the fear of the gods and thus also, potentially, the topic of guilt and a bad conscience.

This sheds important light on the periocope of Acts 17. Indeed, as detailed in chapter 1, scholars have usually found the end of the speech which announces divine judgment to be unexpected in light of the subject of the speech and have wondered how a Greek audience could have made sense of it. This chapter shows, however, that the issues of divine judgment, divine retribution, and the way human beings can avoid it and have peace with the gods, are very much at the center of what talking about *deisidaimonia* entails !

b) The Heart of the Criticism of Deisidaimonia *and Divine Goodness and Justice*

Second, and against much previous scholarship, this chapter suggests that the heart of the philosophical critique of *deisidaimonia* was theological. Whether the Epicureans, the Stoics or the Platonist Plutarch, they all identify the origin of *deisidaimonia* in ignorance about the gods – namely misunderstanding their nature. The fundamental mistake of *deisidaimonia* is that it associates the gods with evil and harm. To quote Plutarch:

The former [the atheists] do not see the gods at all, and the latter [those fearing the gods – δεισιδαίμονας] believe that they are evil. The former disregard them, and the latter conceive their kindliness to be frightful, their fatherly solicitude to be despotic, their provident care to be injurious, their lack of anger to be savage and brutal. […] And in short, atheism is an indifferent feeling towards the divine, which does not apprehend the good (μὴ νοοῦσα τὸ ἀγαθόν), and *deisidaimonia* is a multitude of feelings which consider the good to be evil (κακὸν τὸ ἀγαθὸν ὑπονοοῦσα). (*Superst.* 167D–E [MC])

The fundamental cause of *deisidaimonia* is thus a mistaken theological – or physical, since theology is part of physics – judgment about reality. And for all three schools (if Plutarch is representative of the Platonists), this mistaken judgment is both impious – for it associates the gods with evil – and dramatic for mankind because it maintains it in a state of 'slavery' – a terminology which is again found in the different Hellenistic schools.

Admittedly the literature surveyed in the present chapter remains limited and further study will be necessary to confirm this conclusion, but in the texts examined, fundamentally, Graeco-Roman philosophers denounced *deisidaimonia* not because it represented a piety which was excessive, embarrassing, unworthy of their social status, foreign, or associated with the private cult rather than public worship, but because it reflected a false judgment about the nature of the gods, which both insulted the gods and threw mankind into the slavery of fear and even wicked and shameful practices to avoid the gods' wrath.[92]

As to their solution to this problem and the way human beings can get rid of this sickness, again, the Epicureans, the Stoics and the Platonist Plutarch are united: human beings need to learn the truth about the gods, and this truth fundamentally entails that the gods are not involved or responsible for evil. At the very heart of the philosophical answer to *deisidaimonia* is thus the belief that the gods are good and just, and not responsible for evil. Theodicy, and demonstration of divine goodness and justice, thus had an important place in the philosophical argument against *deisidaimonia*.[93] And it is at this point that the Stoics, the Epicureans and the Platonists departed from each other and argued with each other, for while they agreed that the divine is not (ultimately!) evil, they had a very different understanding of the way the divine interacts with the world and human beings, a view which was precisely the result of their distanciation of the divine from evil.[94]

---

[92] Against what some scholars have claimed there is no trace either of a connection between *deisidaimonia* and unhealthy curiosity (Gray [2005: 113]) or novelty (Jipp 2012: 574) in the literature examined in chapters 3 and 4.

[93] In his study Martin rightly highlights the importance that the belief in good gods has in the philosophical criticism of *deisidaimonia*. He fails, however, to acknowledge the complexity of the philosophical argumentation when he calls this belief the 'Grand Optimal Illusion' because, as he explains, ancient thinkers had 'no new "data," "facts," or "evidence" from nature that could have demonstrated its truth.' (2004: 227). As this chapter shows, not only *did* some philosophers attempt to demonstrate this belief from nature (the Stoics), but all philosophers were perfectly aware of the difficulties involved in claiming the (ultimate) goodness of the gods and had developed a philosophy and arguments which aimed to deal with those difficulties. A similar criticism is made by Gordon (2006: 524–525) in his review of Martin.

[94] Plutarch does believe in evil demons, but he still emphasizes the goodness of the divine hierarchy. For a discussion of how he can maintain a critic of *deisidaimonia* in this context, cf. Van Nuffelen 2011b.

This also sheds light on the pericope in Acts 17. Indeed, as showed by this chapter, for the philosophers, providing an answer to *deisidaimonia* meant demonstrating that the gods are not evil *and yet* superior or excellent beings. To be superior and excellent, they thus also had to be good and somehow involved in maintaining a form of justice by benefiting the righteous and punishing the wicked. This was the heart of the debate, for the Stoics had to demonstrate that the gods are good (and thus righteous) in an evil and unjust world, and the Epicureans had to show how gods who are not involved in the world can still play a role in the justice and moral fabric of the world. And each school accused the other of failing to provide a convincing view of a divinity uninvolved in evil and yet perfectly superior and 'responsible' for some form of justice, and thus either maintaining the risk of *deisidaimonia*, or threatening the moral fabric of society. In any case, demonstrating the justice and goodness of the gods was at the heart of any attempt to show that *deisidaimonia* was not necessary. This important aspect of the debate is in keeping with the thematic tackled in the conclusion of the speech in Acts 17, namely the proclamation of God's coming judgment in righteousness (17:31). The speech does indeed announce a judgment which will embrasse all mankind and through which God will display his righteousness. As suggested by this chapter, in the context of a debate with the different philosophical schools on the nature of God and *deisidaimonia*, any suggestion about the nature of the gods must also deal with the compatibility of its proposal on a theodicy level and find a way to affirm ultimately divine goodness and righteousness in light of contrary evidence.

c) *A Debated and Polemical Subject*

What this chapter also highlights, therefore, is that while Epicureans, Stoics and Platonists were in agreement about the impiety and 'irrationality' of *deisidaimonia*,[95] they were in strong disagreement about the theology which provided a solution to it. Providing a convincing answer to the fear of evil gods necessitated dealing with questions of divine justice and goodness, and as the writings of Philodemus, Cicero and Plutarch show, this was a central and hotly debated subject among the schools. Thus, in an ironic turn, the Stoics and the Platonists were able to denounce the Epicureans as destroying piety, justice and the excellence of god while they eliminated *deisidaimonia*, while the Epicureans and the Platonists criticized the Stoics for supporting a theology which they argued compromised the goodness of god and contributed to *deisidaimonia*.

This draws attention to an important feature of Hellenistic philosophy at the time which concerns us, namely its polemical and competitive nature. As Trapp comments concerning *philosophia* in the Imperial Age:

---

[95] 'Irrationality' is to be understood as 'in opposition to reality' in this context.

It was made up instead, as it had been since the later fourth century BCE, of a multiplicity of reciprocally critical schools of thought (*haireseis, sectae*), each with its own version of the truth about reality, human nature, and happiness, and its own corresponding modulation of the philosophic life, propounded and defended in vigorous reciprocal polemic with its competitors.[96]

This sectarian and polemical outlook remained the dominant philosophical mode in the first centuries CE, as the surviving literature from this period attests: so, Epictetus attacks Academics and Epicureans from a Stoic perspective, Diogenes of Oenanda decries Stoics and Platonists from an Epicurean point of view and Plutarch denounces the self-contradictions of Epicureans and Stoics.[97] As Stowers puts it, '[t]he Hellenistic philosophies conceived themselves as distinct and mutually exclusive *haeresis*, choices, or sects.'[98] This polemical and exclusive outlook, rather than eclecticism or an attempt to seek common ground, dominated the philosophical landscape when Luke wrote Acts 17, and will have important consequences on the way we interpret its use of philosophical arguments.[99]

Indeed, the scholarly focus on the search for common ground between the speech in Acts 17 and Graeco-Roman philosophy dates back to a time when it was thought that eclecticism was common in early Post-Hellenistic times. As this chapter has shown, the Epicureans and the Stoics did use similar arguments in their attack on *deisidaimonia* and to explain the nature of proper worship, such as the fact that the gods do not need human services. But as this chapter has also shown, such common ground would hardly have been interpreted as a theological rapprochment between two philosophical schools which clearly disagreed on the nature of the gods and the solution to *deisidaimonia*, and violently criticized each other on those subjects. In this context of debate about the gods and divine goodness and justice, and given the highly polemical and exclusive outlooks of the philosophical schools at the time, it is unlikely that the few ideas paralleling Stoic or Epicurean philosophy found in the speech in Athens would have been perceived as a rapproachment. The attention to

---

[96] Trapp 2014: 50.
[97] Trapp 2014: 51.
[98] Stowers 2001: 89,
[99] It is Eduard Zeller, who, in his influential *Die Philosophie der Griechen in ihrer geschichtlichen Entwicklung* (1869–82) popularized the idea that eclecticism dominated philosophy between the first century BC and Plotinus. Recent scholarship, however, has challenged several aspects of his thesis (see especially Dillon and Long 1988), noting in particular that most philosophers during this period still maintained an allegiance to a single tradition (Hatzimichali 2011: 14). Thus, in an article published in 1989, Sedley concluded that apart from the 'curious individual' called Potamo of Alexandria, 'no ancient philosopher is an eclectic' (118–119). For a study of Potamo, the only philosopher who seems to have been a self-conscious eclectic, see Hatzimichali 2011.

commonalities and common ground between sects may have more to do with the predisposition of the modern reader than with that of a 1st century audience.

4.3.2 Stoic and Epicurean Philosophers on Traditional Religion and Piety

a) Attitude Towards Traditional Religion

As mentioned above, the philosophical criticism of *deisidaimonia* was not synonymous with the criticism of traditional religion or practices. Indeed, another element highlighted by this chapter with significant consequences for the interpretation of the pericope in Acts 17 is that both Epicurean and Stoic philosophers did not reject the traditional cult, not even its use of divine images.[100] Certainly, some philosophers were probably more critical of the cult than others, and Lucretius or Seneca might well have been more vocal against it than Philodemus or Epictetus respectively. But the evidence given both by the philosophers and their philosophical rivals suggests that they did not oppose the cult in toto and that they engaged in it.

Not only so, but as some recent studies have suggested, the Epicureans, the Stoics and a Platonist like Plutarch saw in religion and some religious practices the reflection of deep philosophical truth about the divine and the nature of things and sometimes even a positive reinforcement of those truths upon the human mind.[101] Thus, as discussed earlier, the Epicureans encouraged participation in the cult with a correct Epicurean view of the gods to reach *ataraxia*. And the Stoics argued that tradition contained some truth because of human preconceptions about the gods, and, although they denounced the errors to which anthropomorphic representations of the gods led, some of them at least, seem to have found some validity in such representations because of the 'kinship' between men and the divine.

Having said that, the philosophers did criticize and reject certain aspects of traditional 'religion.' Typically, the Epicureans rejected divination or a 'crass' interpretation of the myths as incompatible with their view of non-interventionist gods. The Stoics denounced literal interpretations of the myths, the mistaken *identification* of the gods with their statues and the problems of

---

[100] Martin (2004) totally overlooks this state of affairs in his analysis. Hence Gordon (2006: 525) criticizes Martin for not mentioning that all philosophical schools, apart from the Cynics, accommodated the civic cult, and that the Stoics defended civic religion as an approximation of truth.

[101] On Plutarch's belief that traditional beliefs, myths and practices were sources of knowledge when philosophically interpreted, cf. Ferrari 2005: 14; Hisch-Luispold 2014. On religion being a source of knowledge for philosophers in post-Hellenistic times, cf. Van Nuffelen 2011: 4–10. See also Algra (2009: 227), who argues that 'one of the recurrent themes in the polemics between Stoics and Epicureans in the first century BC [...] is the extent to which each of these schools was able to make sense of, or to salvage, the tradition –be it the sociopolitical or the religious tradition.'

anthropomorphism. Importantly for our purposes, the present analysis also highlights that the philosophers clearly identify certain myths and practices as conducive to *deisidaimonia*, because they encourage the belief that the gods are evil and harmful. In particular anthropomorphic representations of the gods, both in myths and statues are regularly singled out as strengthening *deisidaimonia*, since they imply that the gods have human passions. The passage from Plutarch's *De superstitione* quoted earlier, seems to echo this diagnostic. The full text reads:

The former [the atheists] do not see the gods at all, and the latter [those fearing the gods – δεισιδαίμονας] believe that they are evil. [...] Then again, such persons give credence to workers in copper, sculptors of stone and modellers of wax who make statues of the gods in the likeness of human beings (ἀνθρωπόμορφα τῶν θεῶν τὰ εἴδη), and they have such images fashioned, and dress them up, and worship them. But they hold in contempt philosophers and statesmen, who try to prove that the dignity of god is associated with goodness, magnanimity, good will, and solicitude. (*Superst.* 167D–E [MC])

This passage does not represent a rejection of anthropomorphic images.[102] Indeed Plutarch is generally not opposed to the use of images of the gods, although he denounces the assimilation of the statues of the gods with the gods themselves.[103] Rather this passage denounces the deleterious effect those images have on humanity if they are interpreted as representations of the real nature of the gods. In this case, the implication seems to be that anthropomorphic divine representations lead to or strengthen *deisidaimonia*, probably because gods in the likeness of human beings can be petty, angry and wicked.

The most obvious consequence of this conclusion for the exegesis of Acts 17 is that this raises the question as to whether the anti-idol polemic of the speech can really be said to represent a rapprochement with the Epicurean or Stoic philosophy criticism of some aspects of traditional religion.

b) Piety as Right Knowledge of the Divine and Godlikeness

Moving to their teaching about piety, both Epicurean and Stoic philosophers argued that the gods do not *need* the services of mankind, such as the building of houses or sacrifices. This, however, does not seem to have led them to a rejection of all temples and sacrifices altogether. It did, however, lead them to a re-interpretation of the way humanity can have a relationship with the gods and a new understanding of the '*do ut des*' principle with the gods. Thus, the Epicureans reinterpreted the harms and benefits given by the gods along psychological lines: the wicked is harmed by his view of gods who, like him, harm and will harm him possibly eternally in the afterlife; the righteous, however, is

---

[102] Cf. Van Nuffelen 2011: 69. On Plutarch and images: Graf 2005; on Plutarch's religion more generally: Hirsch-Luipold 2014.

[103] See especially *Is. Os.* 379C–D.

benefited by his view of gods like himself, who are righteous and will not harm him. And the Stoics reinterpreted friendship with god as a friendship of the good, with the wise and virtuous benefiting most from god's goodness.

The philosophers then still understood the relationship between human beings and the gods along the lines of a certain reciprocity. This ensured that the gods played a role in preserving justice, giving retribution and rewards to people as they deserved. Furthermore, this reciprocity often took the form of the gods 'treating' people the way they themselves behaved. Thus, for the Epicureans, the wicked are hurt by their view of 'wicked' and 'harmful gods,' while the righteous is not harmed by his view of unharmful gods. And for the Stoics, it is the virtuous who most benefits from god's virtue.

Furthermore, piety was, above all, for both Stoic and Epicurean philosophers (and indeed the Platonists), to have a right opinion about the gods – i.e. about their nature – and then to imitate them as much as possible, becoming like them. Indeed, both philosophical schools, like the Platonists, believed that true piety is expressed above all in imitation of the gods and godlikeness. Importantly, whether it meant believing that the gods are not moved by *ira* or *gratia* and do not interfer in the world (Epicureans), or that the gods express their excellence in *gratia* and providence (Stoics), in both cases it implied embracing that the divine does not harm and is uninvolved in evil. And since piety was expressed by becoming like god, through right reasoning, but also through ethical emulation, piety also meant being righteous and nor harming anyone (Epicureans), and being good and virtuous (Stoics) like the gods. Piety (*eusebeia*) then was indeed, as the philosophers had concluded, the antithesis of *deisidaimonia*. To have peace with the gods then, one is not to serve them as if they were in need of services, or if they were evil or could be bribed, but one ought to imitate them and become like them, good, virtuous, or unharmful.

Consequently, although both Epicurean and Stoic philosophers taught that the cultic traditions received by the ancestors were generally to be followed, they emphasized the necessity to do so with a correct view of the gods for it to be true and useful piety. Furthermore, for both Epicurean and Stoic philosophers true piety is also ethical, and takes the form of the emulation of the divine. Thus, piety is, as Philodemus puts it, virtually the same as justice for the Epicureans; and for the Stoic, to be pious is to be good like the gods.

Again, this historical background sheds interesting light on Acts 17. For it shows that an ethical appeal in the context of a discussion of proper worship of the divine is perfectly consistent with the treatment of the topic among philosophers. Thus, the ethical imperative or call to righteousness implied in the speech of Acts 17 when it calls people to repentance (17:30) or speaks of a coming judgment in righteousness (17:31) is not unrelated to the subject at hand, namely proper worship in light of divine nature.

4.3 Conclusions

Having shed more light on the philosophical context with which the speech is in diaologue in Acts 17, it is now time to examine the argument of the speech in detail.

5. Something New in Athens – Godlikeness and Divine Justice in Light of the Resurrection (Acts 17:22–31)

Having examined in more depth the religious and philosophical context alluded to in the narrative of Acts 17, the present chapter analyses the argument of the speech in Acts 17:22–31. As will be shown, at several points, the historical context discussed in the two previous chapters sheds light on the argument. To facilitate this analysis, it is divided into four sections each focusing on a portion of the speech. The first part discusses the *proemium* of the speech which introduces the subject of the discourse (vv. 22–23). The second section analyses the main body of the argument until v. 28 (vv. 24–28), while a third section is devoted to the examination of verse 29. Finally, the last section examines the conclusion of the speech in verses 30–31. This chapter argues for a new reading of the main thrust of the speech, which makes better sense in the historical and philosophical contexts discussed in the previous chapters, and illuminates its coherence and in particular the function of what has long been called a 'Christian appendix' in the argument.

5.1 Introducing the Subject: *Deisidaimonia* and the Unknown God (17:22–23)

5.1.1 The Altar to the Unknown God and the Concern About Hostile Gods

Exegetes who have taken δεισιδαιμονεστέρους as a criticism in Paul's discourse have usually interpreted it as a denunciation of the 'superstitious' idolatry or polytheism of the Athenians.[1] But as argued in the preceding chapters, *deisidaimonia* was not specifically associated with idolatry or a particular religious practice, nor did it simply describe any form of 'perverted, false or superstitious religion.' Rather, it referred to the fear or concern to avert divine hostility or wrath and maintain peace with the gods. When the philosophers

---

[1] Rowe 2011: 39: 'As Luke tells it, Paul does not think that the Athenians are particularly pious but exceptionally superstitious – or in Jewish theological language, idolatrous.' cf. Gärtner 1955: 238; Jipp 2012: 576–7.

5.1. Deisidaimonia and the Unknown God

criticized *deisidaimonia* then, they were not targeting the worship of idols specifically, although they *did* point out that images played an important role in leading to *deisidaimonia* when not interpreted appropriately and denounced the excess of religious practices to which *deisidaimonia* could lead.

The speech thus begins by pointing out that the Athenians are seemingly (cf. ὡς) very concerned about preventing divine hostility and maintaining a good relationship with the gods, and refers to the altar to the unknown god as evidence of such extreme concern: '...I *even* (καί) found an altar upon which it is written: to an unknown god.' (23). As explained earlier, such altars reflect a concern not to overlook any god and avert actual or potential hostility and harm from an offended deity. The description of the city of Athens as full of idols (16: κατείδωλον) further demonstrates this preoccupation. As the discussion in chapter three has also shown, it is unnecessary to interpret this characterization as a mockery of the Athenians. The term *deisidaimōn* is first of all descriptive of a very common attitude in Graeco-Roman religion, namely the concern to avoid the hostility and wrath of the gods, and it need not imply either that the Athenians are constantly anxious about or terrorized by the gods.

The attitude of the Athenians thus provides an entry point to Luke's discourse, and also opens up the thematic of the speech: the relationship between human beings and the divine. As discussed in the previous chapters, it was the purpose of traditional religion to maintain the *pax deorum*. Likewise, the Stoics and the Epicureans provided their own teaching on the way to maintain a relationship with the gods characterized by peace, and even love and friendship in the case of the Stoics.

At the same time, verse 23 suggests a problem with Athenian worship: indeed, as Luke puts it, the Athenians are worshipping ignorantly (ἀγνοοῦντες). The association of *deisidaimonia* with ignorance echoes the diagnostic of both Epicurean and Stoic philosophers – the two sects with which Paul has been interacting just before the speech – on the question. As discussed in the last chapter, both schools argued that the wise who through philosophy has a right knowledge of the gods and imitates them is not affected by *deisidaimonia* but has a relationship with the gods characterized by peace or friendship. Understanding the nature of the gods was thus crucial to worship them properly and have peace with them.

The beginning of the speech therefore shows that the apostle tackles a 'religious concern' of the Athenians which the philosophers also aimed to address. According to the philosophers, however, Paul is proposing a 'new teaching' on this question (cf. καινὴ διδαχή in v.19). In so far as the apostle is depicted as addressing a topic discussed and debated by the philosophers and echoing their terminology (ignorance), Luke certainly characterizes Paul as a philosophical 'rival' of the Stoic and Epicurean philosophers. Whether the characterization of the Athenians as δεισιδαιμονεστέρους is also ironic because it highlights a failure of the philosophers to eliminate what they aimed to eradicate is more difficult to assess since the audience of the speech and the Athenians generally were not all philosophers. While it is possible that Luke might want to draw attention to the philosophers' lack of success in convincing their compatriots, it is doubtful that philosophers would have felt responsible for the failure of their contemporaries to apply successfully their teaching and get rid of *deisidaimonia*.

5.1.2 The Unknown God and the Subject of the Speech

Having pointed to the 'problem' or 'concern' of Athenian worship, verse 23 then announces the subject (*propositio*) of Paul's proclamation: 'what you worship ignorantly, this I am announcing to you.'

Acts 17:23 διερχόμενος γὰρ καὶ ἀναθεωρῶν τὰ σεβάσματα ὑμῶν εὗρον καὶ βωμὸν ἐν ᾧ ἐπεγέγραπτο· Ἀγνώστῳ θεῷ. ὃ οὖν ἀγνοοῦντες εὐσεβεῖτε, τοῦτο ἐγὼ καταγγέλλω ὑμῖν.

It is hard to underestimate the hermeneutical importance of v. 23 to understand the argument of the speech: what is Paul announcing and how does it relate to current Athenian worship?[2] Rhetorically, verse 23 forms the conclusion of the *exordium*, whose purpose is, according to Aristotle, to 'either excite or remove prejudice, and magnify or minimize the importance of the subject' of the speech.[3] Exegetes thus commonly understand verse 23 as Paul's attempt to remove the suspicion that he is importing new deities to the city (v.18) by connecting his proclamation to an Athenian altar. The consensus of scholarship throughout history has been that the object of Paul's speech is to make known the unknown god to the Athenians, whom Paul then introduces as the Lord of heaven and earth in v. 24.

It is evident that by employing poetic examples from the *Phaenomena* of Aratus, [Paul] approves of the well-spoken words of the Greeks and discloses that through the 'unknown God' the Creator God [τὸν δημιουργὸν θεόν] was in the roundabout way honoured by the Greeks' (Clement of Alexandria, *Stromata* 1.19).[4]

Die Anknüpfung ist hier eine bewusste. Die Rede knüpft ja an die Inschrift eines heidnischen Altares an: ἀγνώστῳ θεῷ – sie setzt also bei den Hörern eine Ahnung von dem wahren Gott voraus, der ihnen nun erst wirklich bekannt gemacht werden soll. 'Was ihr, ohne es zu kennen, verehrt, das verkündige ich euch.' Gleich die ersten Sätze tragen hellenistische Gotteslehre vor, beginnend freilich im alttestamentlichen Stile mit der Verkündigung des einen

---

[2] So Weiser (1985: 468): 'Der Interpretation des Verses 23 kommt für das Verständnis der *ganzen* Rede sowie ihrer theologischen undgeistesgeschichtlichen Beurteilung eine Schlüsselstellung zu. Wie schätzt Lukas die *religiöse* Situation der Athener ein? Wie beurteilt er das, was sie bereits *haben*, und das, was ihnen *mangelt* und was durch das paulinische "Angebot" behoben werden soll?'
[3] Arist. *Rhet.* 3.14.12 (1415b 37-38), quoted in Zweck 1989: 96.
[4] Quoted in Rowe 2011: 35.

Gottes, der als der Schöpfer keines Tempels zu seiner Verehrung bedarf. (Bultmann 1946: 410)

The singular version only of the inscription could be used by the speaker on the Areopagus, however, for he regarded the inscription as evidence of the Athenians' subconscious awareness of the true God. Now he can begin straight away to proclaim this God. (Dibelius 1956a: 41)

Still, this altar shows that Paul introduces no 'new gods': the accusation raised against Socrates cannot validly be made against Christianity. Out of the ignorance of the Athenians concerning this God, it inevitably follows that Paul must proclaim him. (Haenchen 1971: 521)

Er knüpft an das Thema an, um den Monotheismus zu proklamieren. Dieser unbekannte Gott, den sie neben anderen Göttern verehren, v 16, ist in Wirklichkeit der einzige Gott. Die Aufschrift wird zum Ausgangspunkt für die Verkündigung des einen Gottes, des Gottes Israels. (Jervell 1998: 446)

More significant is Paul's attempt to tie this inscription together with a theology of creation. Given the charge of 'newness,' it is unsurprising that Luke depicts Paul's first argumentative move as an effort to rebuff this charge. 'What you worship unknowingly,' this I proclaim to you.' I do not, implies Paul, bring in anything new at all. Rather, the one to whom I testify has preceded me here in Athens. (Rowe 2011: 40)

Many extracts could be added, but those suffice to illustrate that this reading has had an extraordinary longevity and that it is held by a large spectrum of scholars with very different interpretations of the speech and its relationship to natural theology.[5] Athenian self-acknowledged ignorance about the unknown god of the altar thus provides Paul with an entry point (*Anknüpfungspunkt*) to begin his speech, while enabling the apostle to refute the charge of newness. He then proceeds to present this unknown god who is identified with the creator (v.24). To confirm this reading, as mentioned by Dibelius, exegetes also sometimes point to the singular of the inscription: Ἀγνώστῳ θεῷ. Since so far no such inscription has been found in the singular form, it is argued that Luke has transformed it to serve his purpose of introducing the true God to the Athenians.[6]

This *Anknüpfungspunkt*, however, has led to different conclusions about Luke's assessment of Athenian religiosity. Most exegetes see it as an indication that there is at least *something* positive in the Athenians' attitude, even if it

---

[5] Compare, for example, Dibelius, Jervell and Rowe's interpretation. Similar claims can be found in: Zweck 1989: 103; Porter 1999: 119; Barrett 2004: 839; Pervo 2008: 433; Schnabel 2014: 178.

[6] E.g., Pervo 2008: 433, who points to Jerome who corrects the text and comments that in reality such inscriptions were in the plural (*Comm. in Titum* 1:12). See, however, Horst's discussion of the evidence. He concludes that it cannot be excluded that inscriptions in the singular might have existed (Horst 1990: 1451).

needs correction or even repentance. Thus, for Haenchen, Luke depicts the Athenians in an ambiguous position:

> Paul concludes from this devotion that the heathen live at one and the same time in a positive and negative relationship with the right God: they worship him and yet do not know him – they worship him indeed, but along with many other gods![7]

Wilson speaks for many when he writes: 'Luke thinks the Gentiles' basic response [is] correct but misguided.'[8] More critical is Rowe, who underscores that Athenian worship is problematic because it is *in ignorance*.[9]

Those interpretations, however, create a tension in the narrative which has puzzled other interpreters. Indeed, by linking the unknown god worshipped by the Athenians with Paul's God, Luke seems to put the creator God on the same level as the other gods worshipped by the Athenians. As Barrett notes concerning the inscription: 'This, even in the singular, implies polytheism.'[10] Such a reading is in tension with the wider context of the speech and in particular with Paul's anger at idols in v. 16. Even exegetes who interpret the speech in conciliatory terms have noticed this strange contrast. Thus, many years ago Dibelius wrote: 'the difference in tone between 17.6 and 17.22 is bound to strike the reader of Acts.'[11] The attempt of some exegetes to explain this difference in tone in terms of a *captatio benevolentiae* in v.22 hardly solves the issue,[12] and some interpreters have gone as far as qualifying the apostle's strategy as 'intriguing,' shocking or even deceptive.[13]

In light of such tension, some exegetes have concluded that Paul's mention of the altar to the unknown god is simply an *ad hoc* move, and that the altar

---

[7] Haenchen 1971: 521.

[8] Wilson 1973: 214.

[9] Rowe 2011: 41 (his emphasis).

[10] Barrett (2004: 838) goes on saying that 'the speaker makes it monotheist,' but this is precisely what is arguably problematic.

[11] Dibelius 1939: 66; cf. Conzelmann 1966: 219.

[12] *Contra* Conzelmann 1966: 219.

[13] Porter 1999: 119: 'This is an intriguing logical manoeuvre on Paul's part. Paul clearly has in mind the introduction of his God. However, in the way he states the case, it appears at first as if he sees this God as only one of a number of gods, and that he is simply filling in a blank that is still left in the pantheon.' For Baur (1876: 177–178), this link to the unknown god 'violates the truth' and shows the lack of historicity of the account: 'in this case how can we overlook the fact that the Apostle must have been guilty of open violation of the truth if he declared this very God to be the One whom he preached, the true God, the Creator of heaven and earth? If he were only "an unknown God," he would not be distinguished from the rest of the known gods by his individual character, but only by the accidental circumstances that his name was not known, or that no special name had been given him; he would be one of the same class with the rest of the deities of the polytheistic faith, from whom the true God of monotheism is different in every essential point, and it is evident that there may quite as well be several unknown gods of this sort as one.'

5.1. Deisidaimonia and the Unknown God

provides him with a useful place to begin his speech, while raising the interest of his audience. For example, Barrett writes:

[...] it is important not to give too heavy a theological treatment to Paul's (Luke's) sentence; it must be understood as a preacher's *ad hoc* way of introducing his theme, and it would be unfair to hold him bound to all the theological implications of his illustration. The Athenians (those of them who were religiously rather than sceptically disposed) reverenced a considerable number of gods. The preacher could have made a note of many other σεβάσματα bearing the names of particular gods; he picked out this god, whose name was not given because it was not known, as the one whom, to the exclusion of all the others, he intended to proclaim.[14]

Such an *ad hoc* move seems to be also implied by Marshall, who emphasizes however that there was no connection at all between the unknown god whom the Athenian worshiped and Paul's God.

One such had particularly occupied Paul's attention: a wayside altar with the inscription to *an unknown god*. He eagerly seized on this inscription as a way of introducing his own proclamation of *the* unknown God. There was, to be sure, no real connection between 'an unknown god' and the true God; Paul hardly meant that his audience were unconscious worshippers of the true God. Rather, he is drawing their attention to the true God who was ultimately responsible for the phenomena which they attributed to an unknown god. [...].[15]

But the suggestion that the Paul of Luke's narrative would make an *ad hoc* move by linking an altar in a city full of idols to the true God does not sit well with the narrative of Acts where Christians systematically condemn idolatry to the point of putting their life in danger (Acts 14:8–19; 19:23–27). The connection of the altar to the unknown god with Athenian idolatrous polytheistic worship is made clear in the narrative in that Paul mentions the 'altar of the unknown god' as just one example among other cultic monuments which angered him: ... I *even* found an altar upon which it is written (cf. ἀναθεωρῶν τὰ σεβάσματα ὑμῶν εὗρον καὶ βωμὸν ἐν ᾧ ἐπεγέγραπτο· Ἀγνώστῳ θεῷ). It is also noteworthy that the word βωμός used by Luke is a term traditionally used in connection of illegitimate worship in the Greek translation of the Hebrew Bible.[16] Although this is not an absolute proof that Luke uses it with negative

---

[14] Barrett 2004: 839.
[15] Marshall 1980: 286.
[16] The great majority of times, it is explicitly associated with idol worship. It is also used for the altars of Balaam (Num 23), or the altar set up by the tribes of Reuben and Gad (Jos 22). The only place where it is used of God's altar is in Num 3:10. But it is in the context of an 'outsider' approaching the altar and being put to death. Horst (1990: 1452) comments: 'The single occurrence of βωμός in Acts 17:23 is in sharp contrast to the 23 times θυσιαστήριον occurs in the New Testament. This has its background in the LXX. Whereas the LXX translators freely use pagan cultic terminology to designate objects and persons of the Israelite cult, in the case of the word for altar they differentiate. [...] Whereas Jewish contemporaries of the New Testament authors like Philo and Josephus do not follow the LXX in this matter and freely use βωμός for the altar in the Jerusalem temple, the NT keeps strictly to this usage and uses

connotations, for some Hellenistic Jewish writers did use this word to refer to the altar in Jerusalem, it is surprising that Luke would have chosen such a word in light of the important role the LXX plays in his writings. Rowe's emphasis on Athenian ignorance is important, for, as he points out, Paul's allusion to Athenian ignorance is hardly a compliment.[17] But it still suggests that the Athenians did somehow worship Paul's God, a reading in tension with v. 16.

The suggestion defended here is that the speech does not claim to introduce the unknown god of the altar to the Athenians, much less to present him as the Lord of heaven and earth. Indeed, such interpretations are problematic both grammatically and narratively.

A first indicator raising questions for the common interpretation is the lack of grammatical correspondence between the masculine ἀγνώστῳ θεῷ and the object of Paul's proclamation which is identified by neuter pronouns: ὃ οὖν ἀγνοοῦντες εὐσεβεῖτε, τοῦτο ἐγὼ καταγγέλλω ὑμῖν.[18] Few exegetes comment on this lack of agreement. Dupont, however, suggests that this shows an attempt to prevent an exact identification between the object of Paul's proclamation from the unknown god worshipped by the Athenians.[19] Another detail which casts doubt on a direct correlation between the 'unknown god' and the subject of the speech in this sentence is that rather than announcing that he will proclaim the 'unknown god' [ἀγνώστῳ θεῷ], Paul talks about 'unknowing Athenians' [ἀγνοοῦντες]. This, combined with the move from a masculine noun to a neuter pronoun, seems to suggest that the altar to the unknown god is taken as a sign of the Athenian ignorant condition, or their ignorant worship. The altar to the unknown god is thus mentioned because it is symptomatic of the ignorance which characterizes Athenian worship (cf. 'I *even* saw an altar to an unknown god'), and their failure to worship appropriately and thus have peace with the gods; the speech thus aims to proclaim what the Athenians are revering (εὐσεβεῖτε) in ignorance more generally.

βωμός only here.' Luke otherwise uses θυσιατήριον twice, both times to refer to God's altar (Lk 1:11; 11:51).

[17] Cf. Chapter 4. Both Stoics and Epicureans considered ignorance as the root of all evils.

[18] This is the reading of the earliest manuscripts; but the difficulty generated by this formulation is reflected by the substituted masculine pronouns found in many other witnesses (ὅν...τοῦτον). As most commentators note, the earliest and harder reading is likely original, and the masculine forms are readily explained grammatically by the antecedent of the relative pronoun which is usually thought to be θεῷ. Barrett 2004: 838.

[19] Dupont 1979: 419: 'Fortement accentué, le neutre des deux pronoms a pour effet d'établir un écran entre le dieu inconnu adoré par les Athéniens et le Dieu que Paul annonce. L'un n'est pas l'autre ; vis-à-vis de l'un comme de l'autre, les Athéniens sont dans l'ignorance, une ignorance qui concerne "quelque chose" à adorer.' Pervo (2008: 433), Johnson (1992: 315) and Haenchen (1971: 521) do not comment on the neuter; Marguerat (2015: 157) explains it by suggesting that Paul is talking not about a new god, but about the nature of the divine.

5.1. Deisidaimonia and the Unknown God

In addition, and importantly, exegetes have also been too quick in identifying the object of Paul's proclamation (τοῦτο καταγγέλλω) with the God who made the world spoken about starting in v.24. Indeed, there has been an incredibly long and unwavering consensus in scholarship that the subject of the speech is the presentation of Yahweh – the God who made heaven and earth – to the Athenians. But this is problematic in light of the grammar and the narrative context.

Again, the first problem with this interpretation is the lack of grammatical agreement between the object of Paul's message (τοῦτο) with the masculine ὁ θεός which is the subject of verse 24. In fact, the speech here seems to set apart this creator God from what the Athenians worship ignorantly by saying: 'the God who made the world and everything in it, *this one* [οὗτος]…does not dwell in temples made by human hands.'[20] There is in fact, no *a priori* reason to identify the object of καταγγέλλω in v. 23 as the God who created heaven and earth mentioned in v. 24.

A further feature of the dramatic setting of this pericope corroborates this interpretation. Indeed, at no point is there a sign that the Athenians perceived Paul to be the messenger of the Jewish God – Yahweh. Rather they perceive Paul to be either a *spermologos* or a messenger of foreign divini*ties* (in the plural!), and later speak of a new teaching (v.19). Even if there is some kind of misunderstanding going on here, it is highly unlikely that the Athenians, particularly philosophically sensitive and learned Athenians, would have perceived the presentation of the Jewish God Yahweh as a new teaching. Indeed, Luke has indicated that there was a synagogue in Athens, attended by God-fearers, which suggests a certain success of Judaism among locals. He also describes the Athenians as preoccupied with novelty (vv. 17, 21). The audience would thus have been aware of the basic beliefs about the Jewish God and would have associated Paul's message with Jewish teaching if the object of his proclamation was Yahweh.[21]

In other words, neither the grammar of the *propositio* nor the narrative context support the traditional conclusion that the focus of the message of the speech is the creator of heaven and earth whom the Athenians do not know.

So far then, what the neuter pronoun ὅ refers to is unclear and will need to be clarified in the speech. The narrator has, however, given an indication about the focus of Paul's message earlier, in v. 18: ξένων δαιμονίων δοκεῖ καταγγελεύς εἶναι, ὅτι τὸν Ἰησοῦν καὶ τὴν ἀνάστασιν εὐηγγελίζετο. The terminology of καταγγελεύς in v. 18 is precisely picked up by the verb καταγγέλλω in the *propositio* of the speech. As a starting hypothesis then, it is better to

---

[20] The shift from masculine to neuter is also noted by Barrett and Witherington, who follows Polhill. Polhill (1992: 372) explains it as Paul's move to emphasize that 'their worship object was a thing, a "what," not a personal God at all.'

[21] So also Gärtner (1955: 46-7).

propose that the subject of Paul's speech is, as Luke indicates, 'Jesus and the resurrection,' a message which some understood as a proclamation of new or strange divinities, and which Paul introduced as a correction to the ignorant worship of the Athenians (v.29). How this relates to the creator God Paul goes on to speak about in the few next verses is the subject of the next sections.

5.1.3 Summary vv. 23–22

By calling them *deisidaimonesterous*, the speech thus begins by alluding to the Athenians' concern to maintain peace with the gods and their fear of divine hostility, and as a proof of it points to the fact that they even built an altar to an unknown god to make sure no divinity is offended. Using the altar both as a sign of their concern and as a symptom of their (partly self-acknowledged) ignorance, Luke's Paul announces that he is proclaiming to them what they are revering ignorantly, i.e. mistakenly. The mention of the altar to an unknown god thus serves as a symptom both of Athenian extreme concern to maintain peace with the gods and of their ignorance in how to avert divine wrath. As for the object of the speech, the correlation between καταγγελεύς in v. 18 (ξένων δαιμονίων...καταγγελεύς) and Paul's description self-description as announcing (καταγγέλλω) that which (ὃ) the Athenians are revering mistakenly in v. 23 strongly suggests that his message focussed on the proclamation of something which some Athenians perceived to be 'foreign divinities' and which Luke explains by saying that it was in fact 'Jesus and the resurrection'.

5.2 The Creator God's Relationship to Humanity (17:24–28)

5.2.1 The Impossibility to Serve the Creator God Along Traditional Means (vv.24–25)

24 ὁ θεὸς ὁ ποιήσας τὸν κόσμον καὶ πάντα τὰ ἐν αὐτῷ, οὗτος οὐρανοῦ καὶ γῆς ὑπάρχων κύριος οὐκ ἐν χειροποιήτοις ναοῖς κατοικεῖ 25 οὐδὲ ὑπὸ χειρῶν ἀνθρωπίνων θεραπεύεται προσδεόμενός τινος, αὐτὸς διδοὺς πᾶσι ζωὴν καὶ πνοὴν καὶ τὰ πάντα·

As mentioned above, it is common to interpret verses 24 to 25 as a presentation of the only true God who made the whole world to Athenians who have never heard of him. Yet grammatical structure suggests that this is not the line of the argument. Rather, those verses begin as an assertion about a particular God, namely the one who made the world and everything in it. The first part of the sentence thus does not only describe this God, but also singles him out: the God who made the world and everything in it, *this [particular] one…* does not dwell in man-made temples, nor is he served by human hands: ὁ θεὸς ὁ ποιήσας τὸν κόσμον καὶ πάντα τὰ ἐν αὐτῷ, οὗτος ...οὐκ ἐν χειροποιήτοις ναοῖς κατοικεῖ οὐδὲ ὑπὸ χειρῶν ἀνθρωπίνων θεραπεύεται [. . .]. Apprehending this nuance has two important consequences.

First, those verses do not read as if Paul was introducing to his audience a new god about whom they have no notion at all. Rather, the speech seems to assume that his audience has encountered the notion of a god creator of the world and all things or to take it as self-evident; not that everybody in his audience would have embraced this belief – the Epicureans obviously would not – but the notion is not foreign to them.[22] In any case, the speech does not argue for the existence of such a creator god, but takes it as its starting point: the first sentence of the speech thus begins as an assertion about the creator and lord of the world whose existence is presupposed.

Second, and this has been largely misapprehended in scholarship, those verses do *not* constitute an argument for monotheism, presenting the God who made heaven and earth as the only God.[23] Rather, at this stage, Paul is *distinguishing* this God from others: *this* God – namely the one who made everything – does not live in the houses made for him by humanity, nor can man provide for his needs. In fact, at this stage of the speech, those verses seem to assume the existence of other gods, who, unlike the creator God, *are* in need of housing and have needs.

This reading is confirmed by the particular description of the creator God in those verses – which takes the form of two negated clauses ('he does not live in temples made by human hands' and 'he is not served by human hands'). Indeed, those clauses imply a contrast. In light of the context of the speech (cf. v. 16), there is little doubt that Paul is contrasting the creator God with the idols (or the gods) of the Athenians, which 'live' in temples and are served by human hands. Θεραπεύω is characteristic cultic vocabulary, piety being traditionally described as the 'knowledge of how to serve or worship the gods.'[24] Both of those practices – building a house for the idols of the gods and serving them by bringing them offerings – are common expressions of piety in the Graeco-Roman cult. The speech, however, contrasts the creator God with idols: this is not the way one can relate to the creator God – although this might be the way to relate to other gods!

The assertion about the creator God is supported by two causal participial phrases: this God, *because he is the Lord of heaven and earth*, does not live in temples made by human hands and he is not served by human hands as if needing something *because he himself gives life, breath and everything to all*. Those

---

[22] So, for example, Plutarch (Brenk 2012: 80). On creationism in antiquity, cf. Sedley 2007.

[23] *Contra* what many exegetes assert, Paul's speech is not aimed at defending monotheism against polytheism, at least not in the traditional sense implied by interpreters (e.g., Klauck 2000: 74). It does defend monotheism, but indirectly. Or rather, monotheism is an entailment of the speech's argument.

[24] Cf. Sextus Empiricus, *Against the Physicists* 1.123 (=*Adv. Math.* 9.123): ἔστι γὰρ εὐσέβεια ἐπιστήμη θεῶν θεραπείας; Plutarch, *Aem.* 3.2; Diogenes Laertius, 7.119.

verses imply a reversal between God and humanity: 'God *the one who made* (ὁ *ποιήσας*) the world and everything in it, does not dwell in temples *made by human hands* (χειροποιήτοις), and he is not served – i.e. provided for – by human hands (ὑπὸ χειρῶν ἀνθρωπίνων) as if he needed anything because *he himself* (αὐτός) gives life, breath and all to everybody.' In other words, God *has made* the world *in which everything dwells* and he *does not dwell in what humanity makes,* and God *is not served* by human hands, but *he himself gives* everything to everybody. Thus, not only can humanity not relate to the creator God in the way it relates to other gods, but this creator God relates to human beings in the very way they try to relate to their gods: the creator God provides for human beings what they try to provide for their gods or the idols of their gods.

Verses 24–25 therefore present the relationship between God and his creation as a reversal of the relationship which humanity has with its other gods or more specifically, its idols. Whereas humanity usually provides temples and services to the idols of its gods, the creator God provides breath, life and everything to humanity and all. This contrast and reversal are further emphasized in the next verses. In particular, whereas v. 24 insists that 'God does *not dwell* (κατοικεῖ) in man-made temples,' v. 26 describes God arranging conditions of life so that each race of human beings can '*dwell (κατοικεῖν)* upon the whole earth ... having appointed boundaries to their dwelling-place (*κατοικίας*).

5.2.2 *God's Arrangement of Humanity's Conditions to Seek Him (vv. 26–27)*

Verses 26 to 27 then move to describe in more details God's dealings with humanity.

Acts 17:26 ἐποίησέν τε ἐξ ἑνὸς πᾶν ἔθνος ἀνθρώπων κατοικεῖν ἐπὶ παντὸς προσώπου τῆς γῆς, ὁρίσας προστεταγμένους καιροὺς καὶ τὰς ὁροθεσίας τῆς κατοικίας αὐτῶν 27 ζητεῖν τὸν θεόν, εἰ ἄρα γε ψηλαφήσειαν αὐτὸν καὶ εὕροιεν, καί γε οὐ μακρὰν ἀπὸ ἑνὸς ἑκάστου ἡμῶν ὑπάρχοντα.

Those two verses, and in particular the two infinitives (κατοικεῖν and ζητεῖν), are often understood to indicate the purpose for which God created humanity: God made mankind so that it might dwell (κατοικεῖν) upon the whole earth and seek (ζητεῖν) him.[25] But, although this is rarely noticed, this interpretation creates a tension with the latter part of verse 27. As many exegetes argue, the optative mood and the connotation of ψηλαφάω, which is often associated with 'fumbling in the darkness,' indicate doubt about the success of humanity's search for God.[26] Those verses are thus commonly translated in this way:

And he made from one all the people of humanity, so that they might dwell upon the whole face of the earth, having appointed set seasons and limitations to their dwellings, so that they

---

[25] E.g., Barrett 2004: 842; Haenchen 1971: 523.
[26] Barrett 2004: 844; Conzlemann 1987: 144; Jipp 2012: 582.

might seek God, if they might indeed touch and find him, and indeed he is not far from each one of us.

This common reading suggests that God created humanity and assigned it the purpose to dwell upon the earth and seek him, while at the same time expressing uncertainty about the success of humanity's search, even though God is not far from mankind. It thus intimates that God created humanity for two specific purposes – to fill the earth and to seek him – while also expressing serious doubts about the success of this search and thus the fulfilment of God's purposes. While not impossible, this interpretation has the consequence of depicting God more like a *Zauberlehrling* whose creative purposes are likely to fail, than like the provident creator which the speech otherwise seems to imply.

A better reading is possible, however, if the two infinitives are interpreted as indicating the purpose of the entire clauses which precede them. Thus, κατοικεῖν ἐπὶ παντὸς προσώπου τῆς γῆς does not spell out the purpose for which God created humanity (ἐποίησεν), but the purpose which God sought to accomplish by creating, out of a single one, each race of men (ἐποίησέν τε ἐξ ἑνὸς πᾶν ἔθνος ἀνθρώπων). The first part of verse 26 thus does not affirm God's creation of mankind *simpliciter*, but how God creates *all* people of mankind (πᾶν ἔθνος ἀνθρώπων) through *one*, so that it might dwell upon *all* the face earth (ἐπὶ παντὸς προσώπου τῆς γῆς). This exegesis is supported by the repetition of πᾶς: it was God's purpose to fill the *whole* face of the earth with mankind, and thus he created *all* people from one. Another advantage of this reading is that this way v. 26 does not repeat the content of v. 25 – i.e. God gives life to all – by asserting that God created humanity, but it moves on to give additional and different information (cf. τε): and from one human being (ἐποίησέν τε ἐξ ἑνός), God created all races of mankind, so that they would dwell upon all the earth.[27]

Likewise, ζητεῖν τὸν θεόν does not depend upon ἐποίησεν only, but either describes the purpose of ὁρίσας προστεταγμένους καιροὺς καὶ τὰς ὁροθεσίας τῆς κατοικίας αὐτῶν, or of the whole of v. 26. ὁρίσας προστεταγμένους καιροὺς καὶ τὰς ὁροθεσίας τῆς κατοικίας αὐτῶν is often interpreted as a reference to the expression of divine providence in nature which enables or pushes humanity to search for God. Support for this reading is found in the fact that the idea that nature bears witness to God is attested both in Greek philosophical and Jewish literature, and seems to be found also in Acts 14:17 where God's provision of rains and fruitful seasons is presented as God's witness to himself.[28] It should be noted, however, that although this interpretation makes good

---

[27] The expression ἐξ ἑνός is often interpreted as pointing to the unity of mankind (e.g., Pervo 2008: 435). But this nuance does not fit the argument. Rather, as suggested above, it explains the process of creation and the means by which God filled the earth with human beings.

[28] Acts 14:17: καίτοι οὐκ ἀμάρτυρον αὐτὸν ἀφῆκεν ἀγαθουργῶν, οὐρανόθεν ὑμῖν ὑετοὺς διδοὺς καὶ καιροὺς καρποφόρους, ἐμπιπλῶν τροφῆς καὶ εὐφροσύνης τὰς καρδίας ὑμῶν.

sense of προστεταγμένους καιρούς which can refer to the set seasons which witness to God's providence, it is, however, less successful in explaining τὰς ὁροθεσίας τῆς κατοικίας αὐτῶν. Dibelius had argued that this phrase refers to the zones of the earth which are fit for human habitation according to some philosophers.[29] But Eltester contested this interpretation by pointing out that only two zones out of five were thought to be inhabitable, something which conflicts with the speech's claim that God made humanity to dwell upon *all* the earth. Eltester thus suggested that ὁροθεσίας τῆς κατοικίας αὐτῶν is a reference to the biblical description of God's shielding the habitations of human beings against the chaos-threatening sea.[30] But this explanation is not more convincing if we hypothesize that Luke is concerned about narrative realism because the Athenians of the narrative world of Acts would hardly have understood such a biblical allusion.

In this light, it might be better to take ὁρίσας προστεταγμένους καιρούς καὶ τὰς ὁροθεσίας τῆς κατοικίας αὐτῶν as a modifier of the preceding clause commenting on the way God made it possible for humanity to dwell upon the whole earth. προστεταγμένους καιρούς is thus best translated as 'determined seasons' and refers to God's provision of harvest and food at fixed (i.e. regular) times during the year to enable humanity to plan its survival. This understanding of καιρός as an allusion to the provision of nourishment by God at appointed seasons is the same as the one found in Acts 14:17 (καιροὺς καρποφόρους). More tentatively, τὰς ὁροθεσίας τῆς κατοικίας αὐτῶν – i.e. the 'boundaries to their dwelling place' –is likely a reference to God's provision of different lands or regions to different people to ensure each one has a place to live and flourish (i.e. multiply and grow). This reading also coheres well with vv. 24–25, by building upon the idea that God cannot be provided a place to *dwell* and food by humanity and reversing it by describing God's provision of food (through set seasons) and *dwelling places* (through boundaries) for mankind. The participial phrase thus points to the way God arranged the conditions of life for all people, by setting fixed seasons and boundaries to their dwelling places, *making it possible for them to dwell on all the earth.* God thus organizes the indwelling of all the earth by humanity by multiplying mankind through the gift of fruitfulness and life giving 'out of one' (ἐξ ἑνός) and gives them seasons and dwelling places to sustain life and flourish. Κατοικεῖν thus does not so much describe the purpose which God assigns to humanity, but what *he* enables and arranges through a creative action ἐξ ἑνός and the arrangement of 'conditions of life' as is suggested by ὁρίσας προστεταγμένους καιροὺς καὶ τὰς ὁροθεσίας τῆς κατοικίας αὐτῶν.[31]

---

[29] Dibelius 1939: 30–31.
[30] Eltester 1957: 100–102.
[31] Κατοικεῖν thus has the nuance either of purpose or of result/consequence, or, possibly, both: God multiplied mankind with the aim and result that they might dwell upon the all earth.

5.2 God's Relationship to Humanity

The second infinitive clause (ζητεῖν τὸν θεόν) in verse 27 then describes the purpose or result of the whole sentence in v. 26: God from one created all peoples so that they would dwell upon the whole face of the earth, having appointed set seasons and boundaries to their dwelling place, so that they might seek God, if they might feel for him and find him.[32]

According to this reading, then, those verses do not describe the purposes which God assigns to humanity, but how God arranges and enables humanity to fulfil his own purpose, which is to fill all the earth with mankind, and thus, that mankind would seek, touch and find him.

There remains a final intriguing element in those verses, namely the second part of verse 27. Indeed, although this is rarely commented upon by exegetes, the verb ψηλαφάω – to feel – suggests a physical touch, rather than a metaphorical attempt to 'grasp' God intellectually.[33] As commonly noted, the verb is often used to express the 'feeling around' of people fumbling in the dark. In the LXX the verb is used 10 times out of 15 to describe people suffering from blindness and thus feeling their way around in obscurity.[34] Similarly the verb frequently occurs to describe the groping in the dark in Greek literature (e.g. Homer, *Od.* 9.416; Plato, *Phaed.* 99b). The idea that humanity can 'touch' or even 'feel' God in such a physical way is, to my knowledge, unheard of in Jewish thought, although recent scholarship has drawn attention to the corporeality of the God of the Old Testament presupposed and even affirmed in some texts.[35] For example, the fact that some texts speak of the possibility of 'seeing' God physically, or of God being localized in particular places, implies some sort of corporeality. Some recent scholarship on the *imago dei* in the Old Testament also suggests that the Jewish God is sometimes described as manifesting himself very directly and in a physically located and perceptible way

---

[32] According to Turner (1963: 127), εἰ cum optative in Acts 17:27 expresses not so much a real condition as a final clause: 'The other instances of εἰ c. opt. are not so much real conditions as final clauses (Ac 17:27, 27:12), and there are parenthetical phrases introduced by εἰ = *if possible* or *as it were*: εἰ δυνατὸν εἴη (vl. ἦν), εἰ δύναιντο (Ac 20:16, 27:39) and εἰ τύχοι (1 Co 14:10, 15:37). Other clauses introduced by εἰ and dependent on a verb like ζητεῖν are virtually indirect questions, a class. survival: Ac 17:11, 25:20.'

[33] The physical nuance implied in this verb is rightly emphasized by Norden 1913 (cf. Johnson 1992: 316). When it is used metaphorically, ψηλαφάω means 'to test, to examine.' Cf. LSJ s.v.

[34] The verb is used three times to refer to Isaac 'feeling' Jacob (Gen 27:12, 21, 22), twice as part of the curse which will fall upon the Israelites if they disobey the voice of the Lord – i.e. they will grope at noonday as the blind grope in darkness (Dt 28:29 2x), once when Samson asks to feel the pillar on which the house rests (Jdg 16:26), four times to describe the judgment of God who makes people grope at noonday as in the night (Job 5:14; 12:25; cf. Isa 59:10 2x). Also noteworthy in light of the context of idolatry in which the speech is pronounced, is the fact that the verb is used several times in the LXX to describe idols who have hands but cannot 'feel' (LXX Ps 113:15; 134:17).

[35] See Markschies 2016.

through human beings. For example, Stephen Herring has argued that Exodus 32–34 is crafted to show that Moses is the true image of God reflecting divine glory in contrast to the golden calf fashioned by the Israelites.[36]

Better known to the Athenians, however, would have been the fact that idols in Graeco-Roman religion were thought to provide a means of approaching and even 'touching' the gods. In fact, some Hellenistic Greek authors used this argument to defend the use of idols in the traditional cult. As they argued, the materiality of idols enabled the worshippers to 'touch' and 'feel' the gods and to connect to the divine.[37] For example, in his discourse defending the creation of statues of the gods, Dio Chrysostom, an intellectual influenced by Stoicism, points to the necessity of a material and touchable representation of the gods to enable the worshippers to connect to them and worship them.

> For no one would maintain that it would have been better that neither statue (ἵδρυμα) nor picture (εἰκόνα) of the gods be exhibited among men, because we should look only at the heavens. For on the one hand, the sensible person worships all these objects, believing them to be blessed gods as he sees them from afar. But on the other hand, on the account of their inclination towards the gods (τὴν πρὸς τὸ δαιμόνιον γνώμην), all men have a strong yearning (ἔρως) to honour and worship the divine (τιμᾶν καὶ θεραπεύειν τὸ θεῖον) from close at hand, approaching it and touching (ἁπτομένους) it with persuasion (μετὰ πειθοῦς), by offering it sacrifices and crowning them with garlands. For certainly as infant children when torn away from their father or mother have a terrible longing and desire, and stretch out their hands to their absent parents often when they are dreaming, so also do men towards the gods, rightly loving them on account of their beneficence (εὐεργεσίαν) and their kinship (συγγένειαν), being eager in any way to be with them and to interact with them (ὁμιλεῖν). (Dio Chrysostom, 12.60–61 [MC])

As Chrysostom highlights, physical or anthropomorphic representations of the gods aim to facilitate the connection with, and worship of, those divinities.

What exactly is meant in v. 27 by God's desire that humanity might 'touch' him is difficult to ascertain. Our exegesis of verses 26 and 27, however, suggests that God's multiplication of mankind on all the earth and his provision for their life and flourishing aimed to enable them to seek him and even 'get a feel' for him. One might wonder at this stage whether those verses suggest that God intended humanity itself to be a witness to him and the means by which humanity gets to know, find and possibly touch him, just like idols enabled to get a feel for the gods in the ancient world. This would explain the importance of populating the whole earth with mankind in God's provident arrangement. The biblical idea of God creating humanity in his image and ordering it to fill the earth, and the belief shared by some Greek philosophers that humanity contains something divine (Platonists and Stoics) and is meant to be godlike and

---

[36] Herring 2013.
[37] See Stewart 2003. On the defense of the use of idols for worship by Greek intellectuals, see Clerc 1915, especially part 3.

like a statue of the gods (Stoics) certainly add plausibility to this interpretation in the context at hand.[38]

Verse 27, however, describes the human search for God as a feeling around for him in the darkness, and the optative mood casts doubt upon the success of this search. This fits well with the description of the Athenians as ignorant and living in ignorance. In the context of an anti-idol polemic, and for a reader well-versed in the LXX, this description of humanity is also strangely reminiscent of the way the OT describes idols, where the verb ψηλαφάω is used several times to refer to idols who have hands but cannot 'feel' (LXX Ps 113:15; 134:17).

5.2.3 The Witness of Human Life (v. 28)

The reason for the affirmation of God's nearness is then given in verse 28 (γάρ).[39]

ἐν αὐτῷ γὰρ ζῶμεν καὶ κινούμεθα καὶ ἐσμέν, ὡς καί τινες τῶν καθ' ὑμᾶς ποιητῶν εἰρήκασιν· τοῦ γὰρ καὶ γένος ἐσμέν.

It is often commented that ἐν αὐτῷ γὰρ ζῶμεν καὶ κινούμεθα καὶ ἐσμέν (28a) sounds Stoic or Platonic.[40] But so far, no exact parallel has been found in ancient Stoic or Platonic literature. Because the clause sounds pantheistic and poetic, however, many exegetes suggest that Luke took the clause from somewhere and did not create it himself.[41] Whatever its origin, there is no clue in the immediate context provided by the speech nor in the broader narrative of Acts that this formulation should be interpreted along pantheistic lines. Rather, as most exegetes note, in the speech ἐν αὐτῷ means 'by him' or 'through him.'[42] The clause thus underscores that human life, movement and existence comes from, and is sustained by, God. It is worth noticing that this idea is not foreign to Luke and that he expresses similar thoughts in his gospel in the context of a discussion about the resurrection. In Lk 20:38, Jesus concludes his answer to the Sadducee's question with the affirmation:

θεὸς δὲ οὐκ ἔστιν νεκρῶν ἀλλὰ ζώντων, πάντες γὰρ αὐτῷ ζῶσιν.
Now he is not the God of the dead but of the living, for all live by him (or to him).

---

[38] On the Stoic comparison of humanity with a statue of the gods, see 5.3.

[39] As Barrett (2004: 846) notes, another possibility is that v.28 explains v. 27 as a whole.

[40] Pohlenz 1949; Hommel 1955 and 1957; Conzelmann 1987: 144; Haenchen 1971: 524, n.3; Jervell 1998: 449; Marguerat 2015: 161; Jipp 2012: 583.

[41] Pohlenz 1949: 104; Haenchen 1971: 524 (n.3); Barrett (2004: 847) and Pervo (2008: 438) consider it as possible and probable respectively. See however Gärtner (1955: 195) who attributes it to Paul or Luke.

[42] Jervell, 1998: 449; Barrett 2004: 847; Marguerat 2015: 161. Even exegetes who argue that the clause is of Stoic or Platonic origin often comment that in the speech the clause is not used pantheistically.

What is regularly overlooked, however, is that within the argument of the speech of Acts 17, ἐν αὐτῷ γὰρ ζῶμεν καὶ κινούμεθα καὶ ἐσμέν is not simply an affirmation of humanity's dependence upon God, but functions as a proof of God's nearness affirmed in v. 27: 'and indeed he is not far from each one of us; *for* (γὰρ) by him we live, and move and are.' The life and movement of human beings are thus a testimony to God's nearness, because it is through God that humanity lives and moves.

In this light, it is worth reconsidering the possibility that v. 28a is a quotation from Epimenides. This hypothesis, which was accepted by some influential scholars in the first part of the 20th century before the publications of articles by Pohlenz and Hommel in the late 1940s and 1950s, has recently been defended anew by Rothschild.[43] The strongest argument against an Epimenidean authorship is that none of the writings which have come down to us directly from the pen of the church fathers identifies v. 28a as a quotation. In particular, neither Clement of Alexandria (150–215 CE), nor Theodore of Mopsuestia (350–428 CE) or John Chrysostom (347–407 CE) mention v.28a among their examples of New Testament authors quoting Greek philosophers or poets, or in their discussion of Acts 17:28, even though they all note that Paul cites the Greeks in Acts 17:28b and Tit 1:12.[44] Furthermore, Clement and Chrysostom both identify Tit 1:12 as a verse from Epimenides.[45] In the early 20th century, however, J. Rendel Harris discovered a fragment attributing 28a to an encomium pronounced by the legendary son of Zeus, Minos, in a Nestorian commentary entitled *Gannat Busame* or 'Garden of Delights' containing excerpts from the Syrian Fathers. The extract is translated as follows:

'In Him we live and move and have our being.' The Cretans used to say of Zeus, that he was a prince and was ripped up by a wild boar, and he was buried: and lo! his grave is with us. Accordingly Minos, the son of Zeus, made over him a panegyric and in it he said: 'A grave have fashioned for thee, O holy and high One, the lying Cretans, who are all the time liars, evil beasts, idle bellies; but thou diest not, for to eternity thou livest, and standest; for in thee we live and move and have our being.'[46]

---

[43] Rothschild 2014. An Epimenidean background was accepted by none others than Norden (1913: 277 n.1), Lake (1933: 250) and Dibelius (1939: 49–50). Yet after the publication of Pohlenz 1949 and Hommel 1955 and 1957, many exegetes do not even mention the hypothesis (Conzelmann 1987: 144-145) or reject it (Haenchen 1971: 524 n. 3; Barrett 2004: 847). Marguerat (2015: 161) mentions it in a footnote and writes: 'La thèse d'une citation en 28a d'un hymne à Zeus d'Epiménide de Crète (VIe siècle av. J.-C.) a été abandonnée.' Fitzmyer (1998: 610) considers it 'highly unlikely.' Johnson (1992: 316) and Jipp (2012: 853 n.64), however, list it as a possibility.

[44] For a detailed discussion, cf. Rothschild 2014: 8–16.

[45] Tit 1:12: εἶπέν τις ἐξ αὐτῶν ἴδιος αὐτῶν προφήτης· Κρῆτες ἀεὶ ψεῦσται, κακὰ θηρία, γαστέρες ἀργαί. Epimenides was originally from Crete. He is mentioned by Diogenes Laertius 1.112 as one of the seven sages. Clement associates Tit 1:12 to Epimenides in *Stromata* 1.59.

[46] Harris 1906a: 310.

5.2 God's Relationship to Humanity

Harris ascribes the excerpt to Theodore of Mopsuestia, an attribution which would situate it in the 4–5th centuries.[47] According to the fragment, both the quote found in Tit 1:12 and usually attributed to Epimenides – 'the lying Cretans, who are all the time liars, evil beasts, idle bellies' – and the clause found in Ac 17:28a – for in him we live and move and have our being' – appear in a same text, namely a panegyric to Zeus pronounced by his son Minos. As Harris comments, the reference to Minos as the author of the panegyric is reconcilable with an Epimenidean authorship since, as we know from Diogenes Laertius (1.112), Epimenides was the author of a poem in 1000 verses on Minos and Rhadamanthus.[48] Hence his suggestion that Acts 17:28a stems originally from a poem from Epimenides on Minos, which contains a reference to the famous Cretan lie that Zeus has died.

A confirmation of this original context for 17:28a was provided by the publication of Isho'dad's ninth-century Syriac commentary by 'the Westminster sisters' in 1913. The passage reads as follows:

> This, 'in him we live and move and have our being'; and this, 'As certain of your own sages have said, We are his offspring.' Paul takes both of these from certain heathen poets. Now about this, 'In him we live,' etc.; because the Cretans said as truth about Zeus, that he was a Lord; he was lacerated by a wild boar and buried; and behold! His grave is known amongst us; so therefore Minos, son of Zeus, made laudatory speech on behalf of his father; and he said in it, *'The Cretans carve a tomb for thee, O holy and high! Liars, evil beasts, and slow bellies! For thou art not dead for ever; thou art alive and risen; for in thee we live and are moved, and have our being,'* so therefore the blessed Paul took this sentence from Minos.[49]

Isho'dad frequently relies on Theodore of Mopsuestia in his commentary and it is possible that the church father is his source here as well.[50] Furthermore, the *Gannat Busame* relies on Isho'dad's Nestorian commentary at several places, and the latter might well have been its source for this passage as well.[51] In any case, according to Isho'dad, the quotation in Acts 17:28a comes from the laudatory speech attributed to Minos in answer to the well-known Cretan lie that Zeus is dead and buried in Crete.[52] The story of the Cretan lie was well-known in Antiquity, and Callimachus attests to its association with the phrase 'Cretans are always liars' (*Hymn to Zeus* 8).

---

[47] Harris 1906a: 310: 'It certainly is a translation from the Greek and follows immediately on an extract from Theodore.' Cf. Lake 1933: 249.

[48] Harris 1906a: 311.

[49] ET Margaret Dunlop Gibson as cited in Lake (1933: 249), my emphasis. Isho'dad was a Nestorian whose work was discovered by the twins Agnes Smith Lewis and Margaret Dunlop Gibson (i.e. 'the Westminster sisters') on a trip to Saint Catherine's Monastery and was published by them in 1913. Original and context in Gibson 1913.

[50] Lake 1933: 249.

[51] Harris 1911: xviii.

[52] In fact, it apparently comes from the same text from which Tit 1:12 is quoted.

This evidence led scholars such as Norden (1913), Lake (1933) and Dibelius (1939) to endorse an Epimenidean background for 28a. In the late 40s and in the 50s, however, Pohlenz and Hommel argued against this background as part of their contention that the speech – and in particular v. 28a – rather reflect Stoic or Platonic influence.[53] Emphasizing that early exegetes such as Clement or Jerome do not recognize a quote from Epimenides in Acts 17:8a, Pohlenz argued that Isho'dad had interpreted the plural of 'ποιητῶν' in v. 28 literally and, based on Callimachus' verses, invented the attribution to Minos (perhaps based on an apocryphal work), and added the line found in Ac 17:28a in the passage. He writes:

An seine Kallimachosparaphrase schließt nun 'Minos' bei Ischodad und ähnlich im Gannat Busamé unmittelbar die Worte an: *'for in thee we live and are moved and have our being'* und Ischodad vermerkt dazu *'so therefore the blessed Paul took this sentence from Minos.*[54]

Pohlenz disputes the attribution of this verse to a poem of Epimenides on the ground that such an argument – i.e. that Zeus cannot be dead because human beings are alive – and such a pantheistic view are unlikely to have occurred in a poet of the early 5th century BCE, adding that such an explicit association of the pagan Zeus with eternal life and the origin of all life would hardly have been a wise move on Paul's part.[55] For Pohlenz then, the verse 'in him we live and move and are' stems from Posidonius.[56]

Pohlenz's argument, however, is unconvincing. First, his question concerning the judiciousness of Paul's association of life with Zeus in a mission speech is problematic because, as is widely recognized, Ac 17:28b is a quotation from Aratus' *Phaenomena* 5 about Zeus being the father of humanity, and thus also associates the Christian God with Zeus as the originator and provider of humanity's life. Likewise, the suggestion that a 5th-century poet is unlikely to have such a pantheistic worldview is not strong evidence, since the phrase does not have to be interpreted pantheistically.

Above all, however, Pohlenz fails to provide a convincing explanation for the addition of 28a to the story of the Cretan lie by Isho'dad (and by the author of the *Gannat Busame* if he does not rely on Isho'dad), or another Christian

---

[53] Pohlenz's discussion of Isho'dad on Acts 17:28a occurs in a 4 pages-appendix to his article "Paulus und die Stoa," where he discusses the Stoic background of Romans 1 and Acts 17.

[54] Pohlenz 1949: 103 (emphasis his).

[55] Pohlenz 1949: 103: 'Ihm [Harris] sind dann die anderen gefolgt, ohne sich zu fragen, ob denn ein alter Dichter, der gegen die Behauptung vom Tode des Zeus protestieren wollte, Anlaß dazu hatte, unmittelbar die Begründung hinzufügen, daß wir Menschen in Zeus unser Leben haben, oder ob eine derartige Formulierung pantheistischen Weltgefühl für einen Mann aus dem Anfang des V. Jhs überhaupt denkbar ist, ob endlich Paulus wirklich klug daran getan hätte, in einer Missionspredigt für die Heiden einen Vers beifällig zu zitieren, der ausdrücklich für Zeus als Gott der Volksreligion Ewigkeit und den Charakter als Urgrund alles Lebens in Anspruch nahm.'

[56] Pohlenz 1949: 104.

copyist before him. As he himself notes, several church fathers (such as Jerome) had already questioned the wisdom of 'Paul' quoting Κρῆτες ἀεὶ ψεῦσται in Tit 1:12 because it seems to justify belief in Zeus.[57] For Christian commentators to create a story or add this line in the context of a pagan mythological story about Minos and Zeus only to fit the plural of ποιητῶν, then, would certainly have been a daring move. And as mentioned above, several earlier commentators had only identified one quotation of Greek poets in 17:28 without showing concern for the plural form. In any case Isho'dad himself does not express an apologetic concern in his commentary and no particular attention is paid to the plural ποιητῶν.[58] As often in his commentary on Acts, he only explains this background but does not exploit it to make a particular point. The arguments suggested by Pohlenz against an Epimenidean proposal are thus not conclusive.

In addition, a good case can in fact be made for the use of such a quote in Luke's passage. Scholars who have accepted an Epimenidean background to 28a have usually suggested that Luke's use of it could be explained by the fact that, as we know from Diogenes Laertius (*Epim* 3) Epimenides had been called from Crete to Athens to counsel the Athenians on how to stop a pestilence caused by an offended deity.[59] To solve the issue, Epimenides let loose a number of black and white sheep and ordered to build an altar and offer a sacrifice τῷ προσήκοντι θεῷ wherever they lay down. According to Diogenes, this is why there are altars without names (βωμοὺς ἀνωνύμους) in Athens. The mention of a verse by Epimenides thus fitted Paul's discussion of an 'altar to an unknown god' in Athens.[60] Our discussion about *deisidaimonia* as the concern to avert divine hostility would certainly add to the plausibility of this hypothesis.

There is, however, a much stronger argument for linking 28a with the Epimenidean background which has remained surprisingly unnoticed thus far in scholarship. The key lies not so much in linking those verses to Epimenides himself, but to the *context* in which the verse appears according to the *Gannat Busame* and Isho'dad, namely the Cretan lie. As they both suggest, the quote is part of a denunciation of the lie that Zeus is dead, asserting that the highest god is alive and risen and that this is proved by the fact that 'in him we live and move and have our being.' The text thus argues that the life of humanity attests that Zeus must be alive since he is the provider of human life. This fits remarkably well with the context of the quote in the speech in Acts 17. Indeed,

---

[57] Pohlenz 1949: 103.

[58] See Gibson 1913: 29.

[59] On the ancient traditions about Epimenides, including in Plato and Aristotle, cf. Lake 1933.

[60] Harris 1906a: 317; Lake 1933: 251. Rothschild 2014 argues that Luke depicts Paul as a 'new' Epimenides not only in the speech of Acts 17, but throughout the entire narrative of Acts. See my brief review in *JRS* 42 (2016): 43–44.

the assertion 'in him we live and move and are' (28a) is introduced as an explanation or a proof (γάρ) for divine proximity (καί γε οὐ μακρὰν ἀπὸ ἑνὸς ἑκάστου ἡμῶν ὑπάρχοντα): the fact that humanity's life, moving and being comes from God is thus a witness to God's proximity. If the original context of ἐν αὐτῷ γὰρ ζῶμεν καὶ κινούμεθα καὶ ἐσμέν is as suggested by the *Gannat Busame* and Isho'dad then, this would be a very appropriate use of the quotation in a similar context. The story of the Cretan lie about Zeus was very well-known in antiquity, and many authors mention it. Therefore, although Callimachus does not mention Minos' panegyric in his poem, it is not at all unthinkable that another tradition reports the story as suggested by the Syrian fathers, and that Luke used a verse from this particular tradition.[61] That would explain the poetic formulation of 28a.

Such a background for the quote thus confirms that the point of 28a is that humanity's life is ensured by God and that this attests to his nearness. The second part of verse 28 makes a closely connected point. τοῦ γὰρ καὶ γένος ἐσμέν has been identified to be from the *Phenomena* of Aratus, a poet influenced by Stoicism. A very similar clause also appears in the Stoic Cleanthes's *Hymn to Zeus*: ἐκ σοῦ γὰρ γένος εἴσι (*SVF* 1.537), and it is possible that several sources are in mind, but the exact quotation comes from Aratus.[62] The Stoics believed in the kinship of humanity with the divine, a kinship rooted in the fact that both shared in the *logos* – the divine principle. Many exegetes have thus argued that at this point the speech embraces or at least seeks a rapprochement with Stoicism. The kinship envisioned by the Stoics, however, is closely related to pantheism since it is a consequence of the divine principle permeating all things and especially rational creatures. It is a kinship which consists in a rational principle (i.e. the *logos*). The quote thus seems to introduce an idea otherwise foreign to the kerygma in Luke.[63]

In Aratus' poem, however, the 'kinship' of humanity with Zeus does not refer to the *logos* it shares with the highest god, but to humanity's dependence upon Zeus for its life. The text reads:

From Zeus let us begin; him do we mortals never leave unnamed; full of Zeus are all the streets and all the market-places of men; full is the sea and the havens thereof; *always we all have need of Zeus. For we are also his offspring* [τοῦ γὰρ καὶ γένος εἰμέν]; *and he in his kindness unto men giveth favourable signs and wakeneth the people to work, reminding them of livelihood.* He tells what time the soil is best for the labour of the ox and for the mattock, and what time the seasons are favourable both for the planting of trees and for casting all manner of seeds. For himself it was who set the signs in heaven, and marked out the constellations, and for the year devised what stars chiefly should give to men right signs of the

---

[61] For other references to the Cretan lie in antiquity, see Cook 1914 and Rothschild 2014.

[62] Barrett 2004: 848. The full context of the quote in Cleanthes runs: 'For it is right for all mortals to address you:/ for we have our origin in you, bearing a likeness to God,/ we, alone of all that live and move as mortal creatures on earth.' (Thom 2005: 52).

[63] Famously, this is also one of the points which make the speech emphatically 'unpauline.'

seasons, to the end that all things might grow unfailingly. Wherefore him do men ever worship first and last. Hail, O Father, mighty marvel, mighty blessing unto men. Hail to thee and to the Elder Race! Hail, ye Muses, right kindly, every one! But for me, too, in answer to my prayer direct all my lay, even as is meet, to tell the stars. (Aratus, *Phaen.*1–18 [LCL] *my emphasis*)

Despite the pantheistic flavour of the beginning of the poem, τοῦ γὰρ καὶ γένος εἰμέν is used as a metaphor to compare the relationship of dependence of humanity towards Zeus to that of children's dependence upon their father. Douglas Kidd comments:

A[ratus] begins with a short proem, which owes its form to the traditions of Hesiodic epic and its content to contemporary themes of Stoicism. The main section is a hymn to Zeus, the divinity that pervades the whole cosmos and is the source of all forms of life. He is in this sense our father, and acts like a father in helping men to cope with the struggle for existence, especially in agriculture. To this end he has established the constellations in the sky to serve as a guide to the seasons throughout the year, and this is why Zeus is so widely worshipped (1–14).[64]

Aratus now casts his Stoicism in the form of the old mythologies: since we derive our life from Zeus, we may be described as his children. This is an important step in the argument of the proem, because it leads on to the concept of Zeus as also a father, and therefore a kindly influence: καὶ brings out this new point.[65]

γένος is thus used metaphorically with the meaning of 'offspring' and specifically refers to the fact that the origin of human life lies in God and that it is God who continually provides for the needs of its life, just like a father does for his children. The Stoics often used the metaphor of father to argue precisely this point.[66] This metaphorical meaning fits well with the argument of the speech in 17:28, which has just affirmed that humanity depends upon God to live, move and exist. The poem of Aratus was well-known and popular in antiquity, as its translations into Latin and Arabic show, and it is thus plausible that Luke and his readers would have known the original context of the quote.[67] As this context shows, however, the metaphor does not emphasize human kinship with god through the *logos*, but serves to highlight the dependence of human life upon God, and above all the divine goodness and providence which ensures humanity's continuing life and the reason for human worship and praise of the highest god.

---

[64] Kidd 1997: 161.

[65] Kidd 1997: 166. According to Kidd, Aratus also alludes to Epimenides' story about the Cretan lie in l.30.

[66] See Algra 2007b:46–47.

[67] Rowe 2011: n. 5 p. 35. The translation into Latin was made by Cicero. That the poem – and in particular those specific lines at the beginning of the poem – was also known in Jewish circles is demonstrated by its quotation in Aristobulus (2nd c. BC). See Fragment Four in Holladay 1995: 170–171. Aristobulus cites several lines from the opening praise to Zeus – including the line found in Acts 17 – but substitutes 'God' for 'Zeus' in the text.

By quoting from two Greek poets, verse 28 thus affirms that human life and the continuing animation (cf. κινούμεθα) of humanity is a constant witness and testimony to God's proximity (v. 27b).[68] Within the argument of the speech, then, and especially following verses 26–27, verse 28 does not so much aim to argue for humanity's complete dependence upon God as commonly presumed by exegetes, but rather, *assuming it* (note that this common knowledge – if not necessarily acceptance – is demonstrated by the Greek's own poets here!), makes the point that humanity's very life and animation demonstrates the nearness of God and is a witness to him.[69]

5.2.4 Summary vv. 24–28

After pointing to the Athenians' concern about divine hostility and their ignorance as illustrated by their setting up an altar to an unknown god, the speech announces that it proclaims what they are revering ignorantly (vv. 22–23).

It then begins by turning to the creator God, underscoring that this one [god] cannot be served along traditional means – namely by providing him with a temple or with services – because he *himself* (cf. αὐτός) is the Lord of heaven and earth, and in fact provides all with breath, life and everything. The speech thus highlights that the relationship between the creator God and humanity functions as a reversal of traditional worship: God provides for humanity what humanity provides its gods through caring for idols.

Verses 26–27 then further explains how God filled the earth with humanity, multiplying it 'from a single one' and giving them dwelling places and seasons to live and multiply. This, God did, so that humanity might seek him, if it could possibly touch and find him. The reason for this is that God is not far from each one of us, since he provides humanity's life and move, and continually sustains their life like a father (v.28).

Those verses thus continue to depict God's relationship to humanity as one of divine provision – with dwelling places and seasons (food) – for human life, thereby continuing to describe his relationship to man as a reversal of the traditional man-divine (or man-idol) relationship in traditional Graeco-Roman religion. In addition, it explains that God filled the earth with humanity and ensured its life so that it might seek, and possibly 'feel' and find God. Indeed, the

---

[68] This reading is corroborated by Acts 14:17 which also emphasizes divine provision of rain and food – most likely a reference to Gods' life provision. In Acts 14, this is used as an expression of God's benefaction, which witnesses to him: καίτοι οὐκ ἀμάρτυρον αὐτὸν ἀφῆκεν ἀγαθουργῶν, οὐρανόθεν ὑμῖν ὑετοὺς διδοὺς καὶ καιροὺς καρποφόρους, ἐμπιπλῶν τροφῆς καὶ εὐφροσύνης τὰς καρδίας ὑμῶν.

[69] The function of v.28 in the argument is often misunderstood and exegetes overlook its connection with v. 27. So for example, Jipp (2012: 584) writes: 'Paul, thus, invokes the Athenians' poets, with a Stoic emphasis, to support his claim that humanity's desire for God has been implanted within them.'

life and movement of each human being is a witness to God's nearness. Again then, by depicting God as arranging humanity on all the earth to be a witness to him, the speech seems to further assign to humanity a role similar to that which idols played in ancient religion: representing the god in a particular place. Furthermore, one of the purposes of divine representations in the ancient world was precisely so that human beings could 'touch' and connect to the gods. The idea of humanity playing the role of an 'image of the divine' was familiar both to the Jews through the concept of the *imago dei* found in the biblical creation account, and to the Greeks, through Stoic philosophers, who precisely emphasized that it is the role of humanity to be god's worthy image.

The speech thus far has therefore created a narrative which suggests that the creator God's relationship to humanity is similar to, but a reversal of, that which human beings have towards their gods through idols. At the same time, the speech describes humanity's search for God as a feeling for him in the darkness and casts doubt upon the success of this search, thereby suggesting a problem with humanity's witness to God. And indeed, intriguingly, the word used to describe humanity's feel for God - ψηλαφάω – is the same which is the LXX uses to describe idols which have hands but cannot 'feel.' For a reader familiar with the OT, Luke is in fact attributing a characteristic of idols to humanity.

5.3 False Divine Representations (17:29)

5.3.1. Preliminary Remarks on the Logic of Verse 29

V. 29 is marked by the appearance of a neuter substantive (τὸ θεῖον) which probably harks back to the neuter pronouns used to present the subject of the speech in v.23, and thereby signals that the speech reaches its conclusion.

γένος οὖν ὑπάρχοντες τοῦ θεοῦ οὐκ ὀφείλομεν νομίζειν χρυσῷ ἢ ἀργύρῳ ἢ λίθῳ, χαράγματι τέχνης καὶ ἐνθυμήσεως ἀνθρώπου, τὸ θεῖον εἶναι ὅμοιον.

By and large, exegetes have interpreted v. 29 as a denunciation of Athenian idolatry. The verse is considered to be a criticism along the lines of Jewish anti-idol polemics, possibly also echoing some philosophical denunciations of divine representation.[70] As several scholars note, however, the logic of verse 29, which is presented as a consequence of v. 28 (cf. οὖν), is not easy to apprehend. Pervo, for example, points out that the reader has the feeling that one step is missing in the argument from the affirmation of humanity's kinship with God to the rejection of images.[71]

---

[70] E.g., Haenchen 1971: 525; Marguerat 2015: 161–162.

[71] Pervo 2008: 439: 'Just as the creedal affirmation of God as creator discredited the notion of temples, so God's paternity is the ground for rejecting images (v.29). This enthymeme, as it

Exegetes who associate this kinship with rationality have suggested that v. 29 is an appeal to think about God rationally, and thus exclude the association of the divine with material objects.[72] More generally, the move is understood to be an argument from the lesser to the greater: since humanity was made by God, it should not worship something made by man.[73] For example, Barrett writes:

> The argument runs back from men to God: since we are the thinking and feeling persons that we are, we ought not to suppose that the divine being (τὸ θεῖον, rather than τὸν θεόν; on this see below) is made of metal, even precious metal, or of wood. Luke might have balanced θεῖον with ἀνθρώπειον. If human nature is what we know it to be, and if we who have human nature are God's children, the divine nature will be of no lower order. We deny our own proper being if we identify our progenitor with material objects.[74]

For Barrett, the fact that human beings are thinking and feeling and that they are God's children implies that God cannot be of a lower order than human beings, and thus cannot be made of material.

As shall be argued, however, those common explanations are not fully satisfactory. Two clarifications are helpful here to highlight the logic of this verse.

First, it is noteworthy that what is denounced here is not the *identification* of idols with the divine or gods. In other words, verse 29 does not argue, 'we should not think that man-made objects are gods.'[75] The problem denounced is not the direct equation of idols – man-made objects – with gods. The speech is thus not following the move made by many Jewish anti-idol polemics denouncing those who call man-made objects – which typically cannot see, hear or touch – 'gods' (e.g., Dt 4:28; Isa 42:17; 44:9–17; Wis 13:10–14:10; Philo, *Dec.* 7076), a type of argument which, as seen in the previous chapter, is also found in some Graeco-Roman writers who complain about people mistaking the image for the god himself (e.g., Seneca, Plutarch).[77]

Rather verse 29 focuses on what the divine is similar to, or in that case, what the divine is not similar to: οὐκ ὀφείλομεν νομίζειν [...] τὸ θεῖον εἶναι ὅμοιον

---

were, involves a leap. The speaker does not, for example, state that humans were created in the image of God.' See also Jervell (1998: 450): 'Die Schlussfolgerung ist überraschend und nicht ganz einleuchtend [. . .].' And Conzelmann 1987: 145: 'At first the logic is not clear.'

[72] Johnson 1992: 317: 'The implicit appeal is to think of "the divine" (*to theion* used only here in the NT) in terms appropriate to rational creatures.'

[73] Haenchen 1971: 525: 'What originates in our artistic ability and consideration, and therefore stands under us, cannot portray the divine, which stands over us!'

[74] Barrett 2004: 849.

[75] Although this is what Paul is perceived to be saying elsewhere in Acts. Cf. Acts 19:26: Καὶ θεωρεῖτε καὶ ἀκούετε ὅτι οὐ μόνον Ἐφέσου, ἀλλὰ σχεδὸν πάσης τῆς Ἀσίας, ὁ Παῦλος οὗτος πείσας μετέστησεν ἱκανὸν ὄχλον, λέγων ὅτι οὐκ εἰσὶν θεοὶ οἱ διὰ χειρῶν γινόμενοι.

[76] τὰ δ' ὑπ' ἐκείνων δημιουργηθέντα πλάσματα καὶ ζωγραφήματα θεοὺς ἐνόμισαν.

[77] See preceding chapter and Decharme 1904.

[…]. This type of argument is also found in the LXX, for example in Isa 40:18–20:

To whom will you liken the Lord and to what likeness will you liken him? [τίνι ὡμοιώσατε κύριον καὶ τίνι ὁμοιώματι ὡμοιώσατε αὐτόν;] Does not a craftsman make an image [εἰκόνα], or a goldsmith set it by overlaying it with gold and fashioning it as a likeness [ὁμοίωμα]? For the artisan chooses unrotten wood and wisely seeks how he can set his image [εἰκόνα] so that it might not shake. [MC]

Importantly, then, the verse rejects the affirmation that the divine could be similar to, or represented by, objects of gold, silver or stone. It is concerned with divine-likeness and – as suggested also by the quotation from Isaiah – with images of God, rather than mistaken identification of man-made statues with the divine.

Second, although many commentators interpret γένος οὖν ὑπάρχοντες τοῦ θεοῦ as pointing to the faculty of reason of mankind, as discussed earlier, the metaphor rather points to God's providential care to ensure humanity's *life*. The basis of the argument in v. 29 is thus the divine origin of the *liveliness* of humanity, a reading confirmed by the emphasis the rest of the sentence puts on the quality of *lifelessness* of idols by forefronting the material in which they are made: χρυσῷ ἢ ἀργύρῳ ἢ λίθῳ.[78] Indeed, the word order suggests an emphasis as follows:

γένος οὖν ὑπάρχοντες τοῦ θεοῦ οὐκ ὀφείλομεν νομίζειν χρυσῷ ἢ ἀργύρῳ ἢ λίθῳ, χαράγματι τέχνης καὶ ἐνθυμήσεως ἀνθρώπου, τὸ θεῖον εἶναι ὅμοιον.
Therefore, since we are God's offspring, we ought not to believe it is to gold, silver and stone, objects graven by of the art and imagination of mankind, that the divine is similar.

The verse thus smoothly builds upon the assertion in v. 28 that humanity 'lives, moves and is' in God. Since humanity 'moves' and 'lives' in God, we must not believe that the divine is like lifeless objects. Again, the idea follows nicely the quote from Epimenides, which points to humanity's life to denounce the lie about Zeus' death.

The mention of the material out of which statues are made to underscore their lifelessness and thus unworthiness to represent the divine is attested both in Jewish and Graeco-Roman texts. Jewish literature regularly points to the gold, silver or wood out of which idols are made to underscore their lifelessness and inability to move, hear or see. For example, Ps 115:4–8 reads:

4 Their idols are silver and gold, the work of human hands.
5 They have mouths, but do not speak; eyes, but do not see.
6 They have ears, but do not hear; noses, but do not smell.
7 They have hands, but do not feel; feet, but do not walk; they make no sound in their throats.
8 Those who make them are like them; so are all who trust in them. (NRSV)

---

[78] Note that χαράγματι stands in apposition to χρυσῷ ἢ ἀργύρῳ ἢ λίθῳ.

Likewise, it was not uncommon for Graeco-Roman philosophers to point to the material and lifeless quality of divine representations as one of their important limitations as representation of the gods. For example, concerning the statue of Zeus, Chrysostom writes:

> But if, again, anyone thinks that the material used is too lacking in distinction to be in keeping with the god, his belief is true and correct. But neither those who furnished it, nor the man who selected and approved it, has he any right to criticize. For there was no other substance better or more radiant to the sight that could have come into the hands of man and have received artistic treatment. To work up air, at any air, or fire, or 'the copious sources of water,' what tools possessed by mortal men can do that? These can work upon nothing but whatever hard residuary substance is held bound within all these elements. I do not mean gold or silver, for these are trivial and worthless things, but the essential substance, though all through and heavy; and to select each kind of material and entwining them together to compose every species, both of animals and of plants—this is a thing which is impossible even to the gods, all except this God alone, one may almost say, whom another poet quite beautifully has addressed as follows: Lord of Dodona, father almighty, consummate artist. For he is indeed the first and most perfect artificer, who has taken as his coadjutor in his art, not the city of Elis, but the entire material of the entire universe. (Chrysostom Or.12.80–81 [LCL])

Such an assertion shows that lifeless material cannot really represent the divine worthily, even though it is the best a sculptor can do. In this particular case, it emphasizes that only creation – nature – is worthy of representing god and that only the highest god – Zeus – has the ability to create such a representation. Plutarch and Seneca make similar reflections about the superiority of living divine representations.[79] In fact, Plutarch defends the Egyptian practice of worshipping the divine through living animals precisely on the account that, unlike lifeless representations, they are living and thus a better 'mirror' of the divine (*Is. Os.* 382AC).

Furthermore, as illuminated in the last chapter, both Stoic and Epicurean philosophers considered that proper piety was expressed by seeking to be like the gods as much as possible. In fact, Stoic philosophers like Seneca and Epictetus precisely communicate this teaching by contrasting material divine representations with humanity in their teaching on piety, emphasizing that it is more important to 'mould oneself in the likeness of God' than to mould images of gold and silver which cannot really represent the divine. Thus, Seneca writes:

> 'And mould thyself to be worthy of god.'[80] However you will not mould with gold or silver; an image cannot be formed in the likeness of god out of such materials [*non potest ex hac*

---

[79] See for example: Seneca *Ep.* 31.11 or *De Superst.* (*apud Augustine Civ.* 6.10): 'To beings who are sacred, immortal and inviolable, [people] consecrate images of the cheapest inert material.' This materiality does not necessarily lead to a rejection of those images, but it is an acknowledged limitation of those representations.

[80] Virgil *Aen.* 8.364f.

5.3 False Divine Representatoins

materia imago deo exprimi similis]; remember that the gods, when they were well-disposed, were made of clay. (Seneca *Ep.* 31.11 [MC])

And Epictetus makes similar affirmations:

You are bearing God about with you, you poor wretch, and know it not! Do you suppose I am speaking of some external God, made of silver or gold? It is within yourself that you bear Him, and do you not perceive that you are defiling Him with impure thoughts and filthy actions. [...] Nay, if you were a statue of Pheidias, his Athena or his Zeus, you would have remembered both yourself and your artificer, and if you had any power of perception you would have tried to do nothing unworthy of him that had fashioned you, nor of yourself, and you would have tried not to appear in an unbecoming attitude before the eyes of men; but as it is, because Zeus has made you, do you on that account not care what manner of person you show yourself to be? [...] but the works of God are capable of movement, have the breath of life, can make use of external impressions, and pass judgement upon them. Do you dishonour the workmanship of this Craftsman, when you are yourself that workmanship? (Epictetus *Diss.* 2.8.12–23 [LCL])

Again, those passages emphasize the superiority of humanity as an 'image' of god because it is alive and has perceptions. At the same time, it underscores that the Stoics believed that it was humanity's responsibility to mould oneself in the likeness of the gods by pursuing an ethical and wise life. As discussed in the preceding chapter, the Stoics believed that humanity bears a kinship with the divine, a part of the *logos* in its breast. True piety thus consists in living according to this rationality – according to nature, as they often put it – and thus reflect this *logos*.

Such motifs show that a Greek audience would easily have picked on the contrast between γένος οὖν ὑπάρχοντες τοῦ θεοῦ and χρυσῷ ἢ ἀργύρῳ ἢ λίθῳ, namely between the living quality of humanity, and the lifelessness of images. With those two clarifications in mind, we can now attempt to unpack this difficult verse.

5.3.2 The Divine and Man-Made Images

V. 29, harking back to v. 23, denounces what the Athenians 'worship in their ignorance.'

γένος οὖν ὑπάρχοντες τοῦ θεοῦ οὐκ ὀφείλομεν νομίζειν χρυσῷ ἢ ἀργύρῳ ἢ λίθῳ, χαράγματι τέχνης καὶ ἐνθυμήσεως ἀνθρώπου, τὸ θεῖον εἶναι ὅμοιον. (Act 17:29)
Therefore, being the offspring of God, we do not have to believe that what is divine is similar to gold, silver and stone, objects of the art and imagination of man.

τὸ θεῖον most likely recalls the neuter relative pronoun of v. 23: 'what (ὃ) you worship in ignorance, this (τοῦτο) I am announcing to you.' It is common to interpret τὸ θεῖον as pointing to the creator God Paul has been talking about. But the sudden change from the masculine θεός to the neuter τὸ θεῖον suggests that the speech at least temporarily distinguishes God from 'the divine' spoken about more generally here.[81] This confirms that the Athenians are not worshipping the God (θεός) Paul has been talking about in the speech, even indirectly. Indeed, since they use man-made objects to represent and worship 'the divine,' the Athenians cannot be worshipping this God.

The basis of the argument is that humanity's life is provided and guaranteed by God, as suggested by the causal γένος οὖν ὑπάρχοντες τοῦ θεοῦ. To paraphrase the argument then: since we have our life from God, we must not believe that the divine is like the lifeless things made by man.

This is the point to examine in more detail another interpretation of this verse advanced by some scholars, namely that it builds upon an *imago dei* theology and implies that since humanity is God's offspring, it is only humanity which can represent God.[82] The verse would thus read as a contrast between humanity and idols as images of the divine:

Since *we* are the offspring of God, we ought not to believe that it is *to gold, silver and stone, objects of the art and imagination of man*, that the divine is similar.

Several scholars have indeed suggested that Luke uses γένος τοῦ θεοῦ in verses 28-29 as an allusion to the biblical concept of humanity's creation in the image of God (cf. Gen 1:26–27).[83] Jipp sees a confirmation of this reading in the mention of the creation of humanity ἐξ ἑνός which Luke's audience would have linked to Adam, who is precisely created in God's image.[84]

As discussed earlier, the speech does indeed present the creator God's relationship to humanity along lines evocative of, and as a reversal of, the relationship which humanity has with its idols. Despite this, however, the claim that the speech argues that humanity is God's image (or his 'idol') over against man-made idols, goes beyond what the text warrants and appears problematic for three reasons. First, it is questionable that Luke understands γένος τοῦ θεοῦ as a reference to humanity being created in God's image.[85] As discussed earlier, the expression refers to God's provision of life and care for humanity. This idea does not correspond to the way ancient Jewish sources usually interpreted humanity's creation in God's image, although Luke could admittedly be innovative here. While Jewish interpretations vary, they tend to interpret it as humanity's ability either to rule on creation (e.g., Sirach 17:3) or to live an ethical life, i.e. the ability to discern between good and evil (e.g., 2 En 65:2).[86] A second element which mitigates such an interpretation, is the way Luke depicts humanity as 'fumbling' in its attempt to touch and find God. This is not the positive description which we would expect if Luke was suggesting that

---

[81] Nowhere in Luke-Acts is θεῖον used to talk about God.
[82] Nasrallah 2010: 114–115; Jipp 2012: 585; cf. also the brief mention in Jervell 1998: 450.
[83] Jervell 1998: 449; cf. Nauck 1956: 22–23.
[84] Jipp 2012: 585.
[85] Some exegetes explicitly reject this interpretation. Cf. Dibelius 1939: 52.
[86] On the meaning of the *imago dei* in Judaism, cf. Jervell 1960.

5.3 False Divine Representatoins 159

humanity is God's image. Finally, the fact that the speech never explicitly *states* that humanity is God's image raises questions for this exegesis. In fact, as some scholars have noted, what is surprising about v. 29 is precisely that it does *not* say explicitly what we would expect, namely that humanity, and not idols, is the image of God.[87] Rather, it only says, 'since we are God's offspring (i.e. he provides for our life), we must not believe that it is to lifeless objects created by man that the divine is similar.'

Having voiced those caveats, however, this verse *does* suggest that humanity witnesses to God's nature – in this case to his living nature – over against idols. This contrast is strongly emphasized in that v. 29 builds upon v. 28 which has just affirmed that human beings 'live, move and are' in God, a description which contrasts directly with the gold, silver and stone out of which the objects of the art and imagination of man are made. In his study, Gärtner argued that the three verbs used in this line – live, move and are – often occur in biblical anti-idol polemics to describe idols negatively, especially in contrast to Yahweh.[88] Thus idols 'don't live,' but they are dead in contrast to the living God,[89] and they have 'no spirit' in them.[90] Likewise, idols 'don't move' but need to be carried around upon the shoulders of their makers (Isa 46:7). Finally, Jewish traditions often emphasize the non-existence of idols and the fact that they are nothing (1 Sam 12:21). Although v.28a most likely comes from Epimenides then, in the context of an anti-idol polemic, it possibly also evokes biblical and Jewish rhetoric against idolatry. It is easy to see why an author with as much affinity with the LXX as Luke would have found the quotation particularly useful in this context.

There is thus a contrast between human beings and idols in verses 28-29: unlike idols, humanity *does* live, move and exist. The phrase γένος οὖν ὑπάρχοντες τοῦ θεοῦ, however, also stresses another important element: the fact that humanity's life originates with and is guaranteed *by God*. And this stands in strong contrast to the objects of golds, silver and stone, whose creator is *humanity*. The importance of this point in the argument is underscored by the emphasis the verse puts on the creativity of human beings in the production of cultic images, describing them not just as 'made by man,' but as 'carved

---

[87] Conzelmann 1987: 145: 'But the obvious synthesis, that humanity is in the image of the living God, is not spelled out.'

[88] Gärtner 1955: 219–23.

[89] Wis 13:10: 'But miserable, with their hopes set on dead things, are those who give the name "gods" to the works of human hands...' See also Ps 115:5–7 which describes their lack of common signs of life: 'They have mouths, but do not speak; eyes, but do not see. ⁶They have ears, but do not hear; noses, but do not smell. ⁷They have hands, but do not feel; feet, but do not walk; they make no sound in their throats.'

[90] In this respect, it is interesting that Paul's anger at the idols in Athens is described as 'his spirit in him being angered when he sees the city full of idols: παρωξύνετο τὸ πνεῦμα αὐτοῦ ἐν αὐτῷ θεωροῦντος κατείδωλον οὖσαν τὴν πόλιν.

work made by the art and imagination of man' (χαράγματι τέχνης καὶ ἐνθυμήσεως ἀνθρώπου). At the heart of the comparison then, also lie the different creators of humanity and idols. The phrase emphasizes the *divine* origin and guarantee of humanity's life, over against the *human* origin of idols' 'life.' A paraphrase of the verse would thus read:

Therefore, since we are God's offspring and he – and not human beings! – guarantees our life, we do not have to believe that what is divine is similar to lifeless objects, who are, they, the product of the art and imagination of man – and not God.

In this paraphrase, οὐκ ὀφείλομεν is translated with the nuance of 'we don't have to' rather than the usual 'we should not' adopted by most interpreters. Both translations can be justified. Generally, however, ὀφείλω means 'to owe' 'to be bound to' or 'to be obliged to.' It is the vocabulary of debt and refers to what a person is obligated to render to another. While it might seem strange at first to translate ὀφείλω with this nuance at the height of an anti-idol polemic, it would make sense in the context of a discourse concerned with piety and *deisidaimonia* – the fear of the gods. Based on the fact that humanity's life is provided by God – and not man – humanity is not bound to believe that what is divine is similar to lifeless objects – which are, they, made by man – and worship and fear such 'divinities.' On this reading then, verse 29 not only denounces false images of the divine and thus false perception of the divine, but also claims that there is no need to worship or fear such 'divinities,' since God is the provider of human life. The verse thus also addresses the *deisidaimonia* of the Athenians, i.e. their concern and fear of hostile gods.

5.4 Divine Justice and Divine Representation (17:30–31)

τοὺς μὲν οὖν χρόνους τῆς ἀγνοίας ὑπεριδὼν ὁ θεός, τὰ νῦν παραγγέλλει τοῖς ἀνθρώποις πάντας πανταχοῦ μετανοεῖν, ³¹καθότι ἔστησεν ἡμέραν ἐν ᾗ μέλλει κρίνειν τὴν οἰκουμένην ἐν δικαιοσύνῃ, ἐν ἀνδρὶ ᾧ ὥρισεν, πίστιν παρασχὼν πᾶσιν ἀναστήσας αὐτὸν ἐκ νεκρῶν. (Acts 17:30–31)
Therefore, having overlooked the times of ignorance, God now commands all people to repent everywhere, because he has fixed a day on which he is going to judge the inhabited world in righteousness by a man whom he has appointed, giving proof to all by raising him from the dead.

In verses 30 and 31, the speech's argument reaches its climax. Indeed, it picks up the theme of ignorance which the speech claimed to address in the *propositio* (cf. v. 23). Those verses announce the consequence (cf. οὖν) of v. 29 and thus of the whole argument of the speech which has culminated in v. 29. As discussed in the introduction, however, the relationship between this climax and the rest of the speech has often puzzled commentators. Indeed, this conclusion abruptly introduces its only specifically Christian material by mentioning the resurrection of Jesus and the coming judgment through him, a conclusion which seems to have little connection with the rest of the discourse. It thus appears to be, to use Dibelius' famous words, a kind of 'Christian appendix' to an otherwise Hellenistic sermon, or, some might say, to an otherwise Jewish anti-idol polemic.[91] In addition, it is often noted that the mention of a final judgment and the resurrection to an audience such as the Athenians lacks plausibility, since the Greeks did not believe in a final judgment nor in the resurrection.[92] Aeschylus' famous line shows that the Greeks both understood what the concept of resurrection meant – i.e. the physical return to life of the body – and that they did not believe in it.[93]

When the dust has soaked up a man's blood,
Once he is dead, there is no resurrection. (Aeschylus, *Eum*. 647–48)

In that context, Luke's description of the resurrection as a 'proof' is puzzling at best. Thus, more than anywhere else in the discourse, Luke seems to strain historical credibility at this point. Indeed, summing up his assessment of the speech, Pervo writes: 'A cultured Greek would dismiss these brief words as a stylistically inadequate and muddled collection of clichés with an unexpected and improbable conclusion [...]'[94]

At the same time, despite the appearance of specifically Jewish and Christian elements in those final verses, exegetes also often note that even in this part of the speech, the discourse avoids the mention of historical parts of the kerygma which would have been unknown to the audience and thus made little sense to them. Most strikingly, the speech does not mention Jesus' name, nor the fact that he was put to death by the Jews, two elements which otherwise occur almost invariably in the 'missionary' speeches in Acts. This suggests that even in those verses, Luke takes some care to craft a discourse appropriate to his audience, and does not, as a hypothesis suggests, only include this Christian part in the speech mechanically because it is part of a common 'schema' of missionary speeches in Acts.

This section demonstrates the connection of this conclusion with the rest of the speech and argues that, far from being a disconnected part of the speech

---

[91] 'We see that it is a monotheistic sermon and only the conclusion makes it a Christian one. [...] In any case, the specifically Christian content of the speech is presented only in the last two verses.' Dibelius 1956a: 27.

[92] It is often asserted that Stoics would have been more open than Epicureans to the teaching of the resurrection, but this is speculative. While some evidence suggests that some Stoics believed in a time of afterlife before the *ekpurosis*, there is no question of resurrection in Stoicism.

[93] For this view see, for example, Wright's treatment in 2003; contra Porter 1999b.

[94] Pervo 2008: 430. See also Dunn (1996: 237) on v. 30 and the mention of a judgment in righteousness: 'At this point the cameo character of Luke's presentation, simply alluding in a phrase to a whole theme requiring a much fuller exposition, diminishes the credibility of the picture he here paints.'

which would not have made sense to the audience, it represents its climax and follows a logic which – while undoubtedly surprising and even laughable for some of the Athenians – would have been understandable for an audience with philosophical sensibilities.

5.4.1 The Universal Call to Repentance

As a consequence of the denunciation of v. 29 (cf. οὖν), verse 30 proclaims a divine command to repent. This call to repentance begins by asserting that 'God has overlooked the times of ignorance' (τοὺς μὲν οὖν χρόνους τῆς ἀγνοίας ὑπεριδὼν ὁ θεός). The terminology of ἀγνοία recalls the characterization of the Athenians as 'ignorant' (ἀγνοοῦντες) at the beginning of the speech as well as the altar 'to an unknown god' (Ἀγνώστῳ θεῷ). Its connection to v. 29 suggests that it refers specifically to the times characterized by the belief that the divine is like the lifeless objects made by human craft or is represented by them. 'Ignorance' here does therefore not refer to a lack of information, but, as often in the literature, to a distortion or a mistaken notion of the divine: the mistaken belief that the divine is like lifeless objects made by human beings.

The command to repent then most probably refers to the necessity to repent from the belief that the divine is like lifeless objects created by human beings (cf. οὖν in v. 30). Indeed, on the one hand, this belief implies that the divine can be compared to powerless inactive dead objects, a belief offensive in itself, but also a belief which implies that the divine is unable to act to preserve justice.[95] On the other hand, this belief implies that the divine has no power to give life, something which is contradicted by the fact of human life itself (vv. 28–29). It is thus a repentance from false belief about the divine and divine representation.

At the same time, the fact that the reason given for the command to repent is God's coming judgment 'in righteousness' (ἐν δικαιοσύνῃ) probably also implies a repentance from injustice or wickedness more generally. Indeed, the universality of the call to repentance – which implies that it is addressed not only to Athenians worshipping idols but to all humanity – corroborates such an understanding. Furthermore, in Acts the proclamation of the Christian message is generally accompanied by a call to repent from sins and wickedness (Acts 2:38; 3:26; 24:15–16; 24:25; 26:20; cf. Lk 24:46–47).[96] Those elements suggest that the repentance called for in v.29 is also ethical.

---

[95] See 5.4.2.

[96] Despite what is sometimes said in the literature (Vielhauer 1966: 36; Dibelius 1956a: 58), the meaning of μετάνοια as a regret and change from sinful or unrighteous behaviour would have been perfectly understandable to a Greek audience in such a context. See for example, Plutarch: god '[...] distinguishes whether the passions of the sick soul to which he administers his justice will in any way yield and make room for repentance (μετάνοιαν), and for those in whose nature vice is not unrelieved or intractable, he assigns a period of grace....to those whose

As discussed in the previous chapter, piety had important ethical implications for both Stoic and Epicurean (and indeed also Platonist) philosophers, since it took the form of an emulation or assimilation with the divine (i.e. godlikeness). It therefore also implied being righteous like the gods. The move from a denunciation of inappropriate divine representations to a call to repentance from injustice in a speech on piety would thus not have been unexpected for an audience philosophically aware.[97] As we have seen, it was human beings who were to be, ultimately, 'like the gods', for the philosophers, but to be so, they had to emulate their goodness or their righteousness. This behavioral consequence, in turn, implied to have a right view of the nature of the divine, so that the theological and ethical aspects of piety were closely bound together, and could both be understood as 'righteousness towards the gods', namely giving them back their due. The repentance is thus both from a belief in a divine who—like dead objects—is unable to act in justice and give life, and from the practice of injustice itself.

5.4.2 Divine Judgment in Righteousness and the Risen Man

The reason for the call to repentance to the whole world is the proclamation of God's coming judgment of the whole world in righteousness (v. 31: καθότι ἔστησεν ἡμέραν ἐν ᾗ μέλλει κρίνειν τὴν οἰκουμένην ἐν δικαιοσύνῃ). In the context at hand, the words 'in righteousness' (ἐν δικαιοσύνῃ) most likely mean that God will give each person according to what her actions, behaviour or thoughts deserve. Although, unlike many Jews, neither the Greeks generally, nor their philosophers, believed in a coming day of judgment, the idea that the gods exercise post-mortem retribution and reward was common.[98] Furthermore, as the last chapter has highlighted, the philosophical debate on the nature of the gods and *deisidaimonia* precisely involved a discussion of how the gods (or god) are not evil but act righteously towards human beings. The proclamation that God will make things 'right' is thus perfectly appropriate in a discussion about *deisidaimonia* and proper piety.

The next precision about this divine judgment is that it will be 'through a man' (ἐν ἀνδρί). The mention of this 'man' has often seemed without any relation to the rest of the speech to commentators, and they have regularly wondered why the name of Jesus is not mentioned. But the exegesis of the speech suggested thus far in this chapter highlights the logic of the argument at this

---

sinfulness is likely to have sprung from ignorance of good rather than from preference of evil, he grants time for reform; however, if they persist in evil, then to these he assigns suitable punishment.' (*Sera* 551D [LCL]) On the meaning of μετάνοια in Classical and Hellenistic literature, cf. Nave 2002: 40–70.

[97] Philosophically speaking, the lack of ethical godlikeness is the result of false conceptions of the divine.

[98] Also for some Stoics and the Platonists.

point. Indeed, v. 31 finally reveals that God *is represented by a man*, a risen man. This follows nicely from v. 29, which has just denounced the belief that the divine is similar to lifeless objects made by human beings in light of the fact that God provides life to humanity: God's resurrection and appointment of this man to represent him sets this man in stark contrast with the idols denounced in v. 29. Finally then, the speech proclaims what it has been suggesting throughout: humanity *is* meant to be God's image and representative!

Verse 31 thus announces that God will judge in righteousness through a human being who will represent him. It further states that God has given 'proof of this by raising him from the dead' (πίστιν παρασχὼν πᾶσιν ἀναστήσας αὐτὸν ἐκ νεκρῶν). Scholars debate whether the resurrection is the proof that this man has been appointed by God to judge the world,[99] that God will judge the world,[100] or both.[101] The suggestion here is that the resurrection demonstrates (i.e. proves) the godlikeness of the man in question, but also that it serves as a proof of God's righteousness and his coming righteous judgment of the world. The first point, namely that by raising this man from the dead, God proves that this man is godlike and worthy to represent him, will be discussed in the next section. The remainer of this section suggests that the resurrection and appointment of this man as God's judge is also presented as a proof that God will judge the world in righteousness.

First, on one level, and particularly considering the debate about true divine representation between the philosophers, there is likely a theodicic element in the fact that the speech affirms that God's representative in his exercise of justice in the world is, and will be, a living human being, and not dead idols. Indeed, dead idols cannot exercise justice and are anything but threatening. As long as human beings believe that God is represented by dead idols, they are unlikely to take his threat of judgment in righteousness seriously. This problem – namely the fact that false representations of the gods have the regrettable effect of eliminating the moral check of human behaviour – was well-known among Jewish authors and among Greek philosophers.[102] This means that the call to repentance at the beginning of v. 30 is also implicitly a call to repent from the belief in a God who is not righteous, or a God who cannot or does not exercice justice in the world.

---

[99] Barrett 2004: 853; Haenchen 1971: 526; Pervo 2008: 440.
[100] Marguerat 2015: 163.
[101] Jervell 1998: 450.
[102] This is the exactly the point made by the author of the Wisdom of Solomon in 14.29: 'For because they trust in lifeless idols they swear wicked oaths and expect to suffer no harm.' Greek philosophers likewise denounced false divine representation or false ideas about the gods as conducive to the practice of injustice in society. For the problems for morality and justice created by false divine representation and identified by the philosophers, see 4.1.2 b), especially the section "The Gods of the Poets and Other Philosophers as Harmful for Justice."

5.4 Divine Justice and Divine Representation

Furthermore, by pointing out that God has raised a righteous man from the dead and appointed him as his representative in judgment, the speech emphasizes that God has finally found a righteous representative through whom he will exercise his justice.[103] Implicitly, it suggests that before this man there was nobody worthy to be raised from the dead and hold this role of righteous judge. In this sens, this resurrection opens up the possibility for God to judge humanity thoroughly righteously through a human representative itself. At the broader level, it suggests that God, unlike what the world or history might suggest, is righteous: but before the appearance of this man worthy to be raised from the dead there was no representative who could reveal what God is truly like, no real image of him. By raising this man from the dead, God shows that he can only be represented by someone righteous and thus reveals his righteous character.

Finally, the fact that God raises the dead itself opens up the very possibility of post-mortem divine justice. In this sense, the resurrection is not a proof, but a key step in arguing that God is just and will exercise justice in his dealings with humanity: death is not the final word. And the resurrection of this righteous man shows that God gives the righteous what they deserve through the resurrection: eternal life.

On another level, one might wonder if the resurrection of this man and his appointment to represent God as judge does not 'prove' the coming of God's righteous judgment in an additional way, especially in light of the argument of the speech so far. Indeed, one might wonder whether the revelation that God will judge humanity *through a man who represents him* also suggests something about the outworking of God's justice more generally, perhaps something which was unknown so far but which is now revealed or proved through the resurrection and appointment of this man as judge of the world. This reading is suggested by the fact that the speech seems to imply that the "times of ignorance" (v.30) about true divine representation and divine justice have entered a new era now that God has risen a man from the dead. Apparently, something about the outworking of both true divine representation and divine justice are revealed in this resurrection, and this makes the proclamation of this coming divine judgment more convincing than before, and ignorance less excusable than when God overooked it (v. 30: τοὺς μὲν οὖν χρόνους τῆς ἀγνοίας ὑπεριδὼν ὁ θεός). Contextually, this would be pertinent since, as highlighted in the previous chapter, demonstrating that the gods are just and good in their dealings with humanity was key in the philosophical debate about *deisidaimonia* and discussing true piety. Yet this was precisely the difficulty and the point where the different philosophical schools often criticized each other, since the righteousness of the gods was far from obvious in this world.

---

[103] On the righteousness of the risen man, see 5.4.3.

Although this argument is more tentative, it is suggested here that the proclamation that judgment will take place through a risen man reveals that God exercises his righteous judgment towards humanity through humanity itself, and more specifically by letting humanity represent him. Indeed, the whole speech has depicted humanity as having a role and position strickingly remarkable to that of idols representing the gods in the ancient world. In the economy described by the speech, however, God creates and takes care of humanity by giving it the nourishment and dwelling places necessary for life. It has also suggested that God filled the earth with human beings so that they might possibly get a 'feel' for him, strongly suggesting that humanity itself is supposed to be this image of God, representing him. At this point however, the speech has suggested that there is a problem, and the word 'feel' casts humanity rather like the idols who have hands but cannot feel in the Old Testament, showing indeed that humanity has become like the idols it worships, rather than the true images of God they were supposed to be.

Importantly, idol worship has cast humanity in a total reversion of roles: in this economy, humanity takes the place of God by creating idols, and provides food and dwelling places for them. The key problem in this new economy is highlighted by verses 28 and 29: unlike God, humanity can only create lifeless, i.e. dead, things. Considering the argument of the speech, and especially in light of v. 29, the mistaken belief denounced by the speech has tremendous implications: if the divine is similar to lifeless things, then the divine cannot give life to humanity. To believe that the divine is similar to lifeless things is thus a denial of humanity's own life and nature, and to hold to a belief which would imply the death of humanity. Philosophically speaking, the belief of the Athenians denounced by the speech, is a belief which entails the death of humanity and the fact that humanity is like idols. By taking the place of the divine in the economy, humanity has made itself an idol, and implies its own death.

In this context, the resurrection of the righteous man may suggest that death – the mortality of human beings – is the righteous consequence of the disordered economy created by humanity. Indeed, in the economy created by humanity, human beings behave as if they were the divine, even though they can only create dead idols. The proclamation of a righteous divine judgment through a risen man thus ironically highlights the logic of the righteous divine judgment at work in the world as it is: humanity is meant to represent the divine, but it has done so by reversing the divine economy and by taking God's place; therefore, righteously, God lets humanity be judged by its own actions and receive what its belief and actions deserve. Humanity thus ultimately becomes like what it would be if humanity was God: an idol, and, ultimately, a dead idol. The resurrection of the man and his appointment as judge worthy to represent the righteous God thus not only annonces a future judgment in righteousness, but also shows the logic of divine judgment at work before this final judgment: God judges humanity by letting humanity take his place, namely he lets them live the righteous consequence of what they do when they take the place of the divine and create idols.

There is indeed possibly a tension in the argument of v. 29: if humanity's life comes from God and he is eternal, why then does humanity die? Should human beings not live eternally? The answer seems to be that death is the righteous consequence of humanity's false beliefs about God and their worship of dead things. And this false belief seems to be the result of humanity having overturned the divine economy by taking God's place and thereby envisioning the divine as similar to human beings. Indeed, if the gods humanity worships are like human beings, humanity can only be an idol.

In any cases, the speech does suggest that this humanity which worships other gods through idols has itself become an idol, i.e. like the objects made by human creators. It has thus become like what it worships, i.e. mortal, dead, unable to 'feel' God, a teaching found frequently in the Old Testament (cf. Ps 115:4–8), but also, as discussed in the previous chapter, among the Epicureans, who argued that there is a direct correlation between the type of gods a person worships and a person's character. If the expression 'in righteousness' in v. 31 means that God treats or will treat humanity according to what its actions, behaviour and thougths deserve, then the fact that humanity worships gods represented by lifeless things would mean that deserve righteously to die.

In this sense, the resurrection and the appointment of this risen man to represent God reveals the way God judges humanity: by letting it be judged by the type of gods which they worship, i.e. gods which are in the end like themselves, since they (human beings) behave like gods.

Still tentatively, this reading would explain *deisidaimonia* – humanity's fear of evil gods – as the consequence of humanity's own wickedness and injustice. Human beings fear wicked and unjust gods because they themselves are wicked and unjust. As discussed in the preceding chapter, the philosophers – especially the Stoics – apparently made a similar connection when they denounced the way some anthropomorphic representations of the gods were conducive to *deisidaimonia*. For the philosophers, however, such 'anthropomorphisation' of the gods was mistaken, since the gods can only be good and cannot commit evil. In answer to this fear then, as discussed in the last chapter, the philosophers emphasized that the gods are not evil but good and just and thus need not to be feared.

According to Acts 17, however, *deisidaimonia* is not just a cognitive mistake which needs to be treated through right reasoning, but is actually – potentially – a sign of God's righteous judgment: human beings will indeed be judged in righteousness by a god in their own image, and they must therefore repent.

Ironically, this also shows the predicament of mankind as long as it relies on itself. Despite its attempt to imitate God, humanity is not god, and while it might be able to provide houses and food, it cannot provide life to its idols.

Alternatively, as the speech has shown, it is God who alone can provide such things for humanity and thereby represents its source of life. Potentially then, the speech might also be challenging the philosophical belief that humanity's imitation of God could lead anywhere. Fundamentally, only God can make humanity the divine image which it is meant to be. And this is the last point to be discussed below.

5.4.3 The Resurrection and the Proclamation of True Divine Representation

If verse 31 highlights the outworking of God's righteousness, it also reveals the nature of true divine representation, and what God is truly like. Indeed, by announcing that God intends to judge the inhabited world in righteousness *through a man* divinely appointed and risen from the dead, the speech implies that this divinely chosen man is worthy to *represent* God. True divine representation or godlikeness is thus not represented by gold, silver and stone, but by the living risen man. His resurrection by God presents him in powerful contrast with the lifeless idols which are created by men and were denounced as inappropriate divine representations in v. 29.

True godlikeness is thus embodied in a resurrected man. And this human being is characterized by eternal life and righteousness. The righteousness of this man is evident by the role which is given to him, namely to be the one through whom God will judge the world *in righteousness*. To be worthy to be God's representative as the one exercising the judgment of the whole world, this man must be uncharacteristically righteous. In both Jewish and Greek traditions such tasks are indeed attributed to unusually righteous people. The belief that the righteous will judge the world is common in Jewish thought (Dan 7:22; Wis 3:7–8; 1QpHab 5:4). And similar ideas are found in Greek literature, where righteous people are appointed with the task of judging mankind. For example, in Greek mythology both Rhadamanthus and Minos were appointed judges of the dead because of their great justice:

> Moreover, because of his [Rhadamanthus'] very great justice [δικαιοσύνης], the myth has sprung up that he was appointed to be judge in Hades, where his decisions separate the good from the wicked. And the same honour has also been attained by Minos, because he ruled wholly in accordance with law [νομιμώτατα] and paid greatest heed to justice [δικαιοσύνης]. (Diodorus Siculus, 5.79.2 [LCL])

In addition, this man's righteousness is most likely implied by the declaration that God raised him from the dead. Indeed, resurrection into eternal life was for many Jews the reward of righteousness. Luke seems to endorse this belief by putting a similar logic in Jesus' mouth when he speaks of 'those who are considered worthy to attain that age and the resurrection from the dead' (Lk 20:35: οἱ δὲ καταξιωθέντες τοῦ αἰῶνος ἐκείνου τυχεῖν καὶ τῆς ἀναστάσεως τῆς

5.4 Divine Justice and Divine Representation

ἐκ νεκρῶν).[104] And as already mentioned, some Jewish texts reflect the belief that the resurrected righteous will judge the world, and particularly the wicked.

As for the Greeks, although they did not believe in the resurrection, they did, however, consider immortality to be the reward of godlikeness.[105] It is clear that God's resurrection of this man to establish him as judge implies a gift of eternal life and that it is not just a momentary physical reanimation. From a Greek perspective, then, this man has received a kind of immortality which confirms his godlikeness and would imply that he has been divinized. It is thus unsurprising that some of the Athenians believed that Paul was announcing foreign divinities when he was announcing Jesus and the resurrection (v.18). The risen Jesus can easily be interpreted as a new foreign divinity.

The mention of the risen man who will represent God thus follows nicely the call to repent both from belief in divinities which are like lifeless statues and from unrighteousness. Indeed, it highlights that godlikeness – God's true image – is represented by a righteous risen man, not by lifeless objects, nor by humanity generally: the creator God is represented by a man characterized by (eternal) life and righteousness. God's resurrection of this man, and his appointment of him to represent him as judge, is thus a reaffirmation of God's life-giving power affirmed throughout the speech, and the climactic proclamation – and indeed a revelation – of what God is truly like. God is a living and righteous God, and a God who gives life. And this living and righteous God is represented by a man who died and was risen from the dead.

The risen man thus reveals the nature of godlikeness and true piety: the man who was raised from the dead *is* the image of God, and the one human beings should revere instead of lifeless images, in order to worship the true (and righteous) God.

Here lies the logic of v. 23: 'what you revere unknowingly or mistakenly, this I am announcing to you.' As highlighted (implied) by v. 29, the Athenians worship a divinity which is like gold, silver and stone and thus cannot be truly divine. And in this relationship, they try to do for their gods, what God does for them. Instead, the speech calls them to worship the God represented by the risen man, through the risen man. This God is living, righteous, but he is also the one who gives everything to humanity to enable it to be this living image, and the one who raises the dead. Peace with God – or proper relationship to the divine – according to the speech, thus implies to repent from false divine representations and from unrighteousness, and instead believe that the life-

---

[104] The resurrection of Jesus is also linked to his righteousness in the first – and thus highly programmatic – speech in Acts, namely in Acts 2. Cf. Monique Cuany, "The Divine Necessity of the Resurrection: A Re-Assessment of the Use of Psalm 16 in Acts 2," *NTS* 66 (2020): 392–405.

[105] Of course, the nature of this immortality was understood differently by the various philosophers. The Epicureans, for example, did not conceive of this 'immortality' as a form of afterlife. Cf. Warren 2011.

giving and righteous God is represented by the righteous man who died and was risen from the dead by this God.

Finally, the resurrection also stresses God's gift of eternal life as that which makes humanity truly godlike.[106] As v. 29 emphasized, because *God* provides life to humanity, it is not necessary to believe that the divine is represented by what is lifeless. Indeed, God is not like men who cannot give life to the statues they make, but he gives life to what is lifeless.

It is at this point that the speech might well be making the assertion which challenges common philosophical teaching about piety. Of course, the proclamation of the resurrection is already new and challenging on its own. But, again tentatively, in light of the context highlighted by the previous chapter, there might well be here also an implicit criticism of what the philosophers taught: namely their claim that true piety and the path to divine-likeness and peace with the gods consists in imitation of the divine. Indeed, while the speech, like the Stoic philosophers for example, underscores that it is God who provides all for humanity and not human beings who serve him, the speech seems to use this argument differently, namely to contrast divine and human activity and put humanity resolutely on the receiving end in the divine-human relationship.

Indeed, implicitly, the speech highlights and criticizes the fact that humanity has taken up the divine role and acts like God by doing for idols what God is doing for them. So far the philosophers would agree. But the speech goes further in that it shows that by doing so, humanity only manages to create lifeless images which are unworthy to represent God (v. 29); and ironically, humanity itself now ressembles those idols since they have hands but 'cannot feel' God (v. 27). It thus seems that the speech highlights the limitations or the problems inherent in the imitation of the divine for humanity: ultimately, humanity is not able to give life. Although this must remain tentative, there might well be a hint here that divine imitation is impossible. Just like humanity cannot give life to what is lifeless or dead, so also it is unable to 'mould itself' in the likeness of the creator God, as the philosophers were teaching.[107] In the speech, God raises a man into eternal life and into his representative. The whole speech thus focuses on contrasting not just God and idols, but God and humanity. And by proclaiming that God raised a man from the dead, it certainly emphasizes the creative and life-giving power of God in bringing to life this perfect image of himself.

Finally, and although this interpretation must also remain tentative, the speech seems to imply that, by resurrecting this man, God also opened up the

---

The motif of Christians being perceived as 'gods' in human forms appears several times in Acts: Acts 14:11, 28:6, and possibly the fact that the Athenians thought that Paul was announcing new divinities in Acts 17. [106]

[107] I am not hereby implying that the philosophers were teaching that human beings could become like the divine in all aspects.

way for the rest of humanity to receive eternal life. This might be what is also proved by the resurrection (cf. πίστιν). It would explain why, in v. 32, the Athenians understood the speech to speak about 'a resurrection of dead persons' in the plural (ἀνάστασιν νεκρῶν) and not just about 'a resurrection from the dead' (ἀνάστασιν ἐκ νεκρῶν) as would have been the case if the speech only announced the resurrection of Jesus. Such a reading is also suggested by the way Luke summarizes the message in Athens as '*the good news* of Jesus and the resurrection'(τὸν Ἰησοῦν καὶ τὴν ἀνάστασιν *εὐηγγελίζετο*) in v. 18 and possibly by the fact that part of the philosophers had the feeling that Paul was announcing new divinities in the plural. It is, in any case, corroborated by the description of the Christian message elsewhere in Acts as the proclamation of 'the resurrection from the dead in Jesus' (Acts 4:2: καταγγέλλειν ἐν τῷ Ἰησοῦ τὴν ἀνάστασιν τὴν ἐκ νεκρῶν). In this case, what the speech is announcing is that somehow through this risen man, perhaps just like the creator did at the beginning when he created all people from one man so that they might fill the earth with the witness of him (cf.v. 26), God will populate the earth with human beings who are his true representation. For indeed the risen man reveals what the true God is like: he is alive and judges righteously, and, unlike man, *he* has the power to give life.

5.5 Conclusion

The present chapter has argued that the speech in Acts 17 should be understood as a discourse addressing the Athenian concern of maintaining peace with the gods and preventing their hostility through the presentation of the true 'image' of God.

Rather than introducing Yahweh to the Athenians as a new God whom they do not know, or as the God whom they are already unwittingly worshipping, the speech thus aims to present the true image or representation of the creator God, thereby indicating what the creator God is like, and the means by which the Athenians can worship this God 'in knowledge' and have peace with him.

The speech thus begins by emphasizing that the creator God cannot be worshipped along traditional means – i.e. by providing him with temples and services – because *he* provides everything to everybody. This God – through one – created all the nations of men, so that they would dwell upon the whole earth, providing them with set seasons and boundaries to their dwelling. This, God did so that humanity would seek him, if it could possibly touch and find him. The reason for this is that God is not far from each one of us, since he provides humanity's life and move, and continually sustains their life like a father (v.28).

The speech thus strongly denies that humanity can in anyway relate to God the way it relates to its idols (i.e. by providing him with temples and services), and depicts God's relationship to human beings along lines reminiscent of the relationship which human beings have with the idols of their gods: God is the one who provides humanity with seasons so it has food, and with places to dwell, and he is the one who – by creating all people from a single model – makes sure that it fills the whole earth so that humanity can itself 'get a feel for' (touch) him. For indeed, where humanity is, God cannot be far, for it is God who provides the life of humanity. This depiction is reminiscent of the role of divine images in the ancient world and in the Graeco-Roman cult: among other things, their materiality enables human beings to 'touch' and connect to the god, in the best of cases to get a better idea of his attributes, and to worship him approriately. At the same time, the speech never explicitly identifies human beings as God's image, and in fact, the verb used to describe the human search for God – ψηλαφάω – rather suggests the attempt of a blind man to feel its way. As mentioned earlier, intriguingly, ψηλαφάω is also the verb used in the LXX to describe idols which have hands but cannot 'feel' and the speech comes close to imply that human beings are currently similar to idols who have hands but cannot really feel God. The speech thus seems rather to suggest that, while humanity seems to have the role of a witness to the divine in God's creation, yet it is more like an idol (a highly pejorative word for OT readers) in the current state of affairs, than what it is meant to be.

Based upon the claims that God is the provider and sustainer of human life in v.28, verse 29 then argues that humanity need not believe that the divine – what is truly divine and needs to be worshipped and feared – is similar to lifeless gold, silver and stone, which are statues made by men. It has been usual in the exegesis of the speech to affirm that v. 29 is the climax of the speech and that it is at this point that Luke unleashes its attack on Athenian worship. Yet this cannot be sustained in light of the historical context highlighted in the previous chapter. In fact, the claim made in v. 29 is anti-climactic: what it asserts is self-evident, and no philosopher would have disputed such a statement. It is in the following verses that the speech makes a powerful and controversial claim based on v. 29, which then gives v. 29 a new nuance which differs radically from what the Greeks had done with this type of argument.

From a basic and quite logical argument, the speech then moves in vv. 30 and 31 to the heart of its argument and the proclamation and demonstration of the nature of the divine. The climax of the speech thus comes with vv. 30 and 31: God has overlooked the times of ignorance, but he now commands all human beings everywhere to repent because he is about to judge the world in righteousness. The connection of this verse with v. 29 (οὖν in v. 30), suggests that the ignorance concerns the belief that God could be similar to lifeless things. And here indeed the resurrection of this man proves that God is not similar to lifeless things, but to the risen man. At the same time, the content of verses 30 and 31 suggests that this ignorance about godlikeness also concerns his righteousness and his judgment of the world, since this is what the resurrection also proves. And as mentioned earlier, such a climax with the

5.5 Conclusion

demonstration that godlikeness is also righteousness makes perfect sense in the philosophical context at hand: discussion of the nature of the divine and how humanity relates to it implies the demonstration of divine goodness and righteousness in light of an unjust world (for example in light of the fact that wicked human beings are not punished whereas just human beings suffer).

Human beings are thus to repent from believing that the divine can be similar to lifeless (and thus unable to act righteously) things, but also from unrighteousness. Indeed, God is in fact represented by a human being who is very well alive, and through whom God will exercise his justice.

The resurrection thus demonstrates that God's image, his representative, is the risen man. It also demonstrates God's power to create his own image by raising the dead, thereby contrasting him with human creators who only create lifeless things. And it sheds new light on the outworking of his righteousness, thereby proving that God is a righteous. While the purpose of the speech was to 'announce' (cf. καταγγελεύς and καταγγέλλω in v. 18 and v. 23) the true image of God then, the function of this *image* is of course to reveal what *God* is like – his true nature – and to enable humanity to relate appropriately to him. In this respect, the risen man reveals a God who is eternal, life-giving, providing all what humanity needs to live and fill the earth, who creates his own image in humanity, gives life to the dead, and judges in righteousness. The risen man thus reveals God's true nature – his eternal life, his goodness, and his righteousness. And it is through this risen man that true worship of the true God is made possible, and in him that true godlikeness is revealed to humanity.

6. Conclusions – A New Interpretation of the Argument in Athens and Its Relation to Greek Philosophy

As highlighted in the introduction of this book, despite its important role to assess how Luke depicts the relationship between the early Christian movement and Greek 'religion' and culture in Acts, Paul's speech in Athens continues to lead scholars to widely divergent conclusions on this subject and to raise questions as to its cohesion and even coherence. Perhaps most symptomatic of the puzzle raised by the speech is its conclusion. Despite the whole speech's apparent attempt to contextualize its message for its Greek audience, its conclusion – which introduces the only specifically Christian material of the discourse – has felt not only sudden and totally disconnected from the rest of the speech, but also seemed to give up any previous effort at Greek contextualization by announcing the resurrection of a man and a coming divine judgment of the world.

Building upon Rowe's recent remark concerning the necessity to examine ancient philosophies as complex integrated systems before comparing them with Christianity, this project has adopted an approach which examines in much more depth than previous studies the historical religious and philosophical background alluded to by the pericope in Acts 17. This methodological decision was further justified in the second chapter of this project. Indeed, an analysis of the narrative context of the speech in Athens itself suggests that the philosophical and religious historical backgrounds are important to interpret the pericope.

Consequently, the next two chapters of this book focused on analysing and outlining the religious and philosophical background implied by the pericope of Acts 17. This was done first of all by examining the meaning of *deisidaimonia*, the word which Paul uses to characterize the Athenians at the beginning of the speech and as a springboard for his discourse. In addition, chapter four has examined more broadly what Stoic and Epicurean philosophers taught about the traditional cult and the use of images – which is clearly an issue in Acts 17 (cf. vv. 16 and 29) – as well as what they taught more generally about the worship of the gods and being at peace with the divine—which was the aim of traditional religion and which the philosophers tackled under the broader subject of piety (and the rejection of *deisidaimonia*). Retrospectively, those two chapters have served to correct several longstanding mistaken conceptions about *deisidaimonia* and the philosophers' views on the cult and human relationship with the divine, and thus shed new and important light on the historical background alluded to in the narrative of Acts 17. In their conclusions, those chapters have also begun to hint at the way this background information sheds new light on the argument of the speech itself and on its relationship to Stoic and Epicurean philosophy.

The last chapter then proceeded to analyse the speech itself verse by verse. While this examination relied mainly on a careful reading of the material found in those verses (vv. 23–31), it also drew upon the results of the previous chapters at several key places.

This concluding chapter draws together the results of the different chapters in order to answer the two questions raised in the introduction concerning this famous pericope, and to highlight the broader contribution of this project to scholarship. The first question it addresses, unsolved so far in scholarship, concerns the coherence of the speech, and more specifically the relationship of the speech with its 'Christian appendix'. The second issue, which has divided modern scholars for over a century, concerns the relationship of the speech with Greek philosophy and religion. More specifically, and in light of the recent challenge raised by Rowe, it will be asked whether it is appropriate to speak of this speech as a rapprochement with the religion or philosophy of the Athenians.

After tackling those two central issues, this chapter discusses how those results challenge current scholarly assessments about the nature of Christian preaching to the Gentiles in Acts and about the claim that Acts 17 represents a 'foreign body' in Acts. It also considers how this project contributes to the assessment of Luke's attitude towards the Graeco-Roman world and his literary purpose in composing his double-work. A discussion of the implications of those results for the much-debated question of Luke's Paulinism or his picture of Paul must, however, be left for another day.

6.1 A New Reading and Coherence for the Speech: Proclaiming the True Image of God

Perhaps the greatest issue in the interpretation of the speech in Athens concerns its coherence, and in particular the relationship of the main body of the speech with its so-called 'Christian appendix'. As is commonly pointed out, verses 30 and 31 appear to have little connection with the rest of the speech, and introduce for the first time Christian concepts which seem unannounced by the discourse, and hardly understandable by a Greek audience without a lot of elaboration. It should be noted, however, that this perceived incoherence is largely the result of the way the speech is usually (and in fact almost consensually) read, namely as a speech aiming to introduce the one true God – Yahweh – who is unknown to, or worshipped in ignorance by, the Athenians, over against their many gods or idols. According to this usual reading, the main trust of the speech is an anti-idol polemic and the proclamation of Jewish monotheism.

The present project, however, challenges this interpretation and argues that the purpose of the speech is *not* (directly!) the presentation of Yahweh or monotheism, but the demonstration and proclamation of God's true image – the risen man – in the context of a debate about the aversion of divine hostility. This reading gives the speech much more cohesion, and shows that the last verses (vv. 30–31) are not a 'Christian appendix' with little connection with the preceding verses, but that they represent the very climax of the speech's argument and message. This interpretation is supported by a careful reading of the speech's argument (chapter 5), by its immediate narrative context (chapter 2), and by the presupposed philosophical context of this pericope (chapter 3 and 4).

6.1.1 The Argument of the Speech

Turning first to the speech itself, as argued, the mention of *deisidaimonia* at the beginning of the speech is not a criticism of Athenian idolatry nor more generally of its traditional cultic practices as is often assumed by exegetes. Rather, it is an allusion to the Athenians' concern to avert divine hostility or divine retribution through their cultic practices. The broader context of the speech and its springboard is thus the topic of peace with the divine. What is at stake between Paul and the Athenians is not just the true nature of the divine (although it is also that!), but human relationship with the divine, and the aversion of divine hostility, something which sheds light on the so-far unexplained mentions of a call to repentance and divine judgment at the end of the speech.

Then, importantly, the beginning of the speech does not connect the object of Paul's proclamation (cf. the neutral pronoun in v. 23) with the God (masculine) of heaven and earth he begins to talk about in v. 24. Furthermore, the discourse never presents Yahweh as if the Athenians had absolutely no concept of a creator God or never heard of him. Rather, it focuses on outlining the nature of the relationship between this creator God and humanity, and draws conclusions on what this implies – negatively – in terms of worship, and thus peace with him. In a few sentences, it reminds the Athenians that they cannot relate to the God of heaven and earth the way they relate to their 'idols', namely by providing him with a house or food, or anything, and that this God, actually, does for them – i.e. humanity – what they are trying to do for their idols.

The speech further proclaims that through one man, God made all the nations, so that humanity would dwell upon the whole earth. And he appointed seasons and limitations to their dwellings, so that humanity might be able to seek him. Importantly, as this project has argued, vv. 26–27 do not describe the purposes which God assigns to humanity, but how *God* arranges and enables humanity to fulfil his own purposes, which is to fill all the earth with mankind, and thus, that mankind would seek, touch and find him. Indeed, by ordaining seasons and appointing dwelling places, God has provided the conditions of life for humanity, thus ensuring that it can fill the whole earth. Those verses therefore depict humanity as having a function very close to that of a divine image of the creator: God makes all the nations on the model of one image, and then ensures they fill the whole earth, by providing the seasons which bring the food necessary and the dwelling places for their life to be sustainable. He thus arranges the conditions for humanity to seek, 'touch' and find him. At the same time, the speech never explicitly describes humanity as God's image, and its failure to 'feel' him makes it look more like an idol. Yet, as v. 28 emphasizes, humanity's life does attest to God's proximity, since God is the provider of humanity's life. Humanity is thus a witness to God's presence and nature.

A crucial point highlighted in those verses which past scholarship has too often overlooked is the presentation of God as above all the creator, the life-giver, and the life-sustainer of humanity. It is this provision of *life* which mainly characterizes the divine-human relationship, and which makes humanity a witness to God. This is confirmed in verse 29, which contrasts humanity with idols precisely on this point: humanity is God's offspring – namely *God* provides its life, whereas idols are made of lifeless material and are the product of humanity's creation. This emphasis on life and contrast with the lifelessness of idols prepares the proclamation of God raising a man from the dead in v. 31.

The whole speech thus seems to suggest that humanity is the most appropriate candidate to be a divine image, yet it never affirms that it is and suggests that it is failing. It is in verses 30 and 31 that the speech reaches its climax, calling humanity to repent in light of a judgment in righteousness through a man whom God raised from the dead as a proof. The resurrection of this man proves indeed that he is God's representative, and thus his worthy image. The gift of the resurrection and the role which he receives – to judge the world in righteousness – show that this man is eternal and perfectly righteous like God. More broadly, the resurrection of this man proves that humanity is indeed meant to be God's image, while the call to repentance also shows that the rest of humanity is not currently the image it should be.

Verses 30 and 31 thus do represent the climax of the speech. It is only at this point that what God is like is truly revealed and that the ignorance (ἄγνοια) concerning the divine is lifted: God is like the risen man – he is living, eternal, and righteous. At the same time, those verses draw the speech together by announcing, as expected, that God is represented by *a human being, living eternally*. This follows perfectly the claims of verses 28 and 29: since humanity has its life from God, God can only be represented by something living. The proclamation of a man risen from the dead and living eternally is thus in keeping with the main idea of the speech so far: it comes as the climactic proclamation of a God who is by definition the one who gives life and all what is needed for life, and the one who can thus only be testified to by something living (cf. v. 29).

While a few scholars have noticed traces of an *imago dei* theology here and there in the speech, this project shows how this idea runs through the whole speech, from the beginning to its end. At the same time, the present study also argues that there is a tension in the speech, and that the discourse also depicts humanity in terms usually applied to idols in the OT. This study thus departs from the assertions of previous exegetes by arguing that the speech defends the idea that it is the risen man – Jesus – who is presented as this divine image (and probably risen humanity), and not humanity in general in its present situation.

6.1.2 The Immediate Narrative Context

The reading of the speech as a proclamation of the true image of the divine or true divine-likeness rather than Jewish monotheism is further corroborated by the immediate narrative context of the speech. As argued in chapter 2, it is noteworthy that the narrative clearly identifies the idolatry of the Athenians as a direct cause for Paul's proclamation in Athens (vv. 16–17). In this context, it would make sense that the heart of the apostle's proclamation should focus on the question of divine images. So far, exegetes have usually interpreted the speech as proclaiming Yahweh over against the idols of the Athenians as the only true god. But there is absolutely no sign in the narrative context that the polemic centred around Yahweh or a creator God. Rather, the Athenians – who must have known what Jewish 'religion' was about since they were curious (v. 21) and there was a synagogue in Athens (v. 17) – identify Paul's message as something new, and something about 'strange' gods in the plural. Luke comments that they drew this conclusion because Paul 'was preaching as good news Jesus and the resurrection' (τὸν Ἰησοῦν καὶ τὴν ἀνάστασιν εὐηγγελίζετο, v. 18). As has been argued, this assessment makes sense with a message which proclaims the resurrection of the dead, since resurrected people who live eternally could easily have been considered to be 'gods' according to Greek conceptions. In any case, Luke, the author, tells his readers that Paul's message in Athens was Jesus and the resurrection. The narrative context therefore suggests that the heart of the proclamation in Athens was Jesus and the resurrection, and not Jewish monotheism.

6.1.3 The Philosophical Teaching in Early Post-Hellenistic Times

Finally, the analysis of the historical context and the attitude of Stoic and Epicurean philosophers towards divine images also corroborates this new reading. Indeed, unlike what is sometimes assumed in the literature, the philosophers did not reject the usage of divine images. Rather, the philosophers were conscious of the limitations *and* the usefulness of using material, man-made images to express piety. They were thus not against their usage (sometimes even encouraging it), but they were emphatic about the dangers of identifying man-made images with the god itself. In addition, and above all, they were all adamant that piety is above all intellectual and ethical and consists in imitation of the divine. In this context, it would not make much sense for the speech to try to argue that 'idols are not gods, only Yahweh is.'[1] Indeed, no philosophers would have said that idols are 'real gods.' They would, however, have debated on what constitutes true divine-likeness for a human being. In this context, an argument which focuses on true divine representation through humanity is much more pertinent.

To conclude then, as highlighted in the analysis of the speech, there remain parts where the logic of the argument is not totally clear, because the speech is extremely concise. But reading the speech as aiming to proclaiming the risen man as the true image of God over against idols or humanity in general is much more coherent and promising. Indeed, it makes sense of the 'Christian conclusion' and shows that it is not an unrelated appendix, but in fact the climax of the speech. It also has the advantage of making this speech much more in keeping with the apostolic proclamation in Acts, which centres on the proclamation of the resurrection. More on this shall be said in section 3 of this chapter.

6.2 The Speech and the Greeks: A Rapprochement with Greek Philosophers?

Can we speak of a rapprochement between the Christian message and Greek philosophies in the speech? As highlighted in the introduction, it was Rowe's central thesis that the discourse in Athens cannot be seen as a rapprochement with the Greek philosophies of its day because of the nature of ancient philosophy.[2] At the same time, exegetes have criticized him for failing to provide a convincing explanation for the high degree of hellenization of the speech. Indeed, Rowe seemed to imply that the hellenization of the speech is only superficial and for the sake of immediate apologetic purposes. The present study corroborates Rowe's major conclusion in a new way, but challenges his interpretation of the hellenization of the speech. In summary, it shall be argued that while the speech would not have been perceived to represent a 'significant'

---

[1] The fact that idols are not gods, but only Yahweh is, is clearly an entailment of the speech. But not its main argument. On the other hand, the fact that Yahweh created the world and is its life-giver and sustainer is a presupposition of the speech which is never argued for.

[2] For philosophy as an art of life and a life-long commitment to self-improvement so as 'to approximate ever closer to the ideals of character-structure and relation to the world established by the great philosophers,' see also Trapp 2014: 49; Hadot 1995.

theological rapprochement by Greek philosophers, the speech *does* represent a clear rapprochement with its Greek audience, albeit not in the way argued by many past studies. This section ends with a suggestion concerning the challenge the speech is raising against the Greek philosophical teaching of its day.

6.2.1 No 'Significant' Rapprochement From a Philosophical Point of View

Both the analysis of the narrative context of the speech in chapter two and the study of the philosophical background outlined in chapter four suggest that it is fundamentally mistaken and misleading to see the speech in Acts 17 as a rapprochement – or at least a *significant* rapprochement – with Greek philosophy.

With respect to the immediate narrative context, both the Athenians' perception of Paul as announcing 'a new teaching' and their characterization of him as a *spermologos* or a 'proclaimer of foreign divinities' suggest that his message was not perceived as congenial. At best, the term *spermologos* might imply that he used some philosophical language or arguments, but this was obviously not perceived as a rapprochement since the term is derogatory. In fact, the narrative context depicts Paul as *debating* with the philosophers about issues connected to worship before they decided to bring him before the Areopagus. At the same time, by connecting the speech directly to a debate with Stoic and Epicurean philosophers, depicting Paul like a new Socrates and alluding to the *deisidaimonia* of the Athenians, the narrative confirms the importance of the philosophical athmosphere in the periocope. This strongly undermines interpretations of the speech which deny its attempt to intereact with philosophy.

In addition, chapter four corroborates this conclusion in a different and so far unexplored way. Indeed, this chapter has highlighted something too often overlooked in studies of Acts 17, namely the fact that the way the different philosophical schools in early post-hellenistic times interacted with each other was essentially polemical and competitive. Eclecticism, which was once thought to be the hallmark of Hellenistic philosophy at that time, was in fact rare. In this context, the philosophical schools sometimes used similar concepts and agreed on some points considered to be self-evident – such as the eternity of the divine or the fact that it cannot be evil. But they widely disagreed with each other and debated with each other on the rest.

Chapter four illustrates well this situation. It shows that the philosophical teaching of the Epicureans and the Stoics on the gods, *deisidaimonia* and proper worship or piety had several elements in common, and made some similar claims about the gods, yet they taught very different theologies and engaged in serious debate and polemics with each other about the exact nature of the divine and how it relates with humanity. In such a polemical context, the significance of the use of common terminology and arguments to assess theological rapprochement is strongly diminished. For example, both the Stoics and the Epicureans claimed that the gods are not served by human hands and do not need temples. But the Epicureans would hardly have perceived the Stoic affirmation of this claim as a 'theological' rapprochement with their own theology! Rather, this claim was part of philosophical common places about the gods and piety.

In this light, the speech's claims that the divine does not live in temples made by human hands, nor is served by human hands are unlikely to have been perceived as a meaningful rapprochement by the Athenians, much less by any of the philosophical schools.[3] Likewise, the belief that God made the earth and all what is in it was shared by the Stoics and the Platonists, who again engaged in serious debates with each other about the nature of the divine. Consequently, this assertion is also unlikely to have been perceived by the Stoics as a 'significant' rapprochement with their own worldview. The fact that the speech claims several things which were shared by several philosophical schools which hotly debated with each other and engaged in polemics about the nature of the gods, *deisidaimonia* and piety strongly relativizes the significance of this 'common ground' in terms of the speech's relationship with a particular philosophical school or even Greek philosophy more generally.

As discussed in the introduction, studies on Hellenistic Judaism have drawn attention to the dangers of overinterpreting the significance of hellenization in a thoroughly hellenized environment. The present study suggests that the presence of philosophical common places in the Areopagus speech has too often been overinterpreted, especially as rapprochement with the theology of the audience, whereas it would simply have been the common type of vocabulary and arguments used to talk about the subject at hand with a Greek audience. Understanding the background debate and the polemics between Epicurean and Stoic philosophers on the question of piety and the nature of the gods thus helps to explain why they perceived Paul's teaching as alien rather than congenial, even though it *does* contain philosophical common places. What makes a teaching congenial in such a context is not the use of similar arguments and motifs, but the whole complex of theology and worldview in service to which those arguments and motifs are used. Chapter four thus confirms the conclusions highlighted in chapter two, and explains this apparent tension between newness/collision and yet familiarity: the context is a debate between rival views on the divine and how humanity maintains peace with it.

---

[3] Trapp (2014: 51) notes that in the ancient world some people did occasionally try to focus on the common ground found in different philosophical schools rather than commit to a single one. But by and large, the default option, was 'to commit to one school of thought in distinction from the others, and to perpetuate the game of defending one's own and attacking the opposition by all means available.' Cf. Sedley 1989.

This project thus confirms Rowe's conclusion that the speech cannot be interpreted as a theological rapprochement with Greek philosophy – at least not a *significant* one – and that methodologically its relationship with Greek philosophy cannot be evaluated by measuring their continuity and discontinuity with each other at the level of motifs or even arguments.[4]

At the same time, on another level, the speech *does* represent a rapprochement with the audience at hand. And here the present thesis departs from Rowe's conclusion. As mentioned in the introduction, Rowe's reading of the speech failed to account for the strong degree of hellenization of the speech. The present study, however, suggests that the speech shows a very significant rapprochement with the audience at hand by *engaging* the philosophical debates of its day to a great degree on the turf of its narrative audience. This, it shall be argued, explains the very high degree of hellenization of the speech.

6.2.2 A Speech 'at Home' in – and Engaged With – the Debates About Deisidaimonia, Piety and Peace With the Gods Among Stoic and Epicurean Philosophers

Whereas the speech's argument would never have been considered a serious theological rapprochement by a philosophically trained audience, it must nonetheless be considered a rapprochement with the audience at hand for several reasons. First, it is a rapprochement in that it tackles a 'religious concern' *of the Athenian*s which the philosophers also sought to address: *deisidaimonia* and peace with the gods. It thus engages the subject of peace with the divine on the turf of its Greek audience. Furthermore, the argument of the speech suggests an awareness of the presuppositions, terminology, common places, type of arguments and even some of the nuances of the teachings of Greek philosophers related to the subject. Not only so, but the speech uses and builds much of its argumentation using terminology (ἄγνοια, δεισιδαιμονία, τὸ θεῖον) and arguments commonly used in philosophical discussions of this topic.

This is one of the major contributions of the study of the religious and especially the philosophical background implied by the narrative world in chapter four. Indeed, it highlights that many of the topics which appear in the speech and several of the arguments used by the speech are precisely the topics and arguments which are found in the philosophical debates about *deisidaimonia*, piety and the gods in early post-Hellenistic times. In fact, several aspects of the speech which have seemed strange or off the subject to scholars (especially in the Christian conclusion), were very much expected and at home in a debate on this subject with philosophers.

For example, exegetes have long been puzzled by the sudden mention of divine judgment, justice or the resurrection in the conclusion of the speech. But

---

[4] This point had also been emphasized by Conzelmann 1966.

the study of the meaning of *deisidaimonia* and the philosophical debates about it show that to talk about averting divine hostility and how to be free of fearing the gods meant discussing the topics of divine judgment, and the question of the goodness and the justice of the gods. It also regularly meant discussing post-mortem divine retribution or reward. In this context, the subjects of divine judgment, post-mortem judgment or even the resurrection appear not at all off topic. On the contrary, they are very much the type of themes which a Greek audience – even philosophically less trained audience – would have expected and found key in discussing this subject. It was not enough for the philosophers to say that one should not fear the gods: they had to explain why and be convincing. And if both the Stoics and the Epicureans were adamant in claiming that the gods cannot do evil and thus should not be feared, they were also keen to maintain that the gods were *somehow* involved in the administration of justice, and they believed in a form of divine retribution. To think otherwise would have made the gods either less good, or possibly complicit in evil.

Furthermore, the description of the attitude of Stoic and Epicurean philosophers towards the traditional cult and especially towards the use of divine images made in chapter four, shows that the angle taken by the speech makes sense in the context at hand. Indeed, neither the Stoics nor the Epicureans were rejecting the traditional cult, nor the veneration of images, for both philosophical schools could see didactic advantages in the use of such representations. At the same time, the philosophers, especially the Stoics, strongly denounced the identification of the statues with the gods themselves, and they were very aware of the limitation of those images to represent the divine, especially because they were not living images.

Interestingly, the speech in Acts 17 never attempts to convince its audience that idols are not gods. And indeed, it would have been unnecessary to try to convince a philosophically educated audience that idols are not gods: that was not the debated issue. Rather, the speech is discussing godlikeness and how one can truly represent the divine, and this is what was debated among the philosophers. Likewise, it would not have been a very earthshattering claim to say that man-made divine representations are not worthy divine representations. And indeed, although the speech builds upon this assumption (v. 29), it does not stop at this claim – which is a well-shared belief – but goes on to make a truly new and controversial claim: the risen man is the one worthy to be this divine representation.

In sum, those chapters suggest that a Greek philosophically educated audience would have been able to follow much of the argument of the speech. Above all, the philosophers were familiar with the argument that only living beings can worthily represent the divine, just like they were familiar with the idea that humanity is ideally to embody divine-likeness and be a worthy statue of the gods, and they shared the belief that true piety is ultimately at least partly ethical – namely imitation of the gods. This is not to claim that the philosophers would have agreed with the argument of the speech, much less that they would have found the resurrection believable: indeed, many did not (v. 32). But the speech is not, as Pervo argues, 'a muddled collection of clichés with an unexpected and improbable conclusion,'[5] nor is it, as Rowe's and other exegetes' interpretations seem to suggest, a speech which would only make sense to a Christian audience.

The speech thus *does* represent a rapprochement with the Greek audience, and this explains why it is so different from the other speeches in Acts, especially the discourses addressed to the Jews: the speech is clearly tailored to the audience at hand. The subject of divine judgment is tackled from the angle of Graeco-Roman culture – i.e. the question of how to maintain peace with the gods (*pax deorum*) and avert divine hostility. The speech appeals to the philosophical presuppositions of the Greeks about the divine, uses their vocabulary and the arguments they were themselves using when discussing this subject. But rather than a *significant* rapprochement with their theology, it is a rapprochement with their own debates on the questions of *deisidaimonia*, piety and the nature of the gods, and a willingness to use and build upon philosophical common places about the divine and piety in its own argumentation.

It is this willingness to enter the *debate* (as suggested in chapter 2) of the philosophers and the concerns of the Athenians which explains the high degree of hellenization of the speech. In this respect, it is important to note that this rapprochement is more than just 'formal' or 'superficial' with the use of some similar terminology and the occasional common argument, as some exegetes have suggested (Rowe seems to imply this). Rather, this project suggests that it was a real attempt to enter a debate or conversation with Epicurean and Stoic philosophers on their points of contention about piety, the nature of the gods, and the way to avert their hostility. While the terminology and arguments used in the speech must thus not be interpreted as 'significant' theological rapprochement then, those elements, and especially the argument of the speech itself, show a level of engagement with the beliefs and presuppositions of the audience much deeper than what past scholarship has discerned so far. In fact, the speech does not just engage the issue of the use of material divine images in worship, but it tackles also the deeper philosophical issue of godlikeness and divine justice.

6.2.3 A New Teaching in Athens: The Challenge of the Speech to Greek Philosophies

In what way then does the message of the speech depart from the philosophical teaching of its day on peace with the divine and godlikeness, and represent a 'new teaching' (ἡ καινὴ διδαχή v. 19) ? A few suggestions have been made

---

[5] Pervo 2008: 430.

throughout the analysis of the speech in chapter five. The discourse, however, is very brief, and what is suggested in this respect must therefore remain tentative. Perhaps two elements might nonetheless help in this respect. First, the discussion of the teachings of Stoic and Epicurean philosophers on the subject of *deisidaimonia* and relationship with the gods in chapter four provides a foil with which to compare the argument of the speech and identify where it departs from them. And second, in light of the narrative context of the speech in Acts 17, the particular emphases of Paul's discourse are probably the points which the narrator wishes to stress over against the Athenians.

To summarize the teaching of the philosophers, as highlighted in chapter four, the Stoics and the Epicureans denounced *deisidaimonia* as impiety because it is a fear – or sometimes by metonymy practices and beliefs associated with it – based on the mistaken belief that the gods are harmful and evil. Against it the Epicureans emphasized that the gods cannot be influenced by *ira* or *gratia*, and that they therefore do not interfere in human affairs and do not harm. The Stoics, on the other hand, emphasized that god is good and provident, and that a right understanding of the good enables the wise to see that god is not evil.[6]

Conversely, both Stoics and Epicureans taught that true worship, piety or peace with the gods is ultimately expressed and gained by imitating them, namely godlikeness. Although this teaching was also accompanied by a cognitive element – true piety is also expressed by having a right notion of the gods—and a practical element – generally, following the practices of traditional religion as far as they are compatible with a right view of the gods, piety thus had an important ethical overtone in both Stoicism and Epicureanism. For the Stoics, gaining over the goodwill of the gods necessitates to be a 'good' man and practice virtue. For the Epicureans, to benefit from the gods, the philosopher must seek to harm no one and have a 'placated' spirit like the gods. As for the use of divine images to worship the gods, while they were critical of some aspects of the practice and vehemently criticized the assimilation of the statues with the gods themselves, both Epicureanism and Stoicism had not only accommodated it, but even found some truth and positive elements in this practice. At the same time, both Epicurean and Stoic philosophers insisted that the gods do not need the service of human beings, and that true piety first of all constitutes in having a right opinion about the gods, and then in emulating them, i.e., godlikeness. This was the way one could have peace with the gods.

Turning then to the speech, it is noteworthy that its main line of argumentation centres on describing a human-divine relationship in which humanity is decidedly at the receiving end. It is God who provides life, breath and all, and

---

[6] It is important at this point to emphasize that the divine punishment of the wicked or of injustice was not understood as harm or evil by the philosophers. On the contrary, it was seen as justice for the good, and healing for the wicked.

not humanity who can provide anything to God. Furthermore, the speech stresses God's role, not only in providing 'life and breath' (v. 25) to all, but also in providing the conditions which make it possible for humanity to sustain life – namely the seasons, and dwelling places (v. 26). Above all, it also stresses that those conditions, which ensure humanity's life, are what *God* put in place so that humanity would be able to seek and feel God, and indeed so that through this divine provision humanity itself might in some sense be a witness to God (v. 28).

In parallel to that, the speech strongly contrasts divine with human *activity*, underscoring not only that humanity cannot provide or make anything for God, but also that humanity cannot make true divine images through its own creation, since they are lifeless. Thus, v. 29 strongly contrasts two creators: God, the creator of living humanity, with humanity the creator of lifeless images. And it stresses that *because of this reality*, because *God* is the provider of the life of humanity, humanity does not have to believe that the divine is like lifeless things. The basis of the argument is thus the fact that *God* is humanity's life provider (γένος ὑπάρχοντες τοῦ θεοῦ), and not humanity.

By v. 28 then, the speech has been stressing that God is the creator and sustainer of what is supposed to be his image, namely humanity, and that *he* is the one who enables it to have this role through the gift of life. At the same time, the speech has intimated that there are problems with this image, since humanity struggles to get a feel for and find God. It is noteworthy that up to this point (namely v. 28), the speech has not yet affirmed anything really new for a philosophical audience.

What is interesting is what comes afterwards, both in terms of what the speech affirms and what it does not say. Indeed, verse 29 does not go on to affirm, as we would expect by then, that humanity is God's image. Neither does the speech explicitly states that humanity ought to seek divine-likeness and emulate the divine to become a worthy image of the divine. Yet this is most likely what the philosophers would have taught at this point of the speech. As highlighted in chapter four, the Stoics taught that true piety and thus friendship with the gods is reached by 'moulding oneself' into a worthy image of the divine, mainly by emulating the divine ethically. And the Epicureans likewise taught that piety implies to imitate the divine. But the speech does not go down that path. Rather, in v. 29, the speech first stresses a question of *belief* (νομίζειν) in light of *God's* provision of life to humanity. And then verses 30 and 31 go on to affirm that God has raised a human being as a proof of what he is truly like and how he will judge the world. Those verses thus reveal the true divine image and representative: it is the risen man, who will judge the world in righteousness. But they also depict God bringing about this image of himself by raising him from the dead. Verses 29–31 might thus well be an appeal to believe that God can raise humanity from the dead to make it into his worthy image. In this sense, it is an appeal to have 'faith' in this God who has proved (cf. πίστιν, in v. 31) his power to do such a thing through the resurrection, and who, as the creator, has always had this kind of relationship with humanity.

Of course, the speech also calls humanity to repentance, a repentance from false beliefs about God and godlikeness, but also most likely from unrighteousness more generally. There might thus also be an implicit criticism of humanity having failed to truly represent the divine. But the emphasis of the whole speech on God's life-giving power, the focus on the call to belief in v. 29 and the narrative context which identifies the good news (εὐηγγελίζετο, v. 18) of Jesus and the resurrection as the subject of the message suggest that the speech does not just make an ethical call to divine imitation in the manner of the philosophers, but that it calls for a belief in God's divine power to 'make humanity' truly like God through the resurrection.

Although this cannot be affirmed categorically, then, in light of the emphases of the speech and what was taught by the philosophers, one wonders whether the discourse is not challenging the philosophical belief and teaching that humanity can and must emulate the divine and make itself into a divine image. Indeed, the whole speech criticizes the human attempt to take care of the divine or divine images, and highlights its inability to create worthy divine images. In parallel, it highlights that humanity is constantly at the receiving end in its relationship to God, and that it is God's gift of life which is paramount in the creation of a worthy image. Against the philosophical view that humanity ought to imitate the divine in order to be a worthy image and have peace with it then, the discourse seems to emphasizes that humanity must believe that the life-giving God is the one who gives everything to humanity to enable it to be this living image, and that only he can create it. In this context, the resurrection seems to announce that God's gift of eternal life is necessary to make humanity godlike. It seems also that the risen man as the true image of God plays a role in enabling human beings to become like him.

As argued in chapter five then, while the speech, like the Stoic philosophers for example, underscores that it is God who provides all for humanity and not human beings which serve him, it seems to use this argument differently, namely to contrast divine and human activity and put humanity resolutely on the receiving hand in the divine-human relationship. And ultimately, the speech highlights the limitation of the practice of divine imitation: humanity is not able to give life to what is lifeless, only God can.

6.3 Christology and the Proclamation of the Kerygma to the Gentiles in Acts

The interpretation argued for in this project has significant consequences for the assessment of the function of Christology in the speech in Athens and thus also the nature of the Christian proclamation to the Gentiles in Acts. As mentioned several times in this project, it has been a consensus in scholarship that the purpose of the speech is to announce the nature of Yahweh, the creator of heaven and earth. Some scholars have even affirmed that the speech in Athens does not announce Jesus or the gospel at all, but that it only focuses on the doctrine of God. For Jervell, this reflects the fact that for Luke, the gospel is not preached outside of the synagogue. The speech is thus an anomaly in the book (*ein Fremdkörper*) meant to demonstrate 'das Nein der Kirche zum ausserjüdischen Heidentum.'[7] For Schnabel, this absence rather shows that the speech does not represent a typical missionary speech to the Gentiles.

Paul's speech is traditionally regarded as an example of the early Christian missionary preaching before pagan audiences. However, in the context of Acts 17, Paul's speech is a special case of missionary preaching before Gentiles at best: the philosophers and the council members asked Paul to give an account of the deity that he was preaching. In other words, Paul did not explain his message of Jesus, Kyrios and Saviour of the world, when he spoke before the Areopagus; rather, he explained his concept of God. It is not only the historical context but also the flow of the argumentation of the speech itself that indicates that the only topic is the concept and the knowledge of God. Paul explains in his dialogue with the philosophers and council members who are present *one* of the themes that he presented in his public teaching activity, namely his doctrine of God.[8]

Other scholars, however, note that both verses 18 and 31 suggest that Jesus and the resurrection were part of the proclamation in Athens. For them, while the speech focuses on the proclamation of Yahweh, the narrative also makes clear that Jesus was part of the proclamation, although it follows the teaching about Yahweh. On this reading, however, the speech in Athens still differs significantly from other speeches addressed to the Jews in Acts, whose focus is on Jesus. Many scholars explain this difference by the context at hand and the necessity to first correct the Gentile's notion of the divine, before announcing Jesus. Indeed, whereas belief in the one true God can be presupposed with Jewish audiences in Acts, this monotheism must first be affirmed to the Gentile audience in Athens. For example, Dunn writes:

In short, the Christology is subordinated to the theology; the developing Christological distinctives of Christian faith are subordinated to the prior task of winning appropriate belief in God.[9]

While Dunn also notes that 'the focus on resurrection in both 17.18 and 31 confirms that in a Greek context as well as a Jewish (see Ac 2:24; also 4:1–2 and 23.6) the claim that God had raised Jesus from the dead stood at the centre

---

[7] Jervell 1998: 455.
[8] Schnabel 2005: 178. See also Tannehill (1991: n.39, p.414) who argues that the Areopagus speech 'does not represent the full missionary message,' but only reflects 'the special preparation necessary with those not yet ready to understand "Jesus and the resurrection" (17.18).'
[9] Dunn 1996: 231. Cf. Conzelmann 1966: 227–228.

of the Christian gospel,'[10] his commentary reflects the assumption that the proclamation to the Gentiles in Acts began with the proclamation of the Jewish God and monotheism – the first article of faith, and was then followed by the second one on Jesus.

The reading defended in this project, however, challenges this understanding. Indeed, it argues that Christology is the very climax of the speech because it represents the revelation of what *God* is like. In other words, Christology is neither subordinate nor complementary to the proclamation of the nature of God, it *is* the proclamation of the nature of God and how one is to relate to him. The righteous and risen man is the image of God, and it is only in him that true godlikeness and true piety are revealed. The speech is clearly unfinished and makes no meaningful or new assertion before the final verses proclaim the resurrection of Jesus, and therefore the nature of God's righteousness and true piety. Admittedly, the description of God implied in the first part of the speech forms the context in which the Christology of the final verses makes sense. In this sense, theology does open up the way to Christology in Acts 17. But it is the Christological part of the speech which, *in the context of the debates at hand*, represents the crucial and new affirmation about theology in the speech. It is the risen man who reveals God's justice and his goodness, and his power to give life to the dead.

This has important consequences for assessing how the Christian message and movement relate to Judaism and to the Gentiles in Acts, two central questions in Acts scholarship. It is not uncommon to find scholars affirming that the speech in Athens is 'an apology for the Jewish understanding of God'[11] or a defence of monotheism. But the speech significantly departs from classical apologetic Jewish presentations of God by claiming that this God is represented by a man who was risen from the dead and will judge the world. The speech's aim is thus not to proclaim the Jewish God and monotheism *and then* the Christian part of the kerygma, but to proclaim that the true powerful and righteous God is revealed in Jesus. This reading is corroborated by the fact that the Athenians did not perceive the apostle to be preaching Jewish doctrine, but some 'new teaching.' That the author believes that this is the Jewish God of the Old Testament is clear from the broader narrative of Acts. But at no point is he announcing this God apart from his revelation through the resurrected man.

Consequently, and turning to the nature of the kerygma in Gentile contexts in Acts, the speech in Athens suggests that the resurrection of Jesus is not an additional complementary part of the message preached to the Gentiles, but the very means by which the nature of the true God is proclaimed to the nations. This mitigates claims that the proclamation of the gospel to the gentiles in Acts necessitates first the proclamation of the Jewish God and monotheism and that

---

[10] Dunn 1996: 231.
[11] Dunn 1996: 236.

the Old Testament and the synagogue alone can prepare for the gospel as Jervell claims. Rather, Luke has crafted a speech in which the central Christian message is proclaimed to an audience without any Jewish background. Not only so, but even more importantly, an understanding of the issues and debates in Greek philosophy and religion in early Post-Hellenistic times shows that Luke presents the central Christian message as a new teaching about what were also Greek concerns and Greek debated questions: the means of averting divine hostility and having peace with the gods, and the affirmation of the goodness and justice of the gods and their reward of the good, despite the presence of evil and injustice in the world.

This challenges the view that the speech in Acts 17 is a *Fremdkörper* in Acts on the theological level.[12] Of course, comparing Acts 17 with the other speeches in Acts to determine their common points and differences is beyond the scope of the present project. But in light of the thesis of this project, it cannot be affirmed that the speech is a foreign body because it does not proclaim what the other speeches announce, namely 'Jesus and the resurrection.' While the speech in Acts 17 is certainly peculiar *in the way* it approaches its subject because of its audience, it still proclaims the exact same message: Jesus, the resurrection and the coming judgment.

Likewise, as argued in chapter five and although this interpretation remains more tentative, the speech does seem to include the good news by implying that, by resurrecting this man, God also opened up the way for the rest of humanity to receive eternal life. This would explain why, in v. 32, the Athenians understood the speech to speak about 'a resurrection of dead persons' in the plural (ἀνάστασιν νεκρῶν) and not just about 'a resurrection from the dead' (ἀνάστασιν ἐκ νεκρῶν) as would have been the case if the speech only announced the resurrection of Jesus. Such a reading is also suggested by the way Luke summarizes the message in Athens as '*the good news* of Jesus and the resurrection'(τὸν ᾿Ιησοῦν καὶ τὴν ἀνάστασιν **εὐηγγελίζετο**) in v. 18 and possibly by the fact that part of the philosophers had the feeling that Paul was announcing new divinities in the plural. The Christological focus of the speech highlighted by the present project certainly suggests that v. 18 is a trustworthy summary of the content of the message in Athens according to Luke.

---

[12] For Jervell, the speech in Athens is a 'foreign body' in terms of both content (i.e. theology) and form (language and style). Cf. Jervell 1998: 452. As argued in section 6.2, the speech is indeed peculiar in Acts in terms of its form.

6.4 The Christian Movement, Graeco-Roman Culture and the Purpose of Acts

In conclusion, a final word must be said about the way this project contributes to the scholarly discussion on Luke's attitude towards Graeco-Roman culture and his purposes in composing his double-work. As highlighted in the introduction, Acts 17 has been a key text to assess those perennial questions in Lukan scholarship and has been used to support very different theses concerning the attitude of the Christian movement towards Graeco-Roman culture in Acts. It would be inappropriate to make general claims about Acts based solely on the analyse of this pericope, but two points can be made here to guide further research.

First, as highlighted in one of the preceding sections, the present project demonstrates the problems with Jervell's thesis, namely that the Areopagus speech represents the 'no' of the church to *ausserjüdisches Heidentum*. This project thus corroborates the assessment of many who have criticized Jervell for underestimating the importance of the mission to the Gentiles in Luke's literary project.[13] In particular, it suggests that the 'good news' of the resurrection of Jesus was announced to an audience of Gentiles *who had no connection with Judaism and were steeped in paganism*, as an answer to their apparent fear of the gods and concern to maintain peace with them. Not only so, but although the speech assumes an OT worldview, the message makes little appeal to specific Jewish knowledge and rather builds upon Greek philosophical commonplaces about piety and the nature of a creator god endorsed by some philosophers.

On the other hand, the reading suggested by this project also challenges the view that Luke depicts the Christian movement and message as peacefully accommodationist of Graeco-Roman culture. In fact, the interpretation suggested in this project argues that the speech is not only a critique of idolatry or polytheism, but a call addressed to *all* to repent from mistaken beliefs about God and godlikeness, and to repent from unrighteousness. It thus articulates a much more fundamental criticism than the question of the materiality of divine representations, and includes the philosophers in its criticism. What Acts 17 calls for is more than the removal of idols, something which some philosophers might well have accommodated, but a repentance and new vision of God, his representative and divine-likeness.

Finally, this project raises questions for the claim that the Areopagus speech illustrates Luke's apologetic purposes, because it seeks to 'defend' or 'legitimate' the Christian message and movement by showing that it shares much common ground with the best of Greek philosophy.[14] Indeed, as highlighted in

---

[13] Cf. Butticaz 2011: 15.
[14] Malherbe 1989: 152; Jipp 2012.

the discussion of the meaning of the hellenization of the speech, not only do the Athenians of his narrative not perceive Paul to bring a teaching congenial to their own, but the historical background shows that the commonplaces invoked by the speech would not have been understood as significant rapprochement. Likewise, it is unlikely that the speech aims to convince the philosophers of inconsistency with their own beliefs because they still engage in the Graeco-Roman cult, since both the Epicureans and the Stoics had rationales for doing so.

Most importantly, the speech does actually present something new and hardly believable which challenges common philosophical conceptions, even if it proceeds within some accepted Greek common places. This is confirmed by the mockery of part of the Greeks at the end of the speech. All those elements suggest that the speech is not concerned primarily with proving its legitimacy through a rapprochement, but with the proclamation of a *novum* which, while in agreement with several Greek common places and presented as an answer to a Greek concern, departs from, and challenges, both Stoic and Epicurean teaching in important ways. Luke thus rather presents the Christian kerygma as a rival to the Stoic and Epicurean teaching on the question of peace with the divine. At the same time, Luke *does* paint the Christian message as the answer to what were also Greek questions. In this sense, this passage probably has an apologetic value, although what is meant by this word would need to be carefully defined.

It is of course not possible to conclude from this very limited study that Luke is not concerned with apologetic purposes towards the Graeco-Roman world in his work. Above all, the word 'apologetic' can be understood along different lines, and need not be incompatible with, for example, a proselytic endeavour.[15] But this study certainly constitutes a warning against too quickly interpreting any kind of 'hellenization' or use of 'Greek' motifs as signs of an apologetic endeavour in a defensive sense.[16] It is still a widespread assumption in Acts scholarship that the early Christians would have felt the need to respond defensively to the majority culture or legitimate themselves with respect to, or through the script of, this majority culture.[17] In the case of the Areopagus speech, however, while Luke presents the Christian message as a rival to Greek philosophical traditions and is concerned to convince its Greek audience by using common Hellenistic terminology and arguments, the specific nature of the argumentation seems to be more dictated by the subject and the audience at hand rather than by a concern for legitimacy or defensive apologetic. Indeed,

---

[15] On this subject, cf. Carleton Paget 2010: esp. 164.

[16] See, for example, Aitken (2004: 339) who criticizes Hengel's book because it still presumes that 'a writer in Greek would have apologetic purposes whether addressing Jews or Greeks,' and not allowing 'for other possible explanations.'

[17] E.g., Malherbe 1989.

the speech not only does not shy away from proclaiming the new and culturally most shocking aspect of the Christian message to its Greek audience, but it actually climaxes on it: '… and of this God gave proof, by raising him from the dead' (v. 31).

Bibliography

Primary Texts

Aratus. *Phaenomena: Edited with Introduction, Translation and Commentary*. Edited by Douglas A. Kidd. Cambridge: Cambridge University Press, 1997.
Arius Didymus. *Epitome of Stoic Ethics*. Edited by Arthur J. Pomeroy. Atlanta, GA: Society of Biblical Literature, 1999.
Augustine. *De civitate Dei. Book X. Edited with an Introduction, Translation and Commentary*. Edited and translated by Patrick G. Walsh. Oxford: Aris & Phillips, 2014.
Callimachus, Lycophron and Aratus. Translated by A.W. Mair and G.R. Mair. LCL 129. London: William Heinemann, 1921.
Cleanthes. *Hymn to Zeus: Text, Translation, and Commentary*. Edited by Johan C. Thom. STAC 33. Tübingen: Mohr Siebeck, 2005.
Cicero. *On Old Age. On Friendship. On Divination*. Translated by W. A. Falconer. LCL 154. Cambridge, MA: Harvard University Press, 1932.
–. *On the Nature of the Gods. Academics*. Translated by H. Rackham. LCL 268. Cambridge, MA: Harvard University Press, 1933.
–. *M. Tulli Ciceronis De natura deorum*. Edited by Arthur Stanley Pease. 2 vols. Darmstadt: Wissenschaftliche Buchgesellschaft, 1968 [1955].
Cornutus. *Cornuti Theologiae Graecae Compendium*. Edited by Carolus Lang. Leipzig: Teubner, 1881.
Dio Chrysostom. *Discourses 1-11*. Translated by J. W. Cohoon. LCL 257. Cambridge, MA: Harvard University Press, 1932.
Diodorus Siculus. *Historical Library*. Translated by Russel M Geer, C. H. Oldfather, Charles L Sherman, Francis R. Walton, and C. Bradford Welles. 12 vols. LCL. Cambridge, MA: Harvard University Press, 1967–1984.
Diogenes Laertius. *The Lives of Eminent Philosophers*. Translated by R. D. Hicks. 2 vols. LCL 184–5. Cambridge, MA: Harvard University Press, 1979–1980.
Epictetus. *The Discourses as Reported by Arrian*, The Manual, and Fragments. Translated by W.A. Oldfather. 2 vols. LCL. Cambridge, MA: Harvard University Press, 1956–1959.
Epicurea. Edited by Hermann Usener. Cambridge: Cambridge University Press, 2010 [1887].
Fragments from Hellenistic Jewish Authors. Vol. III. Aristobulus. Edited by Holladay, Carl R. Atlanta: Scholars, 1995.
Ishoʻdad of Merv. *Commentaries of Ishoʻdad of Merv, Bishop of Ḥadatha (ca. 850 A.D.): in Syriac and English*. Vol 4: *Acts of the Apostles and Three Catholic Epistles*. Edited and translated by Margaret Dunlop Gipson. Cambridge: Cambridge University Press, 1913.
Josephus. *Jewish Antiquities*. Edited by William Whiston. London: 1828.
–. *Jewish Antiquities*: Books XII–XIV. Translated by Ralph Marcus. LCL. Cambridge, MA: Harvard University Press, 1957.
Lucian. Translated by K. Kilburn. Vol. 6. LCL 430. Cambridge, MA: Harvard University Press, 1963.

Lucretius. *De rerum natura Libri Sex. Edited with Prolegomena, Critical Apparatus, Translation and Commentary.* 3 vols. Edited by Cyril Bailey. Oxford: Clarendon Press, 1947.
–. *De rerum natura.* Translated by W. H. D. Rouse and revised by Martin F. Smith. LCL 181. Cambridge, MA: Harvard University Press, 2002.
Philodemus. *On Piety: Critical Text with Commentary.* Part 1. Edited by Dirk Obbink. Oxford: Clarendon, 1996.
–. *On Piety.* Part 2 = P. Herc. 1428 = Henrichs, A. 1974. "Die Kritik der stoischen Theologie im PHerc. 1428." *CErc* 4: 5–32.
–. *De dis, book I =* Diels, H. 1916. "Philodemus über die Götter, Erstes Buch." APAW, Philosophisch-historische Klasse, Nr. 7 (Text und Erläuterung).
–. *De dis, book III =* Diels, H. 1917. "Philodemus über die Götter, Drittes Buch." APAW, Nr. 4 (Text) und 6 (Erläuterung).
[–]. [*On Choice and Avoidances*]: *Edited with Translation and Commentary.* Edited by Indelli, Giovanni and Voula Tsouna-McKirahan. La scuola di Epicuro 15. Naples: Bibliopolis, 1995.
Plutarch. *Lives.* Translated by Bernadotte Perrin. 11 vols. LCL. Cambridge, MA: Harvard University Press, 1914–26.
–. *Moralia.* Translated by Frank Cole Babbitt, William C. Helmbold, Philip H. De Lacy, Herbert B. Hoffleit, Edwin L. Minar, F. H. Sandbach, Harold North Fowler, Lionel Pearson, Harold Cherniss and Benedict Einarson. Vol. 1–55. LCL. Cambridge, MA: Harvard University Press, 1967–1984.
Seneca. *Epistles.* Tramslated by R. M. Gummere. Cambridge, MA: Harvard University Press, 1917–1925.
–. *Moral Essays.* 3 vols. LCL. Translated by J. W. Basore. LCL 75–77. Cambridge, MA: Harvard University Press, 1928–1935.
Strabo. *Geography.* Translated by Leonard Jones. 8 vols. LCL. Cambridge, MA: Harvard,
Stoicorum Veterum Fragmenta (*SVF*). Edited by Hans F. A. von Arnim. 4 vols. Leipzig: Teubner, 1903–1924.
The Hellenistic Philosophers. Edited by A. A. Long and David Sedley. 2 vols. Cambridge: Cambridge University Press, 1987.
Theophrastus. *Characters.* Edited by James Diggle. Cambridge: Cambridge University Press, 2004.

Commentaries

Barrett, C. K. 2004. *A Critical and Exegetical Commentary on the Acts of the Apostles.* Vol.2: *Introduction and Commentary on Acts XV–XXVIII.* ICC. London: T&T Clark.
Bauernfeind, Otto. 1980. *Kommentar und Studien zur Apostelgeschichte.* Tübingen: Mohr.
Beyer, Hermann Wolfgang. 1949. *Die Apostelgeschichte.* 5th ed. Göttingen: Vandenhoeck & Ruprecht.
Conzelmann, Hans. 1987. *Acts of the Apostles: A Commentary on the Acts of the Apostles.* Hermeneia. Philadelphia: Fortress.
Dunn, James D. G. 1996. *The Acts of the Apostles.* Epworth Commentaries. Peterborough: Epworth.
Fitzmyer, Joseph A. 1998. *The Acts of the Apostles: A New Translation with Introduction and Commentary.* AB 31. New Haven: Yale University Press.

Foakes-Jackson, F.J. and Kirsopp Lake, eds. 1922–1939. *The Beginnings of Christianity.* Part I. *The Acts of the Apostles.* 5 vols. London: Macmillan.
Gaventa, Beverly Roberts. 2002. *The Acts of the Apostles.* ANTC. Nashville, TN: Abingdon.
Haenchen, Ernst. 1971. *The Acts of the Apostles: A Commentary.* Oxford: Basil Blackwell.
Holladay, Carl R. 2016. *Acts. A Commentary.* Louisville: Westminster John Knox.
Jervell, Jacob. 1998. *Die Apostelgeschichte.* KEKNT 3. Göttingen: Vandenhoeck & Ruprecht.
Johnson, Luke Timothy. 1992. *The Acts of the Apostles.* SP 5. Collegeville, MN: Liturgical Press.
Marguerat, Daniel. 2007. *Les Actes des Apôtres (1–12).* Vol. 1. Genève : Labor et Fides.
–. 2015. *Les Actes Des Apôtres (13–28).* Vol. 2. Genève : Labor et Fides.
Marshall, I. Howard. 1980. *The Acts of the Apostles: An Introduction and Commentary.* Leicester: Inter-Varsity Press.
Pervo, Richard I. 2008. *Acts: A Commentary.* Hermeneia. Philadelphia: Fortress.
Polhill, John. 1992. *Acts.* NAC 26. Nashville: Broadman Press.
Schnabel, Eckhard J. 2012. *Acts.* ZECNT. Grand Rapids: Zondervan.
Schneider, Gerhard. 1980. *Die Apostelgeschichte: Einleitung. Kommentar zu Kap. 1,1 – 8,40.* Vol. 1. HThKNT 5. Freiburg: Herder.
–. 1982. *Die Apostelgeschichte: Kommentar zu Kap. 9,1 – 28,31.* Vol. 2. HThKNT 5. Freiburg: Herder.
Tannehill, Robert C. 1986–1990. *The Narrative Unity of Luke-Acts: A Literary Interpretation.* Vol. 1–2. Philadelphia: Fortress Press.
Walaskay, Paul W. 1998. *Acts.* Louisville: Westminster John Knox Press.
Weiser, Alfons. 1985. *Die Apostelgeschichte: Kapitel 13–28.* ÖKTNT 5.2. Würzburg: Gütersloh und Echter.
Wendt, Hans Hinrich. 1913. *Die Apostelgeschichte.* Von der 5. Auflage an neu bearbeitet. Göttingen: Vandenhoeck & Ruprecht.
Zahn, Theodor. 1921. *Die Apostelgeschichte des Lucas. Zweite Hälfte Kap. 13–28.* First and second edition. Leipzig: Deichert.

Secondary Literature

Adams, Sean A. 2012. "The Genre of Luke and Acts: The State of the Question." Pages 97–120 in *Issues in Luke-Acts: Selected Essays.* Edited by Sean A. Adams and Michael Pahl. Piscataway, NJ: Gorgias Press.
Aitken, J.K. 2004. Review of Martin Hengel, *Judentum und Hellenismus. JBL* 123:331–41.
Alexander, Loveday. 1999. "The Acts of the Apostles as an Apologetic Text." Pages 15–44 in *Apologetics in the Roman Empire: Pagans, Jews, and Christians.* Edited by M. Edwards et al. New York: Oxford University Press.
Algra, Keimpe. 2003. "Stoic Theology." Pages 153–178 in *The Cambridge Companion to the Stoics.* Edited by Brad Inwood. Cambridge: Cambridge University Press.
–. 2007a. *Conception and Images: Hellenistic Philosophical Theology and Traditional Religion.* Amsterdam: Koninklijke Nederlandse Akademie van Wetenschappen.
–. 2007b. "Epictetus and Stoic Theology." Pages 32–55 in *The Philosophy of Epictetus.* Edited by Theodore Scaltsas and Andrew S. Mason. Oxford: Oxford University Press.
–. 2009. "Stoic Philosophical Theology and Graeco-Roman Religion." Pages 224–251 in *God and Cosmos in Stoicism.* Edited by Ricardo Salles. Oxford: Oxford University Press.

André, J.-M. 1983. "Sénèque théologien: l'évolution de sa pensée jusqu'au *De superstitione*." *Helmantica* 34: 55–71.
Attridge, Harold W. 1978. "The Philosophical Critique of Religion under the Early Empire." *ANRW* 16.1: 45–78.
Babut, Daniel. 1969. *Plutarque et le stoïcisme*. Paris: Presses universitaires de France.
–. 1974. *La religion des philosophes grecs*. Paris: Presses universitaires de France.
–. 2004. "Notice." In Plutarque. *Oeuvres Morales*, vol. XV.1, Traité 70, *Sur les contradictions stoïciennes*. Traité 71, *Synopsis du traité Que les Stoïciens tiennent des propos plus paradoxaux que les poètes*. Edited by M. Casevitz and Daniel Babut. Collection des Universités de France. Paris: Belles Lettres.
Balch, David L. 1990. "The Areopagus Speech: An Appeal to the Stoic Historian Posidonius against Later Stoics and the Epicureans." Pages 52–79 in *Greeks, Romans, and Christians: Essays in Honor of Abraham J. Malherbe*. Edited by David L. Balch, Everett Ferguson and Wayne A. Meeks. Minneapolis: Fortress, 1990.
Baldassarri, Mariano. 1996. "Inquadramento filosofico del *De superstitione* Plutarcheo." Pages 373–387 in *Plutarco e la religione*. Edited by I. Gallo. Naples: M. D'Auria.
Barclay, John M.G. 1996. *Jews in the Mediterranean Diaospora: From Alexander to Trajan (323 BCE–117 CE)*. Edinburgh: T&T Clark.
Barnes, T.D. 1969. "An Apostle on Trial." *JTS* 20: 407–419.
Baroja, Julio Caro. 1974. *De la superstición al ateísmo: meditaciones antropológicas*. Madrid: Taurus.
Barrett, C. K. 1974. "Paul's Speech on the Areopagus." Pages 69–77 in *New Testament Christianity for Africa and the World*. Edited by Mark E. Glasswell and Edward W. Fasholé-Luke. London: SPCK.
Baur, Ferdinand Christian. 1876 [1845]. *Paul The Apostle of Jesus Christ: His Life and Work, His Epistles and His Doctrine*. Vol. 1. 2nd Edition. London: Williams and Norgate.
Beck, Mark, ed. 2014. *A Companion to Plutarch*. Chichester: Wiley-Blackwell.
Benveniste, Emile. 1969. *Le vocabulaire des institutions indo-européennes*. Vol. 2. Paris: Editions de Minuit.
Beurlier, Emile. 1896. "Saint Paul et L'Aréopage," *Rev. d'hist. et de litt. rel.* 1: 344–66.
Bobzien, Susanne. 1998. *Determinism and Freedom in Stoic Philosophy*. Oxford: Clarendon.
Bowden, Hugh. 2008. "Before *Superstitio* and After: Theophrastus and Plutarch on *Deisidaimonia*." Pages 56–71 in *The Religion of Fools? Superstition Past and Present*. Edited by S.A. Smith and Alan Knight. Past and Present Supplement 3. Oxford: Oxford University Press.
Bremmer, Jan. 1998. " 'Religion,' 'Ritual' and the Opposition 'Sacred vs. Profane.'" Pages 9–32 in *Ansichten griechischer Rituale: Geburtstags-Symposium für Walter Burkert, Castelen bei Basel, 15.bis 18. März 1996*. Edited by Fritz Graf. Stuttgart: Teubner.
Brenk, Frederick E. 1977. *In Mist Apparelled. Religious Themes in Plutarch's Moralia and Lives*. Leiden: Brill.
–. 2012. "Plutarch and 'Pagan Monotheism.'" Pages 73–84 in *Plutarch in the Religious and Philosophical Discourse of Late Antiquity*. Edited by Lautaro Roig Lanzilotta and Israel Muñoz Gallarte. Leiden: Brill.
Bultmann, Rudolf. 1946. "Anknüpfung und Widerspruch," *TZ* 2: 401–418.
Butticaz, Simon. 2011. *L'identité de l'Eglise dans les Actes des Apôtres. De la restauration d'Israël à la conquête universelle*. BZNW 174. Göttingen: De Gruyter.
Calderone, Salvatore. 1972. "*Superstitio*," *ANRW* 1.2: 337–396.

Carleton Paget, James. 2010. "Jewish proselytism at the time of Christian origins: chimera or reality?" Pages 149–183 in *Jews, Christians and Jewish Christians in Antiquity*. Tübingen: Mohr Siebeck.

Clerc, Charly. 1915. *Théories relatives au culte des images chez les auteurs grecs du IIme siècle*. Paris: Fontemoing.

Collins, John J. 2000 [1983]. *Between Athens and Jerusalem: Jewish Identity in the Hellenistic Diaspora*. 2nd ed. Grand Rapids: Eerdmans.

Collins, John J. and Gregory E. Sterling, eds. 2001. *Hellenism in the Land of Israel*. Notre Dame, IN: University of Notre Dame Press.

Conzelmann, Hans. 1960 [1954]. *The Theology of St. Luke*. Translated by Geoffrey Buswell. London: Faber.

–. 1966. "The Address of Paul on the Areopagus." Pages 217–230 in *Studies in Luke-Acts*. Edited by Leander E. Keck and J. Louis Martyn. Nashville: Abingdon.

Cook, Arthur Bernard. 1914. *Zeus: A Study in Ancient Religion*. 2 vols. Cambridge: Cambridge University Press.

Cuany, Monique. 2016. Review of Clare K. Rothschild, *Paul in Athens*. The *Religio*us Context of Acts 17. *JRelS* 42: 43–44.

–. 2020. "The Divine Necessity of the Resurrection: A Re-Assessment of the Use of Psalm 16 in Acts 2." *NTS* 66: 392–405.

Davies, Janson. 2009. "Religion in Historiography." Pages 166– in *The Cambridge Companion to the Roman Historians*. Edited by Andrew Feldherr. Cambridge : Cambridge University Press.

Decharme, Paul. 1904. *La critique des traditions religieuses chez les Grecs des origines au temps de Plutarque*. Paris: A. Picard.

Dibelius, Martin. 1956a [1939]. "Paul on the Areopagus." Pages 26–77 in *Studies in the Acts of the Apostles*. Edited by Heinrich Greeven. Translated by Mary Ling. London, SCM.

–. 1956b [1949]. "The Speeches in Acts and Ancient Historiography." Pages –185 in *Studies in the Acts of the Apostles*. Edited by Heinrich Greeven. Translated by Mary Ling. London, SCM.

Dillon, John. 2002. "Plutarch and God: Theodicy and Cosmogony in the Thought of Plutarch." Pages 223–237 in *Traditions of Theology: Studies in Hellenistic Theology, its Background and Aftermath*. Edited by Dorothea Frede and André Laks. Leiden: Brill.

–. 2014. "Plutarch and Platonism." Pages 61–72 in *A Companion to Plutarch*. Edited by Mark Beck. Chichester: Wiley-Blackwell.

Dillon, John M. and A. A. Long, eds. 1988. *The Question of 'Eclecticism': Studies in Later Greek Philosophy*. Berkeley: University of California Press.

Dupont, J. 1984. "Le discours à l'Aréopage (Ac 17, 22–31), lieu de rencontre entre christianisme et hellénisme." Pages 24–36 in *Nouvelles études sur les Actes des apôtres*. LeDiv 118. Paris: Cerf.

Eltester, W. 1957. "Schöpfungsoffenbarung und natürliche Theologie." *NTS* 3: 93–114.

Engberg-Pedersen, Troels, ed. 2001. *Paul Beyond the Judaism/Hellenism Divide*. Louisville: Westminster John Knox Press.

Erbse, Hartmut. 1952. "Plutarchs Schrift ΠΕΡΙ ΔΕΙΣΙΔΑΙΜΟΝΙΑΣ." *Hermes* 80: 269–314.

Erler, M. 2002. "Epicurus as *Deus Mortalis: Homoiosis Theoi* and Epicurean Self-Cultivation." Pages 159–181 in *Traditions of Theology: Studies in Hellenistic Theology, its Background and Aftermath*. Edited by Dorothea Frede and André Laks. Leiden: Brill.

–. 2009. "Epicureanism in the Roman Empire." Pages 46–64 in *The Cambridge Companion to Epicureanism*. Edited by James Warren. Cambridge: Cambridge University Press.

Ferrari, Franco. 2005. "Der Gott Plutarch's und der Gott Platons." Pages 13–26 in *Gott und die Götter bei Plutarch: Götterbilder – Gottesbilder – Weltbilder*. Edited by in Rainer Hirsch-Luipold. RVV 54. Berlin: Walter de Gruyter.

Festugière, A.-J. 1946. *Epicure et ses dieux*. Paris: Presses universitaires de France.

Foerster, Werner. 1964. "δεισιδαίμων, δεισιδαιμονία." Page 2 in vol. 2 of *Theological Dictionary of the New Testament*. Edited by Gerhard Kittel and Gerhard Friedrich. 10 vols. Translated and edited by Geoffrey W. Bromiley. Grand Rapids: Eerdmans.

Frede, Dorothea. 2002. "Theodicy and Providential Care in Stoicism." Pages 85–117 in *Traditions of Theology: Studies in Hellenistic Theology, its Background and Aftermath*. Edited by Dorothea Frede and André Laks. Leiden: Brill.

Gallo, Italo, ed. *Plutarco e la religione: atti del VI Convegno plutarcheo (Ravello, 29–31 maggio 1995*. Napoli: M. D'Auria, 1995.

Garland, Robert. 1992. *Introducing New Gods: The Politics of Athenian Religion*. Ithaca: Cornell University Press.

Gärtner, Bertil E. 1955. *The Areopagus Speech and Natural Revelation*. Translated by Carolyn Hannay-King. Vol. 21. Acta Seminarii Neotestamentici Upsaliensis. Uppsala: C. W. K. Gleerup.

Given, Mark D. 1995. "Not Either/or but Both/and in Paul's Areopagus Speech." *BibInt* 3: 356–372.

Görgemanns, Herwig, ed. 2003. *Plutarch, drei religionsphilosophische Schriften: Über den Aberglauben, Über die späte Strafe der Gottheit, Über Isis und Osiris*. Düsseldorf: Artemis und Winkler.

Gordon, Richard. 2006. Review of D. Martin. *Inventing Superstition. From the Hippocratics to the Christians*. *Gnomon* 78: 251–526.

–. 2008. "*Superstitio*, *Superstitio*n and *Religio*us Repression in the Late Roman Republic and Principate (100 BCE–300 CE)." *Past & Present Suppl*. 3: 72–94.

Graf, Fritz. 2005. "Plutarch und die Götterbilder." Pages 251–266 in *Gott und die Götter bei Plutarch: Götterbilder – Gottesbilder – Weltbilder*. Edited by in Rainer Hirsch-Luipold. RVV 54. Berlin: Walter de Gruyter.

Gray, Patrick. 2004. *Godly Fear: The Epistle to Hebrews and Greco-Roman Critiques of Superstition*. Leiden: Brill.

–. 2005. "Athenian Curiosity (Acts 17:21)." *NovT* 47: 109–116.

Grodzynski, Denise. 1974. "*Superstitio*." *Revue des études anciennes* 76: 36–60.

Gruen, Erich S. 1998. *Heritage and Hellenism: The Reinvention of Jewish Tradition*. Berkeley, CA: University of California Press.

Hadot, Pierre. 1995. *Philosophy as a Way of Life: Spiritual Exercises from Socrates to Foucault*. Oxford: Blackwell.

Harnack, Adolf von. 1913. *Ist die Rede des Paulus in Athen ein ursprünglicher Bestandteil der Apostelgeschichte?* TU 39/1. Leipzig: Hinrichs.

Harris, J. Rendel. 1906a. "The Cretans Always Liars." *Expositor* 7.2 (1906): 305–7.

–. 1911. "Introduction." Pages xi-xxxii in *Commentaries of Isho'dad of Merv, Bishop of Ḥadatha (ca. 850 A.D.): in Syriac and English*. Vol 1: *Translation*. Edited and translated by Margaret Dunlop Gipson. Cambridge: Cambridge University Press, 1911.

Hatzimichali, Myrto. 2011. *Potamo of Alexandria and the Emergence of Eclecticism in Late Hellenistic Philosophy*. Cambridge: Cambridge University Press.

Hengel, Martin. 1974. *Judaism and Hellenism: Studies in their Encounter in Palestine during the Early Hellenistic Period*. London: SCM.

Herring, Stephen L. 2013. *Divine Substitution: Humanity as the Manifestation of Deity in the Hebrew Bible and the Ancient Near East.* FRLANT 267. Göttingen: Vandenhoeck & Ruprecht.
Hershbell, J. P. 1992a. "Plutarch and Epicureanism." *ANRW*.36.5: 3353–3383.
–. 1992b. "Plutarch and Stoicism." *ANRW* 36.5: 3336–3352.
Hirsch-Luipold, Rainer, ed. 2005. *Gott und die Götter bei Plutarch: Götterbilder – Gottesbilder – Weltbilder.* RVV 54. Berlin: Walter de Gruyter.
–. 2014. "Religion and Myth." Pages 163–176 in *A Companion to Plutarch*. Edited by Mark Beck. Chichester: Wiley-Blackwell.
Hirzel, R. 1912. *Plutarch.* Leipzig: Dietrich.
Hommel, Hildebrecht. 1955. "Neue Forschungen zur Areopagrede Acta 17." *ZNW* 46: 145–78.
–. 1957. "Platonisches bei Lukas: Zu Acta 17.28a (Leben-Bewegung-Sein)." *ZNW* 48: 193–200.
Horst, Pieter W. van der. 1990. "The Altar of the 'Unknown God' in Athens (Acts 17:23) and the 'Cult of the Unknown Gods' in the Hellenistic and Roman Periods." ANRW 18.2:426-56.
Houte, Maarteen Stijn Adriaan van. 2010. "Seneca's theology in its philosophical context." Ph.D. thesis, University of Utrecht.
Janssen, L. 1975. "Die Bedeutungsentwicklung von *superstitio*/superstes." *Mnemosyne* 28: 135–89.
–. 1979. "'*Superstitio*' and the Persecution of Christians." *VC* 33: 131–59.
Jervell, Jacob. 1960. *Imago dei. Gen 1,26f. im Spätjudentum, in der Gnosis und in den paulinischen Briefen.* Göttingen: Vandenhoeck & Ruprecht.
–. 1972. *Luke and the People of God: A New Look at Luke-Acts.* Minneapolis: Augsburg Publishing House.
Jipp, Joshua W. 2012. "Paul's Areopagus Speech of Acts 17:16–34 as Both Critique and Propaganda." *JBL* 131: 567–88.
–. 2017. Review of C. Kavin Rowe, *One True Life: The Stoics and Early Christians as Rival Traditions. BBR* 26:445–448.
Jobes, Karen J. 1994. "Distinguishing the Meaning of Greek Verbs in the Semantic Domain for Worship." Pages 201–211 in *Biblical Words and Their Meaning: An Introduction to Lexical Semantics,* by Moisés Silva. Grand Rapids: Zondervan.
Kerferd, G.B. 1977–1978. "The Origin of Evil in Stoic Thought." *BJRL* 60: 482–94.
Klauck, Hans-Joseph. 1997. "Religion Without Fear: Plutarch on Superstition and Early Christianity." *Skrif en Kerk* 18: 111–26.
–. 2000. *Magic and Paganism in Early Christianity: The World of the Acts of the Apostles.* Edinburgh: T&T Clark.
Koets, Peter John. 1929. *Deisidaimonia: A Contribution to the Knowledge of the Religious Terminology in Greek.* Purmerend: J. Muusses.
Lebram, J.-C. 1964. "Der Aufbau der Areopagrede." *ZNW*: 221–243.
Lake, Kirsopp. 1933. "Note XX. Your own Poets." Pages 246–251 in *Beginnings of Christianity,* vol. 5. Edited by F. J. Foakes-Jackson and Kirsopp Lake. 5 vols. London: Macmillan.
Lane Fox, R. J. 1997. "Theophrastus' Characters and the Historian." *Proceedings of the Cambridge Philological Society* 42: 127–170.
Liebersohn, Yosef Z. 2012. "Seneca and the Problem of Theodicy in Stoicism: 'The e contrario Answer'." *The Ancient World* 43: 133–150.
Long, A. A. 2002. *Epictetus: A Socratic Guide to Life.* Oxford: Clarendon.

–. 1968. "The Stoic Concept of Evil." *Philosophical Quarterly* 73: 329–343.
–. 1988. "Socrates in Hellenistic philosophy." *CQ* 38: 150–71
Lozza, G. 1996. "Tyrannis e *deisidaimonia* in Plutarco." Pages 389–94 in *Plutarco e la religione*. Edited by I. Gallo. Naples: M. D'Auria.
MacGillivray, Erlend D. 2012. "The Popularity of Epicureanism in Elite Late-Republic Roman Society." *The Ancient World* 43: 151–172.
Malherbe, Abraham J. 1989. " 'Not in a Corner': Early Christian Apologetic in Acts 26:26.' Pages 147–163 in *Paul and the Popular Philosophers*. Minneapolis: Fortress.
Manning, C.E. 1996. "Seneca and Roman religious practice." Pages 311–319 in *Religion in the Ancient world: new themes and approaches*. Edited by Matthew Dillon. Amsterdam: A.M. Hakkert.
Mansfeld, Jaap. 1999. "Theology." Pages 452–478 in *The Cambridge History of Hellenistic Philosophy*. Edited by Keimpe Algra, Jonathan Barnes, Jaap Mansfeld and Malcolm Schofield. Cambridge: Cambridge University Press.
Marguerat, Daniel. 2004. *The First Christian Historian: Writing the 'Acts of the Apostles.'* SNTSMS 121. Cambridge: Cambridge University Press.
Markschies, Christoph. 2016. *Gottes Körper: Jüdische, christliche und pagane Gottesvorstellungen in der Antike*. München: C. H. Beck.
Martin, Dale B. 2004. *Inventing Superstition: From the Hippocratics to the Christians*. Cambridge, MA: Havard University Press.
–. 1997. "Hellenistic Superstition: The Problems of Defining a Vice." Pages 110-27 in *Conventional Values of the Hellenistic Greeks*. Edited by P. Bilde et al. Aarhus: Aarhus University Press.
Mason. Steve. 2012. "Speech-Making in Ancient Rhetoric, Josephus, and Acts: Messages and Playfulness, Part II." *Early Christianity* 3: 147–171.
Merckel, Cécile. 2012. "Seneca theologus: La religion d'un philosophe romain." Ph.D. thesis, Université de Strasbourg.
Moellering, H. Armin. 1963. *Plutarch on Superstition*. Rev. ed. Boston: Christopher.
Nasrallah, Laura S. 2010. *Christian Responses to Roman Art and Architecture: The Second-Century Church amid the Spaces of Empire*. New York: Cambridge University Press.
Nauck, Wolfgang. 1956. "Die Tradition und Komposition der Areopagrede: eine motivgeschichtliche Untersuchung." *ZTK* 53: 1152.
Nave, Guy D. 2002. *The Role and Function of Repentance in Luke-Acts*. Leiden: Brill.
Nongbri, Brent. 2013. *Before Religion: A History of a Modern Concept*. New Haven: Yale University Press.
Norden, Eduard. 1913. *Agnostos Theos: Untersuchungen zur Formengeschichte Religiöser Rede*. Leipzig: Teubner.
Opsomer, Jan. 1996. "Divination and academic 'scepticism' according to Plutarch." Pages 164–94 in *Plutarchae lovaniensia: a miscellany of essays on Plutarch*. Edited by Luc Van der Stockt. Studia Hellenistica 32. Leuven: s.n.
–. 2014. "Plutarch and the Stoics." Pages 88–103 in *A Companion to Plutarch*. Edited by Mark Beck. Chichester: Wiley-Blackwell.
Otto, Walter. 1909. "*Religio* und *Superstitio*." *AR* 12: 533–54.
Pérez, Jiménez A. 1996. "*Deisidaimonia*: el miedo a los dioses en Plutarco." Pages 195–225 in *Plutarchae lovaniensia: a miscellany of essays on Plutarch*. Edited by Luc Van der Stockt. Studia Hellenistica 32. Leuven: s.n.
Phillips, T. E. 2006. "The Genre of Acts: Moving Towards a Consensus?" *Currents in Biblical Research* 4: 365–96.

Pià, J. 2011. "Philosophie et religion dans le stoïcisme impérial romain. Etudes de quelques cas: Cornutus, Perse, Epictète et Marc Aurèle." PhD. Thesis, Université de Paris IV, La Sorbonne.
Plümacher, Eckhard. 1972. *Lukas als hellenistischer Schriftsteller: Studien zur Apostelgeschichte.* Göttingen: Vandenhoek & Ruprecht.
Pohlenz, Max. 1949. "Paulus und die Stoa." *ZNW* 42: 69–104.
Porter, Stanley E. 1999. *The Paul of Acts: Essays in Literary Criticism, Rhetoric and Theology.* WUNT 115. Tübingen: Mohr-Siebeck.
–. 1999b. "Resurrection, the Greeks and the New Testament." Pages 52–81 in *Resurrection.* Edited by Stanley E. Porter, Michael A Hayes, and David Tombs. JSNTSup 186. Sheffield: Sheffield Academic Press.
Rese, Martin. "Die Aussagen über Jesu Tod und Auferstehung in der Apostelgeschichte – Ältestes Kerygma oder lukanische Theologumena? " *NTS* 30: 335–353.
Roig Lanzilotta, Lautaro and Israel Muñoz Gallarte, eds. 2012. *Plutarch in the Religious and Philosophical Discourse of Late Antiquity.* Leiden: Brill.
Rothschild, Clare K. 2014. *Paul in Athens: The Popular Religious Context of Acts 17.* WUNT 341. Tübingen: Mohr Siebeck.
Rowe, C. Kavin. 2009. *World Upside Down: Reading Acts in the Graeco-Roman Age.* New York: Oxford University Press.
–. 2011. "The Grammar of Life: The Areopagus Speech and Pagan Tradition." *NTS* 57: 31–50.
–. 2016. *One True Life: The Stoics and Early Christians as Rival Traditions.* New Haven: Yale University Press.
Russell, D. A. 2001. *Plutarch.* 2nd ed. London: Bristol Classical Press.
Russell, D. C. 2004. "Virtue as 'Likeness to God' in Plato and Seneca." *JHPh* 42: 241–260.
Sandnes, Karl Olav. 1993. "Paul and Socrates: The Aim of Paul's Areopagus Speech," *JSNT* 50: 13–26.
Schmid, Wilhelm. 1943. "Die Rede des Apostels Paulus vor den Philosophen and Areopagiten in Athens." *Philologus* 95: 79–120.
Schnabel, Eckhard J. 2005. "Contextualizing Paul in Athens: The Proclamation of the Gospel Before Pagan Audiences in the Graeco-Roman World." *Religion & Theology* 12: 172–190.
Schubert, Paul. 1968. "The Place of the Areopagus Speech in the Composition of Acts." Pages 235–61 in *Transitions in Biblical Scholarship.* Edited by J. C. Rylaarsdam. Essays in Divinity 6. Chicago: University of Chicago Press.
Sedley, David. 1989. "Philosophical Allegiance in the Greco-Roman World." Pages 97–119 in *Philosophia Togata: Essays on Philosophy and Roman Society.* Edited by Miriam Griffin and Jonathan Barnes. Oxford: Clarendon.
–. 1999. "The ideal of godlikeness." Pages 309–28 in *Plato 2: Ethics, politics, religion, and the soul.* Edited by Gail Fine. Oxford: Oxford University Press.
–. 2007. *Creationism and its Critics in Antiquity.* Berkeley: University of California Press.
Silva, Moisés. 1994. *Biblical Words and Their Meaning: An Introduction to Lexical Semantics.* Grand Rapids: Zondervan.
Setaioli, Aldo. 2004. "Interpretazioni stoiche ed epicuree in Servio et la traditizione dell'esegesi filosofica del mito e dei poet a Roma (Cornuto, Seneca, Filodemo), I," *International Journal of the Classical Tradition* 10: 341–367.
–. 2007. "Seneca and the divine: Stoic tradition and personal developments." *IJCT* 13: 333–368.

Smith, Morton. 1975. "*De superstitione* (Moralia 164A–171F)." Pages 1–35 in *Plutarch's Theological Writings and Early Christian Literature*. Edited by Hans Dieter Betz. Leiden: Brill.
Soards, Marion L. 1994. *The Speeches in Acts. Their Content, Context, and Concerns*. Louisville: Westminster/John Knox Press.
Spicq, Ceslas. 1994. *Theological Lexicon of the New Testament*. Translated and edited by James D. Ernest. 3 vols. Peabody: Hendrickson.
Stenschke, Christoph W. 1999. *Luke's Portrait of Gentiles Prior to Their Coming to Faith*. WUNT 2/108. Tübingen: Mohr-Siebeck.
Sterling, Gregory E. 1992. *Historiography and self-definition: Josephos, Luke-Acts, and apologetic historiography*. Leiden: Brill.
Stewart, Peter. 2003. *Statues in Roman Society: Representation and Response*. New York: Oxford University Press.
Stowers, Stanley K. 2001. "Does Pauline Christianity Resemble a Hellenistic Philosophy?" Pages 81–102 in *Paul Beyond the Judaism/Hellenism Divide*. Edited by Troels Engberg-Pedersen. Louisville: Westminster John Knox Press.
Summers, Kirk. 1995. "Lucretius and the Epicurean Tradition of Piety." *Classical Philology* 90: 32–57.
Tannehill, Robert C. 1991. "The Functions of Peter's Mission Speeches in the Narrative of Acts." *NTS* 37: 400–414.
Trapp, Michael. 2014. "The Role of Philosophy and Philosophers in the Imperial Period." Pages 43–57 in *A Companion to Plutarch*. Edited by Mark Beck. Chichester: Wiley-Blackwell.
Trier, Jost. 1931. *Der deutsche Wortschatz im Sinnbezirk des Verstandes. Die Geschichte eines sprachlichen Feldes*. Heidelberg: Carl Winters.
Turner, Nigel. 1963. *Syntax*. Vol 3 of *A Grammar of New Testament Greek*. Edited by James H. Moulton. Edinburgh: T&T Clark.
Van Kooten, George H. 2010. "Is Early Christianity a Religion of a Philosophy? Reflections on the Importance of 'Knowledge' and 'Truth' in the Letters of Paul and Peter." Pages 393-408 in *Myths, Martyrs, and Modernity: Studies in the History of Religions in Honour of Jan N. Bremmer*. Edited by Jitse Dijksa, Justin Kroesen and Yme Kuiper. Leiden: Martinus Nijhoff/Brill.
Van Nuffelen, Peter. 2011. *Rethinking the Gods: Philosophical Readings of Religion in the Post-Hellenistic Period*. Cambridge: Cambridge University Press.
–. 2011b. "Plutarch of Chaeronea: 'History as a basis for a philosophy that has theology as its end.'" Pages 48-71 in *Rethinking the Gods: Philosophical Readings of Religion in the Post-Hellenistic Period*. Cambridge: Cambridge University Press.
–. 2011c. "Plutarch: A benevolent hierarchy of gods and men." Pages 157-175 in *Rethinking the Gods: Philosophical Readings of Religion in the Post-Hellenistic Period*. Cambridge: Cambridge University Press.
Versnel, H.S. "δεισιδαιμονία." In the Oxford Classical Dictionary, accessed online 7.7.2017 at http://classics.oxfordre.com/view/10.1093/acrefore/9780199381135.001.0001/acrefore-9780199381135-e-2073
Vielhauer, Philipp. 1966. "On the 'Paulinism' of Acts." Pages 33–50 in *Studies in Luke-Acts*. Edited by Leander E. Keck and J. Louis Martyn. Nashville: Abingdon.
Warren, James. 2009. "Removing Fear." Pages 234–248 in *The Cambridge Companion to Epicureanism*. Edited by James Warren. Cambridge: Cambridge University Press.
–. 2011. "Epicurean Immortality." *Oxford Studies in Ancient Philosophy* 18: 231–61.

Winter, Bruce W. 1996. "On Introducing Gods to Athens: An Alternative Reading of Acts 17:18–20." *TynB* 47: 71–90.
Wilson, Stephen G. 1973. *The Gentiles and the Gentile Mission in Luke-Acts.* SNTSMS 23. Cambridge: Cambridge University.
Wright, N. T. 2003. *The Resurrection of the Son of God.* London: SPCK.
Wycherley, R. E. 1968. "St. Paul at Athens." *JTS* 19: 619–621.
Zeller, Eduard. 1869–82. *Die Philosophie der Griechen in ihrer geschichtlichen Entwicklung.* 3 vols. Leipzig.
Zweck, Dean. 1989. "The Exordium of the Areopagus Speech, Acts 17.22, 23." *NTS* 35: 94–103.
–. 1985. "The Function of Natural Theology in the Areopagus Speech." Th.D. dissertation. Lutheran School of Theology at Chicago.

Index of References

Old and New Testament

Genesis
1:26–27   158
27:12   143
27:21–22   143

Exodus
32–34   144

Numbers
23   135
3:10   135

Deuteronomy
28:29   143
4:28   154

Joshua
22   135

Judges
16:26   143

1 Samuel
12:21   159

Job
5:14   143
12:25   143

Psalms
113:15   143, 145
115:4–8   155, 167
115:5–7   159
134:17   143, 145

Isaiah
40:18–20   155
42:17   154
44:9–17   154

46:7   159
59:10   143

Daniel
7:22   168

Luke
1:11   136
11:51   136
20:35   168
20:38   145
24:46–47   162

Acts
1   1
2   169
2:24   189
2:38   162
3:26   162
4:1–2   189
13:47   2
14:8–19   135
14:11   170
14:15–17   1
14:17   141, 142, 152
17:11   143
18:12–13   39
19:23–27   135
19:26   154
20:16   143
23:6   188
24:2–4   39
24:14   43
24:15–16   162
24:25   162
25:20   143
26:20   162
27:12   143
27:39   143

28	1, 37		*1 Corinthians*	
28:4	37		14:10	143
			15:37	143
Romans				
1	11, 148		*Titus*	
			1:12	146, 147, 149

Apocrypha, Pseudepicrapha et Qumran Scrolls

Wisdom			17:3	158
3:7–8	168			
13–15	9		*2 Enoch*	
13:10	159		65:2	158
13:10–14:10	154			
14:29	164		*1QpHab*	
			5:4	168
Sirach				

Ancient Authors

Aeschylus			*De civitate Dei (Civ.)*	
			6.10	108, 156
Eumenides (Eum.)			6.10.1	108
647–648	36, 161		6.10.2	108, 112
			6.10.3	109
Aratus			6.10.4	112
			6.10.5	109
Phaenomena (Phaen.)			6.10.6	108
1–18	150–151		6.10.6–7	108
5	148			
			Calllimachus	
Aristotle				
			Hymn to Zeus	
Rhetorica (Rhet.)			8	147
3.14.12 (1415b 37–38)132				
			Cassius Dio	
Arius Didymus				
			52.36.1–2	38
Epitome of Stoic Ethic				
10χ	57		Chrysippus	
Athenaeus			*Fragmenta moralia*	
			394.16	104
Deipnosophistae (Deipn.)			408.4	104
8	104		409.16	104
8.344C	34		411.8	104

Augustine

Cicero

De divinatione (Div.)
1.87	94
2.19	117
2.83	117
2.83–85	117

De natura deorum (ND)
1.41	112
1.45	88, 91, 94
1.55–56	93, 117
1.54	89
1.85	94
1.116	95
1.116–117	96
1.117	58, 88, 97, 104
1.121	97
1.122	98
2	110
2.10	89
2.12	111
2.19	117
2.58	110
2.62	37, 114
2.63–64	106
2.70–71	105, 112
2.71	111
2.71–153	110
2.71–72	104
2.83–85	117
2.140	110
2.147	110
2.154–167	110
2.163	111
3.52	118
3.78	118
3.82–83	118
3.90	118
3.93	118

Clement of Alexandria

Stromata
1.19	5, 132
1.59	146
5.12.76	113–114

Cornutus

Theologiae Graecae Compendium
35	57

Demosthenes

Contra Boeotum I (1 Boeot.)
19.281	38

De corona (Cor.)
18.127	34

Dio Chrysostom

Orationes (Or.)
12.44	113
12.59	113
12.60	113
12.76–77	113
12.60–61	144
12.80–81	156
12.48.5	81
13.35.5	81
31.146.7	81
32.5.2	81
32.9	34
54.3	42
61.9	81
75.5.3	81
77/78.30.1	81
fragment 6	81

Diodorus Siculus, 61, 63

1.2.2	64
1.65.2	64
1.70.8	60
1.79.2	60
1.83.8	60
1.92.5	64
1.93.3	64
1.96.5	64
3.6.3	60
4.8.5	64
4.18.22	64
4.39.1	64
4.46.4	64
4.51.1	60
4.51.3	62
4.52.2	64
5.7.7	64
5.27.4	60

5.63.3	60	19.5	34
5.79.2	168		
7.12.7	64	*De Thucydide (Thuc.)*	
8.12.8	65	42–46	28
8.15.2	64		
8.15.5	64	Epictetus	
11.89.6	60		
11.89.8	60	*Dissertationes (Diss.)*	
12.20.3	64	2.8.12–23	157
12.57.4	64–65	2.8.15–7	113
13.12.6	65	3.1.37	111
13.86.3	60	3.2.4	111
14.77.4	63	3.21.12–16	111
15.53.4	65	3.7.26	111
15.54.4	60		
17.41.5–6	60–61	*Enchiridion (Ench.)*	
17.41.6	60	31.1–4	116
17.41.8	60	31.2	111
18.61.3	61–62	31.5	111
19.108.2	60		
20.14.5	60	*Fragments (frag.)*	
20.43.1	60	32	111
21.17.4	64		
23.11.1	65	Epicurus	
27.4.5	60	*Epistle to Herodotus (Ep. Hdt.)*	
27.4.8	60	81	88
32.12.1	60, 63	76–78	92
32.12.3	60		
33.5.2	65	*Epistle to Menoeceus (Ep. Men.)*	
34/5.10.1	60	123	90, 95, 100–101
34/5.2.47	60, 63	123–124	94
36.13.2	60	124	102

Diogenes Laertius

		Kuriai Doxai (KΔ)	
1.112	146–147	1	90–91
2.20	42		
2.21	42	Epiphanius	
2.40	42		
2.45	42	*Adversus haereses*	
2.122	42	3.2.9	224
7.119	139		
10.4–9	93	Herodotus	
10.10	94	6.58	33
10.123	90	Homer	
10.139	90		
		Odyssea	
		9.416	143

Dionysius of Halicarnassus

Antiquitates romanae (Ant. rom.)

Josephus

Against Apion (Ag. Ap.)
1.208	69
1.212	70
1.224	73
2.130	49, 83
2.262–268	38
2.263	42

Jewish Antiquities (Ant.)
1–5	33
4.31	72
5.116	72
5.327	72
6.78	73
6.90	73
6.127	72
6.265	72
7.269	73
8.121	72
8.13	73
8.208	72
10.42	69
11.239	73
12.255	73
12.259	73
12.278	73
12.304	73
12.5	70
12.6	70
12.259	71
13.243	73
14.226	71
14.228	71
14.232	71
14.234	71
14.237	71
14.240	71
14.72	73
15.277	70
16.172	73
18.11	43
19.290	71, 80

Jewish War
1.108	69
1.110	69
1.113	69
1.630	73
1.633	73
2.119–166	43
2.174	70
2.230	70
4.393	73
7.430	73

Justin

Apologia i (1 Apol.)
5.4	42

Apologia ii (2 Apol.)
10.5–6	42

Lactantius

Divinae Institutiones (Inst.)
3.17.7	92

De ira Dei
13.19	92

Livy
45.27.11	33
9.29.10	89

Lucian

De saltatione (Salt.)
45	36

How to write history
58	28

Lucretius

De rerum natura
1.102–111	88
1.102–116	98
1.104–106	88
1.146–158	88
1.44–48	91
1.62–69	89
1.80–101	89
2.1090–92	89
2.646–651	91
5.1198–1203	95
5.195–324	92
5.8	96
5.82–90	92

5.84–90	89	Col. 76–77	102
6.68–78	102	Col. 77, 2233–41	102
6.73–78	95	Col. 78, 2263–5	95, 102
		Col. 79, 2278	94
		Col. 80, 2313–20	103

Pausanias

1.17.1   33, 35, 49, 83

De pietate (ap. P. Herc. 1428)
Col. 4.16–26   112
Col. 13–15   103
Col. 14.32–15.8   97

Philo

Decalogue (Dec.)
7076   154

Dis   88

Quod Deus sit immutabilis (Deus)
164.1   58

*On Choices and Avoidances
(P. Herc. 1251)* 90
Col 10.12–15   87

Philodemus of Gadara

Plato

De musica
Col. 4.6   94

Apologia (Apol.)
17c	42
19d	42
24bc	42
28e–30e	42
29d	42
33a	42
38a	42

De pietate
Col. 3–36, 72–1022	93–94
Col. 20, 558–9	94
Col. 25, 701–702	44
Col. 27, 765–73	101
Col. 28, 798	94
Col. 28, 808–10	94
Col. 31, 873–898	102
Col. 31, 879–82	94
Col. 32, 910–1	94
Col. 36–59	100
Col. 37, 1045–9	102
Col. 39–40, 1127–46	100
Col. 39–40, 1127–46	94, 96
Col. 39–40, 1127–55	100
Col. 40, 1135–6	87
Col. 46–47, 1306–1344	98
Col. 49, 1395–1402	96
Col. 49–50, 1412–1425	99
Col. 53, 1505–32	93
Col. 60–86	100
Col. 64, 1850	94
Col 71, 2032–260	95
Col 76, 2203	95

Euthyphro (Euthyphr.)
1c	42
2c	42
3b	42

Leges
4.715 E–716A   98

Phaedo
99b   143

Respublica (Resp.)
454a   42

Adversus Colotem (Adv. Col.)
1124E–1125A   98

Aemilius Paullus (Aem.)
1.5	80
3.2	139

Alcibiades (Alc.)
36   34

An vitiositas ad infelicitatem sufficiat (An vit.)
500A   80

Apophthegmata laconia (Apoph. lac.)
238D1   77

Aratus (Arat.)
53.2.3   76

Camillus (Cam.)
19.8.4   76
21.3.1   78
6.6   78

Cimon (Cim.)
13.6   35

Comparatio Lycurgi et Numae (Comp. Lyc. Num)
1.1.5   77

Conjugalia Precepta (Conj. praec.)
140D8   80

Consolatio ad Apollonium
120B4   77
108F8   77

Crassus (Crass.)
16.6.7   78

De Iside et Osiride (Is. Os.)
11   75
354E   78
379C–D   127
382AC   156

De latenter vivendo (Lat. viv.)
1128D8   80

De recta ratione audiendi (Rect. rat. aud.)
43D11   77

De sera numinis vindicta (Sera)

548CD   92
549E   78
551D   163
555A3   76, 80

De Soicorum repugnantiis (Stoic. rep.)
1034B–C   113
1048   119
1049A–D   119
1049D–E   119
1049F–1050D   119
1050D–1051A   119
1051DE   97, 110
1051E   110
1052B   97

De superstitione (Superst.)
165EF   77
165B   107
165BC   57, 76, 79
165D   57, 76
166B7   77
167D–E   123, 127
168BC   76
168C   76
168F6   80
169A   77
169C   70, 72, 77
169F–170A   107
170A   105
170B   76
171F   58
171F5   77

Lysander (Lys.)
25.2.4   77

Marcius Coriolanus (Cor.)
25.2   78
25.3   78

Moralia (Mor.)
1051E   75

Nicias (Nic.)
23.1.4   77

Non posse suaviter vivi sedundum Epicurum (Suav. viv.)

1092B	88	12.24.5	81
1092AB	88	16.12.9	81
1100F	87–88, 99		
1101D9	57, 76		
1101DE	82, 122	Seneca	
1102B	94		
1102BC	97	*De beneficiis*	
1105C	99	1.3.2–4.6	106
1105C–1106A	99	1.6.2	111
1091BC	96	1.6.3	116
		4.28.1–4	116

Numa (Num.)

8.3.9	77	*De clementia*	
14.2.9	77	2.5.1	107
22.7.10	77		

De providentia

1.4–6   116

Pericles (Per.)

6.1   77

Epistulae morales (Ep.)

22.15	107
31.11	156–157
95.49	109–110
95.49–50	114–115
121.4.2	107
123.16	107

Publicola (Publ.)

21.2.1   77

Quaestiones romanae et graecae (Quaest. rom.)

277F4	76
272B9	78

Naturales quaestiones (Nat.)

7.1.2.78   107

Quomodo adolescens poetas audire debeat (Adol. poet. aud.)

Thyestes (Thy.)

34E6	77	678	107

Romulus (Rom.)

Sextus Empiricus

11.5.3	76	*Adversus physicos*	
22.1, 79		1.123	139
24.2.1	77	1.124	96

Solon (Sol.)

12.6.1   77

Sophocles

Fragments (frag.)

Oedipus coloneus

67.2	77	260	49, 83

Polybius

Stobaeus

4.20.2	81	II, 147, 1–3	58
5.10.6	81		
5.12.1	81	Strabo	
6.56.8	81		
9.19.1	81	1.2.8	66, 67, 68
10.2.9	81	3.2.13	68

4.1.13	66	*Peloponnesian War*	
5.4.5	66	1.22.1	28
6.2.3	68	2.60–4	28
7.3.3	67–68	7.42	61
7.3.4	67	8.66	61
12.73	67		
13.1.26	68	Virgil	
15.1.60	68	*Aeneid (Aen.)*	
16.2.36	68	8.364–365	156
16.2.37	67		
		Xenophon	
Theophrastus		*Memorabilia (Mem.)*	
Characters		1.1.1	42
16	53–54	1.1.3	42
16.1	57	1.1.10	42
		Apologia Socratis (Apol.)	
Thucydides		10–11	42

Index of Authors

Aitken, J.K. 25, 192
Algra, Keimpe 112–116, 126, 132
Attridge, Harold W. 109, 111, 112

Balch, David 6, **8**, 15
Barclay, John M.G. 24
Barnes, T. D. 40
Barrett, C. K. 14–17, 20, 35, 41, 85, 133, 134, 135, 137, 145, 154
Baur, F. C. 23, 35, 134
Baroja, Julio Caro 81–82
Bremmer, Jan 56
Brenk, Frederick 50, 75–6, 79
Bultmann, Rudolf 14, 133

Conzelmann, Hans 1, 11, **12–14,** 20, 48, 134, 145, 154, 159, 182, 189

Davies, Janson 81
Dibelius, Martin 1, 4, **6–8,** 9–11, 26, 28, 35, 41, 50, 83, 133–134, 142, 148, 158, 161, 163
Dunlop Gibson, Margaret, and Agnes Smith Lewis 147
Dunn, James D. G. 4, 16, 22–23, 35, 38, 42, 44, 161, 189
Dupont, Jacques 2, 8, 11, 12, 136

Eltester W. 7, 142
Erbse, Hartmut 75

Festugière, A.-J. 82, 101
Fitzmyer, Joseph A. 2, 29, 146

Gärtner, Bertil E. 5, **8–11,** 41, 130, 137, 145, 159
Gray, Patrick 49, 51, 54, 55, 58, 74, 75, 87, 123
Grodzynski, Denise 51, 82, 86–87

Gruen, Erich 25

Haenchen, Ernest 4, 12, 14–15, 20, 33, 49, 53, 55, 133, 134, 136, 146, 154
Harnack 1, 6
Harris, Rendel J. 146–148
Hengel, Martin 24, 25, 192
Hommel, Hildebrecht 7, 145, 146–148

Jervell, Jacob, 3, 35, 38, 48, 49, 133, 145, 154, 158, **188, 190, 192**
Jipp, Joshua W. 4, **14–18,** 20–21, 123, 130, 145, 146, 158, 158, 192
Johnson, Luke Timothy 1, 2, 29, 38, 48, 146, 154

Koet, Peter J. 48, 50, **51–55**, 63, 71, 75, 86

Lake, Kirsopp 146, 147, 148, 149

Marguerat, Daniel 2–3, 11, 17, 26, 28–29, 33, 41, 42, 145, 146
Martin, Dale B. 48, 50, 51, 53, 55, 58, 59, 61–63, 75, 79, 86, 117, 121, 123, 124, 126
Moellering, H. Armin 48, 49, 52, **53–55**, 75

Nauck, Wolfgang 9, **10–12,** 13, 24, 158
Nongbri, Brent 56
Norden, Eduard **5–6**, 11, 143, 146, 148

Opsomer, Jan 29, 75, 120

Pervo, Richard I. 10, 23, 44, 133, 145, 154, 161, 184
Plümacher, Eckhard 28
Pohlenz, Max **6–8**, 145, 146, **148–149**

Rothschild, Clare K. 2, 5, 8, 34, 146, 149, 150
Rowe, Kavin 2, 3–4, 14, **19–22**, 23, 26, 29, 30, 32, 33, 49, 130, 133, 134, 136, 174, 175, 179, 182, 184

Schnabel, Eckhard J. 2, 16–17, 20, 38, 188
Schneider, Gerhard 2, 27
Schubert, Paul, 2, 26
Smith, Morton 74–75
Smith Lewis, Agnes, and Margaret Dunlop Gibson 147
Soards, Marion L. 1, 26, 28
Stenschke, Christoph W. 9

Sterling, Gregory E. 18

Tannehill, Robert C. 26–27, 188
Trapp, Michael 43
Tier, Jost 52

Vielhauer, Philipp 2, 7, 163
Van Kooten, George 43

Walaskay 8, 29
Wycherley, R.E. 33

Zahn, Theodor 35–36
Zeller, Eduard 125
Zweck, Dean 5

Subject Index

Academics 41, 75, 97–98, 117–118, 125; *see also* Platonists
Adam 19, 22
Aeschylus 36, 161
Agnostos Theos (by Eduard Norden) 5–6
Anknüpfungspunkt 3, 19, 44, 133; *see also* Rapprochement, theological
Antipater of Tarsus 104
Anthropomorphic image/representation of the gods, *see* Image/representation of the gods, anthropomorphic
Anti-idol polemic, *see* Polemic, anti-idol
Apologetics 8, **16–18**, 20, 23, 31, 149, 180, 189, **192–193**
Appendix, Christian 130, 161, 175, 176
Aratus 5, 7, 12, 22, 132, 148–151
Aristobulus 11, 12, 151–152
Asebeia, *see* Impiety
Atheism 17, 29, 52, 57–58, 75, 97, 100
Augustine 108

Begleitmotiv 5–6, 11

Callimachus 148, 150
Captatio benevolentiae 30, 48–49
Celsus 86
Characters (by Theophrastus) 53–54, 56
Chrysippus 104, 106, 110, 112
Cicero 58, 87, 88, 96, 104–105
Cleanthes 106
Clement of Alexandria 5, 113–114, 132, 146, 148
Common ground 7, 10, 12, 14, 16–18, 21–23, 24, 25, 41, 46, 140, 201, 202, 214
Common places, philosophical 18, 35, 41
Conscience, bad (troubled) 76, 80, 104, 122

Contextualization, of the Christian message 174, *see also* Preaching, to the the Gentiles in Acts
Cornutus 106
Creation, doctrine of 16
– ~ of the Stoics 93
Culture, Graeco-Roman (Gentile, Pagan) 25, 174–175, 192–193
– Acts 17 as Christian encounter with ~ 1–2, 15, 184
– christianity as fulfillment of ~ 17
– Luke–Acts' attitude towards ~ 2–4, 18, 31, 174–175, 189, 191–193
– philosophy and religion in ~ 43
– proclaiming foreign divinities in ~ 38
– the christian movement and ~ 191–193
– the christian movement as subversive of ~ 4, 19
– trials in ~ 40
– ~ as preparation for the gospel 3
Curiosity, Athenian 39, 49, 123, 178
Cynics 34, 126

De Iside et Osiride (by Plutarch) 75
De pietate (by Philodemus) 96, 100
De superstitione (by Plutarch) 50, 55, **74–79**, 107, 127
De superstitione (by Seneca) 104, 108–112
Deisidaimonia
– ancient definitions of 56–58
– ~ as criticism of Graeco-Roman religion 121, 126, 176
– ~ as criticism of idolatry 121, 130, 176
– ~ as superstition 31, 48–49, 53–56, 82
– contrasted with piety 57, 165, 185
– ~ criticized by Hellenistic philosophers 85–87, **121–126**, 131, 182–183, 185

Subject Index

- in ancient historians and geographers 60–74
- in Graeco-Roman religion 63–64, 81–83, 121, 131
- in Epicurean philosophers 45, 85, 87–103, **121–126**, 175, 180–181, 185
- in Jewish religion 67, 69–72
- in Stoic philosophers 104–121, **122–126**, 167, 175, 180–181, 185
- in Plutarch 74–80, **121–126**
- modern studies of ~ 52–57
- ~ of the Athenians in Acts 17 30–31, 130, 160, 180

Dio Chrysostom 8, 34, 42, 81, 113, 144, 156,
Diodorus Siculus 30, 33, 50, 59, **60–65**
Diogenes of Oenanda 125
Dionysius of Halicarnassus 20, 28, 34
Divine image, *see* Image, divine
Divine-likeness ; *see* Godlikeness
Divinization 37, 169, 170

Eclecticism 9, 125, 180
Empire, Roman 2, 29, *see also* Stoicism in Roman Empire, Epicureanism in Roman Empire
Epictetus 31, 33, 44, 97, 104, 111, 113, 114, 116, 125, 126, 157
Epicureanism
- in Roman Empire 29–30
- on fear of death 45, 88, 90

Epicurus 87–102
Epimenides 8, **146–149**, 151, 155, 159
Epistle to Menoeceus 88
Eulabeia 31, 52, 58, 82
- in Diodorus Siculus 64–65
- in Josephus 72–73
- in Plutarch 76–78

Eusebeia 52, 58–59, 62, **80–82**, 128
- in Diodorus Siculus 64–65
- in Josephus 72–74
- in Plutarch 77
- in Strabo 65–68

Euthyphro (by Plato) 95

Foreign body, *see* Fremdkörper
Foreign gods/divinities, *see* Gods, foreign
Fremdkörper (Acts 17 as   ) 7, 26, 175, 188, 190

Gannat Busame 146–150
God, unknown 42, 44, 49, 130, 132, 133–138
- altar to an ~ 45, 83–84, **130–138**, 149, 152, 162

Gods/divinities
- foreign (new) 16, 34–38, 132–133, 137–138, 139, 169, 171, 178, 180
- anthropomorphic 92, 106; *see also* Images/Representation, divine

Godlikeness (Divine-likeness) /Imitation of the gods
- for Epicureans 31, 95–96, 101, 103, 128, 163, 179, 183, 185
- for the Stoics 31, 110–111, 114–116, 120, 128, 144–145, 156–157, 163, 179, 183, 185
- ~ in Acts 17 155, 173, 183–187, 189
- the resurrection as demonstration of ~ 164, 168–170, 178, 189
- piety as ~ 128, 163

Graeco-Roman cult, *see* Religion, Graeco-Roman
Graeco-Roman culture, *see* Culture, Graeco-Roman
Graeco-Roman world, *see* Culture, Graeco-Roman
Grammar of Graeco-Roman religion, *see* Religion, Graeco-Roman
Grundmotiv 5–6, 11

Hades, *see* Underworld
Hellenization 5, 7, 9, 10, 20, 21, 22–25, 179–182, 184, 192
Heracles 37, 64, 78
Historicity of Acts 17 23, 134, 161; *see also* Narrative realism
Historiography 27–28
History in Acts 13
Homoiōsis theōi, see Godlikeness
Hostility, divine (of the gods), 31, 60–68, 70–73, 76, 78, 80–84, 89, 103, 121–122, 130, 131, 138, 149, 152, 160, 171, 176, 183, 184, 190
Hymn to Zeus (by Aratus) 150–151
Hymn to Zeus (by Callimachus) 148
Hymn to Zeus (by Cleanthes) 150

Idols (statues of the gods)

220 Subject Index

- Athens as full of ~ 33, 46, 131, 135
- contrasting ~ with God 139–140, 152–153, 155–156, 170, 176, 178, 183
- contrasting ~ with human beings 158–159, 160, 164, 166, 169, 177
- humanity as ~ 166–167, 170, 178
- *see also* Image/representation, of the gods
- *see also* Image of God

Idolatry
- ~ of the Athenians 4, 35, 130, 176, 178
- *see also* Polemic, anti-idol

Ignorance
- ~ of the Athenians 4, 17, 22, 44–45, 46, 49, 84, 131–138, 145, 152, 157, 158, 160, 162, 172, 176, 177
- *deisidaimonia* and ~ 45–46, 90, 109, 122, 131
- philosophical criticism of ~ 45, 49, 90, 122, 131, 136, 182
- times of ~ 162, 165, 172, 177

Image/representation, of the gods (statue of the gods)
- anthropomorphic ~ 108–109, 112, 120, 126–127, 144, 167
- Epicureans on ~ 30–31, 94, 103, 126, 174, 178–179, 183, 185, 189
- philosophers on ~ 85, 121, 126, 131, 153, 156, 179, 183
- role of ~ in Graeco-Roman religion 144, 152–153, 172
- Stoics on ~ 29–31, 108, 111–114, 120, 126–127, 144–145, 174, 178–179
- worship of ~ as superstition 54, 85
- *see also* Idols
- *see also* Image of God

Image of God (*Imago dei*) 178
- Jewish understanding of ~ 158
- Moses as ~ 143–144
- humanity as ~ 164, 166, 169–170, 172, 177
- humanity as ~ among philosophers 156–157, 183
- humanity created in the image of God 7, 10, 154, 158–159
- the risen man as ~ 164–165, 166–167, 168–169, 171, 173, **175–179**, 183, 186–187, 184, 189

Imitation of the gods, *see* Godlikeness

Impiety 52, 102
- as the other extreme of *deisidaimonia* 57–58
- *deisidaimonia* as ~ 81, 108, 123–124, 185
- Epicureans accused of ~ 93–94, 96–103, 125
- trials for ~ 38–39, 44

Isho'dad 147–150

Jerome 148–149
John Chrysostom 35, 146
Josephus 30, 33, 38, 43, 59, **69–74**, 83, 86, 121, 135
Judaism 9, 14, 24, 137, 191
- Christianity's relation to ~ 3, 14, 189
- Hellenistic ~ 6, 7, 10–12, 24–25, 181
- Diaspora ~ 9, 24–25
Judgment, divine 7, 22, 31, 122, 143, 161, 163, 164, 166, 167, 172, 174, 176, 182, 183, 184; *see also* Punishment, divine
- post-mortem 79, 183
- through the risen man 166, 168–169
Justice, divine 102, 130, 160, 162–163, 165, 182–183, 190
- post-mortem 163, 165

Kerygma 161, 187, 192; *see also* Preaching
Knowledge of God 4, 5, 6–8, 9, 11, 13, 171, 188
- Acts 17 as discourse on ~ 4, 5
- ~ among philosphers 116, 120, 131
- *see also* Theology, natural

Legitimization of Christianity 18, 191–192; *see also* apologetics
Lives (by Plutarch) 59, 75, 77
Lucian 27–28, 36, 86
Lucretius 31, 87–91, 93, 95, 96, 126,

Minos 34, **146–149**, 168
Missionary speech, *see* Speech in Acts
Monotheism 6, 12–13, 16, 53, 81, 133, 134, 139, 161, 176, 178, 188–190
Morality 63, 64, 82, 165

Narrative criticism 25, 27, 30, 32

Narrative realism (verissimilitude) 10, 16, 22, 23–24, **25–29**, 36, 49–50, 142, 161
New gods, *see* Gods, foreign
Nicias 65
Non posse suaviter vivi secundum Epicurum (by Plutarch) 99

Panentheism 7
Pantheism 6, 12, 112, 145–148, 150–151
Paulinism of Luke 175
Pausanias 83
Pax deorum (peace with the gods) 30, 81–84, 121–122, 128, 130–131, 138, 169–171, 174, 176, 181–182, 184–187, 190–192
Philo 81, 135
Philodemus 31, 87, **93–103**, 124, 126,
Philosopical common places, *see* common places, philosophical
Philosophy, ancient
- ~ as art/way of life 19–20, 43, 179
- grammar of ~ 19–21
- nature of ~ 19–21, 23–24, 30, 43, 179
- rapprochement with ~ 19
Piety
- Athenian in the ancient word 38, 48–49, 83
- *deisidaimonia* as perverted 45, 57–58, 109, 185
- *deisidaimonia* as the opposite of ~ 81, 116, 123, 128
- Epicureans on proper ~ 93–96, 100, 103–104, 126–129, 174, 180–181, 185–186
- Stoics on proper ~111–116, 120–121, 126–129, 179, 180–181, 185–186
- ~as divinelikeness or imitation of the gods 156–157, 163, 169, 170, 179, 184–186, 189
- ~ and righteousness 67

Platonist 58, 79, 92, 99, 110, 120, 122, 123, 124, 125, 126, 128, 145, 163; *see also* Academics
Platonism 43, 74
Plutarch 139
- on *deisidaimonia* 30, 50, 55, 57–59, 70, 74–81, 82, 86, 87, 107–108, **122–126**, 127

- on the Stoics 16, 113, 117, 119–121, 125
- on the Epicureans 16, 92, 96, 98–100, 125
- on traditional religion 126–127, 155–156
- on divine representations 126–127, 154–156
Poets, Greek
- the New Testament quoting ~ 5, 10, 23, 146–150, 152
- Epicureans on ~ 99–100, 102–103
- Stoics on ~ 106, 109, 156
Polemic, anti-idol
- Acts 17 as ~ 4, 8, 49–50, 120, 127, 130, 134, 154, 161, 176, 191
- Jewish ~ 6, 8, 11, 19, 33–34, 154, 160
- in Acts 17 15, 33, 143, 145, 153–154, 160
- in Acts 135
Polybius 54, 81
Points of contact, *see* Common ground
Posidonius 7, 148
Prayer of Manasseh, 13
Preaching
- Acts 17 as example of ~ in early Christianity 7, 188
- Apostolic ~ 6, 9, 179
- ~ in Acts 26, 28, 35, 36, 37, 179
- ~ to the Gentiles in Acts 175, 178, 187–192
- Jewish ~ in Hellenistic setting 6, 9, 10–12
- *see also* Kerygma
- *see also* Speeches, missionary
Proof, of divine existence 6, 9
Providence, divine 17, 155, 171–172, 186–187
- Epicurean criticism of ~ 92, 94, 98–100
- Stoic belief in ~ 110, 116–119, 128
- Criticism of Stoic vision of ~ 92–93, 117–119
- Appointment of seasons as ~ 6, 140–142, 152
Punishment/retribution, divine
- according to Epicureans 128
- according to the Stoics 119–120
- *deisidaimonia* as ~ 76

- fear of ~ 60, 63, 66–69, 73, 80–82, 88, 102, 104, 109, 176
- post-mortem ~ 64, 74–75, 79, 88–89, 99, 102, 109, 122, 128, 163, 183
- ~ of the wicked 64, 75, 92, 98–99, 100–103, 120, 163, 185
- see also Judgement, divine

Rapprochement, theological
- ~ with Greek philosophy 3, 9, **19–21**, 24, 85, 125–126, 127, 150, 175, **179–184**, 192–193
- ~ with popular religion 8

Religion
- Athenian ~ 4, 15
- deisidaimonia as meaning ~ 69, 71, 72, 73, 77, 82
- distinction between ~ and philosphy in ancient world 43
- eusebeia as meaning ~ 83
- Jewish ~ 67, 178
- of the philosophers 15, 75
- see also Religion, Graeco-Roman

Religion, Graeco-Roman/traditionnal 55, 62, 64, 139, 153, 175, 185, 190
- attitude of the philosophers towards ~ 14–16, 29, 31, 85–86, 108, 192
- deisidaimonia in ~ 82, 131
- grammar of ~ 30, 51, 53, 55, 56, 59, 81–82
- Epicureans on ~ 29, 93–96, 103, 126–127, 174–175, 183
- philosophical criticism of ~ 14–18, 29, 85, 86, 121–122, 126–127
- relationship of the speech in Acts 17 with ~ 174–175
- the Stoics on ~ 29, 108, 111–116, 120, 126–127, 174–175, 183

Repentance
- call to ~ in Acts 17 11, 13, 14, 162, 172, 176
- call to repentance in Acts 162–163, 187, 191
- in Plutarch 162–163

Resurrection
- as center of apostolic preaching in Acts 179, 188–189
- as proof 161, 164, 171–172, 177, 186–187
- as subject of the speech in Acts 17 138, 179, 187, 189–190
- in Greek culture 36, 161
- of/from the dead 37, 168–169, 171, 178, 190
- of Jesus 37, 171

Retribution, divine, see Punishment, divine

Rhadamanthus 34, 147, 168,

Seasons, divine appointment of 5, 6, 140–143, 151–153, 171–172, 176–177, 186

Self-contradiction
- in the use of deisidaimonia 50
- of philosophers 15–16, 99
- of the Athenians 39
- of the Epicureans 125
- of the Stoics 113–119, 125

Self-definition, of christianity 18

Seneca 31, 87, 104, **107–111**, **112–116**, 126, 156–157
- on deisidaimonia 104, **107–109**,
- on divine representatoin 154–157
- on traditional religion and piety 111–115, 126, 155, 156–157
- on piety as divinelikeness 156–157
- ~ 's critic of allegorical interpretation 106

Sibylline oracles 11

Socrates 38–39, 42–44, 46, 133, 180

Speeches
- in Acts 1, 5, 25–28, 184, 188, 190
- in ancient historiography 27–28
- missionary ~ in Acts 1, 5, 14, 23, 26, 148, 161, 188

Spermologos 9, 16, 34, 37, 39, 40–41, 137, 180

Stoicism
- in Roman Empire 29–30

Strabo 30, 59, **65–69**, 72, 73, 121, 135, 217

Superstition 82, 86–87, 108
- Athenian piety as ~ 48, 84
- Christianity as no ~ 17
- deisidaimonia as meaning ~ 48–50, 52–56, 82
- modern criticism of ~ 50, 53–55
- modern definition of ~ 54
- philosophical criticism of ~ 31, 49

- veneration of images as ~ 17, 54
- *see also deisidaimonia*

Theodicy 102, 120, 123, 124, 164
Theodore of Mopsuestia 146–147
Theology, natural 7, 9, 11, 14, 141–143;
  see also Knowledge of God
Theophrastus 51, 53–54, 56–57
Theosebeia 52, 64, 68, 72
Thucydides 27–28, 61
Trial
- Paul on ~ in Acts 17 21, 38–40, 42–44
- ~ narratives in Acts 1
- ~ for impiety 38, 42, 44, 93
- ~ of Socrates 42–44
Tyndareus 36

Underworld (Hades) 34, 66, 107, 168

Varro 58, 87, 108

World, Graeco-Roman, see Culture, Graeco-Roman
Wrath, divine 30, 33, 36, 117, 122, 123, 130, 131, 138
- traditional religion and ~ 81–82, 84
- *deisidaimonia* as fear of ~ 63, 71, 76–77
- Epicureans on ~ 90–93, 94, 96, 98, 100, 103
- the Stoics on ~ 107–109
- *see also* Hostility, divine

Zeno 106, 113–115